HOUSE DANCE

Dance Music Played on the Anglo-German Concertina

By Musicians of the House Dance Era

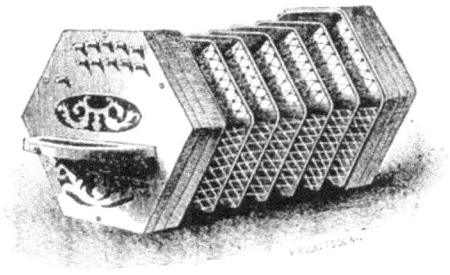

Dan M Worrall

Rollston Press

House Dance: Dance music played on the Anglo-German concertina by musicians of the house dance era

By Dan M Worrall

All rights reserved. No part of this book may be reproduced, scanned, transmitted or distributed in any printed or electronic form without the prior permission of the author except in the case of brief quotations embodied in articles or reviews.

Second Edition Copyright © 2022 Dan M Worrall

ISBN-13: 978-1-953208-03-3

All titles are in the public domain unless otherwise noted.

ROLLSTON PRESS
1717 Ala Wai Blvd #1703
Honolulu, HI 96815
USA
info@rollstonpress.com

Praise for the first edition of *House Dance*

This book is so much more than its title suggests and these words hardly do it justice. Suffice it to say, it is a fascinating experience of reading and listening and…you will find yourself coming back to it again and again.

Michaél Ó Raghallaigh, *Béaloideas: The Journal of the Irish Folklore Society*, 2012

We live in an age in which modern technology is taken for granted. And yet every so often something pops up which seems to use technology in a new way and makes one feel so glad that we live in the 21st century. This disk is just such a product. It is, as it proclaims on the cover, a digital book with embedded sound files, dedicated to an exploration of the use of the Anglo-German concertina in the house dance era. I have to tell you that it is a stunning product. It is the ability to read the book on screen and listen to the audio samples at the same time which turns a first-class piece of musicology into a very special experience.

Chris Metherell, *English Dance and Song* (EFDSS, London), Autumn 2012

[We] have the real music, 'rescued' from archival recordings …of surviving players from the music archives of libraries and folk music organizations of the main countries in which the bright, cheerful music of the 'Anglo' concertina remained an important element in preserving the music and culture of rural and pioneering societies…

Bob Bolton, *Mulga Wire* (Australia), October 2012

It makes for a wonderful experience to read through the generally brief chapters and to listen to the audio files, an experience I would recommend to every concertina player interested in the historical dimensions of the instrument, its repertory, and its origins. With this CD-ROM, Dan Worrall has made a striking contribution to the world of the Anglo-German concertina and its enthusiasts.

Gage Wetherill, *Papers of the International Concertina Association* (UK), 2013

Most people today, if asked to exemplify the differences in English and Irish anglo-concertina styles, would probably think of players such as John Kirkpatrick and Noel Hill - each of whom plays the same instrument in a very different way. But listening to the musical examples here you can see that English and Irish styles were not always so different - nor so different from playing styles on the opposite side of the world.

Andy Turner, *Musical Traditions* (online), 2012

Table of Contents

Preface to the Second Edition
Preface

PART I. The concertina in the world of the house dance

Chapter 1. Introduction 15

Chapter 2. Old-style octave playing on the Anglo concertina 21

Chapter 3. In their own words: playing for house dances 27

Chapter 4. Nineteenth century social dances 37

Chapter 5. A global music 63

Chapter 6. A harvest lost: the banning of house dancing in early twentieth century Ireland 73

PART II. The musicians: An archive

Chapter 7. Australia 93

    Dooley Chapman 99
    George Bennett 105
    Con Klippel 112
    Jim Harrison 115
    Charlie Ordish 118
    Fred Holland 120
    Clem O'Neal 122
    Susan Colley 126
    Ernie James 128
    Percy Yarnold 130

Chapter 8. Ireland 133

Group 1: Musicians of the house dance repertoire
Mary Ann Carolan 141
Ella Mae O'Dwyer 144
Katey Hourican 149
Terry Teahan 150
Stack Ryan 153
Jim Droney 156
Martin Howley 159

Group 2: Musicians of the céilí dance era
Elizabeth Crotty 162
William Mullaly 167
Michael Doyle 169
Patrick Flanagan 172
Tom Barry 173

Chapter 9. England 177
William Kimber 182
Scan Tester 188
Ellis Marshall 195
Fred Kilroy 198
Eric Holland 204
Bill Link 207

Chapter 10. South Africa 211
Faan Harris 218
Chris Chomse 224
Kerrie Bornman 227
Hans Bodenstein 228
Willie Palm 234
Pietie Prinsloo 235
Silver de Lange 236

Chapter 11. Modern players in the old style 239

Australia: Ian Simpson, Ray Simpson, Keith Klippel, Peter Ellis, Dave de Hugard 240
England: Will Duke, Dave Prebble, Harry Scurfield 246
Ireland: Sean O'Dwyer 248
South Africa: Stephaan van Zyl 249

PART III - Tutorial

Chapter 12. Playing in octaves: a brief tutorial 251

Chapter 13. Resources 269

Discography 270

About the Author 288

Preface to the Second Edition

This book was first published in 2011 by Rod Stradling of Musical Traditions (Stroud, Gloucestershire, UK) as a CD-ROM that included both text and imbedded musical recordings, which showcase the earliest players of the Anglo-German concertina from around the world. At the time of publishing, CD-ROMs were standard practice for documents seeking to imbed music and videos into text, but the following decade has not been kind to CD-ROMs, and such technology has all but disappeared in everyday use. Most new PCs, for example, do not even include a slot for CDs. As a practical matter, the 200 or so sound files included here, gathered from sound archives all over the world, were in danger of disappearing as a collection. As a result, those readers and concertina players living in, for example, County Clare, Ireland would have few options for hearing many old, privately made recordings from South Africa or Australia, and vice versa.

With Rod Stradling's kind consent, I explored other options for preserving and publishing this collection. Gary Coover, owner of Rollston Press, suggested imbedding QR codes for sound files into a printed text. Those QR codes point to a private site elsewhere on the web for retrieval of each sound file. Alex Holden, a co-editor of *The Concertina Journal*, provided space on his server for the sound files, and created individual QR codes for each recording. Readers now may simply aim their digital phones at the QR codes as if taking a photograph of them, and push a button to hear each individual sound file. The result is this second edition of *House Dance*, published by Rollston Press.

Technology continues to evolve at an astonishing clip. For any readers who come upon this book in a future century, at a time when its pages are yellow with age, and wonder where the sound files went, copies of the original CD-ROMs are on file at the Irish Traditional Music Archives in Dublin, the Vaughan Williams Memorial Library of the English Folk Dance and Song Society in London, and the National Library of Australia in Canberra. With any luck, someone will have the ability to read them!

But in the meantime, I hope you enjoy this collection of early music on the concertina, as well as the thoughts on the fascinating era in which they were recorded. Any profits generated by this book will be applied to the operation of the non-profit, online *Concertina Journal* (www.concertinajournal.org).

Dan M. Worrall

February 20, 2022
Fulshear, Texas

How to listen to audio files in this book by scanning the QR codes with a smartphone:

- Open the camera app and select the rear facing camera.
- Hold your device so that the QR code appears in the viewfinder in the camera app, as if preparing to take a picture of it.
- Your smartphone should automatically recognize the QR code and show a notification.
- Tap the notification to open the link associated with the QR code.
- The link opens an audio file that can be played.

Preface

This book and its archive of recordings is organized as follows:

Part I includes an introduction followed by:

> **a)** a chapter that describes the old 'octave' manner in which concertinas were played in the era of the house dance;
> **b)** a description of the old house dances in Ireland, Australia, England and South Africa in the words of the musicians who played for them;
> **c)** a discussion of the dances that were popular and their rhythms;
> **d)** an exploration of the cultural links of this globally shared repertoire; and finally
> **e)** a discussion of efforts to ban the house dance and ballroom-style dancing in early twentieth century Ireland, and their subsequent effects on the traditional music repertoire and styles of concertina playing there.

Part II contains an archive dedicated to the musicians of earlier times who played the Anglo concertina, and to recordings of their music. There are some 172 tracks from 36 old time concertina players. The musicians are grouped by country, and there is a biographical description for each musician, followed by some recorded tunes from his or her playing, and a brief discussion of some of the techniques used in playing them. Audio examples of dance tunes that are embedded throughout Part I are drawn from the archive of recordings contained in Part II, so the reader will note a certain amount of repetition in some of the pieces between the two parts.

The musical examples in the archive of Part II are primarily drawn from field recordings, many of which are little-known and rare, of musicians who played German and Anglo-German concertinas in Australia, England, Ireland, and South Africa during the latter part of the heyday of the instrument, which occurred from the 1860s to about 1920, at a time when social dances held in houses, woolsheds, and barns provided a very popular pastime for people in working class urban, rural and frontier areas. As mentioned above, each of the thirty-four musicians whose recordings are featured here were active players before the year 1920. The earliest-born of these musicians arrived in 1866, and all were born before the end of the first decade of the twentieth century. Most of them spent the early parts of their musical lives playing for social dances.

The rather arbitrary cutoff date of 1920 for musicians was chosen as being approximately the end of the heyday of the Anglo concertina, as well as an approximate date for the beginning of the decline of the early ballroom dance genre, the popularization of which the concertina had played such a large role in the late nineteenth century. Clearly, the playing of the concertina for rural ballroom-style dances lived on much longer in Australia and South Africa than it did in England and Ireland, but even in the latter two countries there were small pockets of players well into the twentieth century. But overall, things changed for the worse everywhere for the concertina when the jazz age and the widespread use of recorded music arrived, and in most areas the house, barn and woolshed dances that had been so prevalent in rural areas declined and disappeared.

The recordings of this archive all *postdate* 1920, however. Some few were made in the 1920s and 1930s (especially those in South Africa), but most were made after various efforts at folk and traditional music revivals were begun after the end of World War II. A handful of these recordings was made as late as the 1980s. Thus, many if not most of the field recordings were made when a particular musician was well advanced in age; some sources were recorded well into their nineties. In addition, a significant number of these musicians had not played for decades before someone thrust a concertina into their hands and asked for some music from the old dances. As a result, there is a large variety of quality here not only in the field recording process but in the technical polish of the music provided.

Tracks were chosen for their significance in illustrating either old styles of concertina playing or the house dances themselves, not recording quality or the (apparent) skill of the musician. Most of the musicians were prominent players for house dances when they were in their prime, and were, in nearly all cases, much better players than the field recordings would show. The music they recorded provides a unique window into the past, even if that window has a small cobweb or two on it.

No claims are made here to this archive being completely encyclopedic in including every concertina player from the house dance era, although every effort has been made to include something from every eligible performer whom I could find. Only in one instance was a known performer left out because of a lack of permission from a copyright holder; in a few other cases some known field recordings were left out because those recordings could no longer be found by their owners. A check of most performers whom one might think ought to have been included will, it is hoped, find that the performer in question was a bit too young to have been playing before 1920. Still, there are many, many individuals out there with recordings of relatives on family history tapes that are simply not known to the author.

Part II also includes a chapter of recorded tunes from players of today who still play in the old octave manner. There are 14 tracks from ten such modern-day musicians.

For those interested in learning how to play in the old octave style, nine lessons with examples are provided in Part III, so that one can better understand and recreate the Anglo concertina styles of the historical house dance era. There is also a brief discussion of resources for further information on period music and dance.

Acknowledgements

The project began as an adjunct to my 2009 book, *The Anglo-German Concertina: A Social History* (www.Amazon.com, 2 volumes). The last chapter of that work treated the subject of the playing styles of early recorded players from the only four countries where such recordings are available (England, Ireland, Australia, and South Africa). Although the book included a number of transcriptions made from these recordings, many if not most of the recordings themselves are from either privately held or hard-to-find sources, and were thus somewhat difficult for readers to find. I began to look for a way to make audio examples of the transcriptions available, and this current work is the result. I gratefully acknowledge the generosity of individuals, institutions and companies that have allowed audio or visual archival materials to be included in this collection, or have brought them to my attention. These include:

Australia: The National Library of Australia, including Kevin Bradley, Rob Willis, and Emma Sekuless; Chris Sullivan; Peter Ellis; Warren Fahey; Bruce Kurtz; Alan Musgrove; Bob Campbell; Bob Bolton and the Sydney Bush Music Club; Dave de Hugard.

England: The English Folk Dance and Song Society (and Talking Elephant Records), including Katy Spicer and Malcolm Taylor; Mark Davies; Roger Digby; Vic Smith; Topic Records and Tony Engle; Tony Marshall; Folksound Records, including Graham Bradshaw and Alan Day.

Ireland: *Raidió Teilifís Éireann*, including Malachy Moran and John Glendon; *Comhaltas Ceoltóirí Éireann*, including Siobhán Ní Chonaráin and Peter Denmead; Jim Carroll; Jim MacArdle; Free Reed Records and Neil Wayne; Shaun Jordan; the late John Joe Healy; Joe Queally.

South Africa: *Tradisionele Boeremusiekklub van Suid-Afrika*; Sean Minnie; Stephaan van Zyl; Danie Labuschagne; Kalie de Jager; Wilhelm Schultz; Rob Allingham.

Warren Fahey first suggested the idea of a digital book with embedded sound files rather than a paper tome, but it would never have come to fruition without the encouragement and effort of Rod Stradling at Musical Traditions. The text benefitted greatly from comments made by Sean Minnie, Wilhelm Schultz, Peter Ellis and Tim Collins. Thanks are also due to a number of individuals and organizations that have allowed the use of illustrations in my series of concertina history books; these are listed in the individual illustration captions. Finally, the project would never have advanced without the support and encouragement of my wife, Mary Ryan Worrall.

Dan M. Worrall
November 24, 2011
Fulshear, Texas

Chapter 1. Introduction

House dance culture and the concertina

During the concertina's heyday, a rural 'house dance' culture existed in Europe and its colonies around the world. Rural social dances were held in houses, barns, woolsheds, or - in frontier areas - even on wagon-sails spread on the ground under the stars. The most popular dances at these occasions were the quadrilles, waltzes, polkas, schottisches, galops, varsovianas, mazurkas, and barn dances that were all the rage before World War I.

Most of these dances were derived from local European folk dances that were introduced to high society ballrooms. They rapidly spread to middle and lower class urban haunts, and to rural and frontier areas. These dances are here casually termed 'early ballroom' dances to distinguish them from the jazz- and Latin-derived 'late ballroom' dances that came after WWI, and after the heyday of the concertina. Both types of ballroom dance were largely supplanted by the rock and roll phenomenon of the late twentieth century.

The advent of cheap, mass-produced musical instruments, chiefly fiddles, tin whistles, accordions, mouth organs and concertinas built in German factories, helped the latest dance music to spread from high society ballrooms to the musicians of working class urban, rural and frontier areas, where it thrived. The pace of early ballroom dance is typically relaxed, and hence its music lent itself very well to being played on concertinas as well as on closely related button accordions.

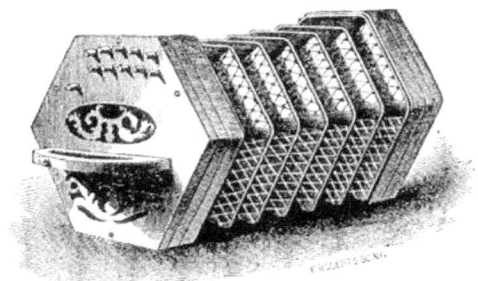

THE GERMAN CONCERTINA.

The musicians who played these popular free-reed instruments played an oversized role in both the global propagation of early tunes for each new dance style (polka, schottische, etc.) as well as the local composition of new tunes for them. Musicians also drew upon other popular sources for inspiration, including tunes from English music halls and American minstrel shows. More than in any previous era, ballroom dance music was becoming global popular music, while still retaining some measure of local identity.

On the continent, the button accordion as well as Chemnitzers and Bandoneons were the free reed instruments most encountered among musicians playing for dances. In Great Britain and its Empire, however, the smaller, typically hexagonal-ended German and Anglo-German ('Anglo') concertina - the focus of this collection - was as popular or more popular than the accordion, especially in the middle to late nineteenth century.

In particular, the concertina was a key part of social dances in England, Ireland, Australia, New Zealand, and in Dutch (Boer) portions of South Africa. It was also a popular instrument for dances in Canada and the United States, but to a somewhat lesser extent than were accordions and stringed instruments.

The octave technique

Although the musicians of various countries who are featured in these early recordings were separated by thousands of miles of land and ocean, and played in their youth for dances in an age that pre-dated broadcast and recorded music, they nonetheless exhibit remarkable similarities in their technical approach to playing dance music on the concertina.

This similarity in approach mirrors an equally similar musical purpose: playing for dancing in noisy, crowded areas. House dances were lively affairs which often lasted all night, and the music was typically provided by a solo concertina player, or perhaps a concertina-fiddle duet. Musicians needed to play simply, accurately and rhythmically to meet the demanding needs of dancers, they needed to play their music loudly enough to be heard in an age before electronic amplification, and they needed to have the stamina to play for much longer periods of time than most dances last today.

A style of playing evolved that consisted of playing the Anglo with double noting, with each hand playing the melody independently of the other, the left hand playing the melody an octave lower than the right. This so-called 'octave' or 'double-note' style, of which more below, was best adapted to these conditions, and evolved more or less independently in each of the four focus countries.

In contrast, in the global folk music revival of the past half century or more, most 'traditional' music is now played for listening in pubs, concert halls, and festivals rather than for dancing, and as a result the Anglo concertina has come to be played at a more rapid tempo and ever more complexly in terms of added ornaments, chords and/or phrasing in Ireland, England and South Africa, displaying a different take on such modernity in each country.

As a result, the earlier and nearly universal 'octave' style that was employed for house dances a century and more ago has all but disappeared among most players today. Very few modern concertina players are technically proficient in playing the old manner, nor typically are most skilled in playing for dances; the world of the house dance has long since passed away.

Hence, this collection of early recordings provides modern Anglo players a window into a largely forgotten world. Moreover, the close similarity in musical repertoire, dances, and concertina playing techniques across the globe that was so evident during the concertina's heyday is often overlooked today as folk revival musicians strive to mark the musical boundaries of each country's national identity.

The repertoire of the house dance

The house dance repertoire comprises a significant part of what is termed the traditional music of England, Australia, and Boer South Africa. Its ballroom dance music forms a large proportion of the so-called English country music genre, which also includes remnants of still earlier step dances and country dances. In Australia and among the Boers of South Africa, ballroom dance tunes comprise the majority of 'bush music' and *boeremusiek*, respectively.

These were the dances of these countries' frontier and colonial past, as well as that of frontier America and colonial New Zealand, where recordings of early concertina players have not survived. In Ireland, on the other hand, the early ballroom dance repertoire is decidedly under-represented in modern traditional music circles.

In the late nineteenth century, house dances that featured various ballroom dances were the dominant form of rural Irish social dance, largely supplanting earlier step dances in even the most remote parts of Gaelic Ireland. They came to be suppressed and even banned as 'foreign' and immoral in the early twentieth century by the Catholic church, the Gaelic League, and the young Irish government.

This anti-foreign crusade was well underway in the early years of the Irish concertina players whose recordings are presented in this archive. These recordings show a split between those (mostly women) who remembered the repertoire of the earlier house dances and those (mostly men) who cast their musical lot with the céilí dances that were designed by cultural authorities to replace them.

As a result of the anti-foreign crusade, by today the traditional music repertoire in Ireland has become decidedly lean in schottisches, barn dances, mazurkas, waltzes, old quadrille tunes and the like relative to that of all other countries where ballroom dance had been popular. Instead, middle twentieth century and later Irish musicians have focused sharply upon the step dance music of the pre-Famine era, notwithstanding the obvious fact that reels, jigs and hornpipes were once equally 'foreign' imports.

Beyond the old-fashioned repertoire and the equally old-fashioned manner in which the concertina was played, there is a refreshing, pretension-free ethos of the musicians themselves that emerges from their playing. In general these were rural people playing in a simple fashion for a shared musical and community purpose. In this music there is none of the rapid-fire and technically ornate virtuosity that is to be found in so many performances of traditional music today, and little to none of the constant strumming of guitars or drums as accompaniment in commercial performances; rather, this was the era of solo instrumentalists playing for dancers. There were no competitions to inject complexity into the melodies, nor, one might imagine, would these players be much impressed if there had been.

From the unusual and at times eccentric settings of many of the pieces one can get the feeling that aural transmission of tunes from other musicians, not standard settings taken from recordings or tune books, was king. It was the last hurrah for 'traditional' dance music (not that these musicians would have been familiar with that term) in the era when such music and dance was the recreation of the majority in rural communities, rather than of the minority that it has been in most places ever since. It is music worth hearing.

Chapter 2. Old-style octave playing on the Anglo concertina

The German concertina was intended by its makers and early promoters from its inception to be an instrument for ballroom dance music, and the two earliest known tutors for the instrument, those of Johann Höselbarth and Carlo Minasi (ca.1837, published in Germany, and 1846, London, respectively) featured a selection of ballroom dance tunes including schottisches, polkas, waltzes, a march, and a galop. Playing the concertina for house dances created a demand for greater volume that was partly filled by playing the instrument doubly, in octaves. This 'octave' style of playing, where two notes an octave apart are played in unison, was one of the earliest ways of playing the instrument, although it is largely lost among modern players. Minasi, who wrote the earliest known English language tutor for the instrument, featured instruction for playing in the octave manner in his 1846 tutor.

Musicians would play the concertina in a double-handed way, playing the melody separately on each hand, the right hand playing it an octave above the left. The fingers of each hand form a 'Z' pattern as they play a scale in octaves (see top part of illustration below).

A more common approach, especially with beginning players, is to play the melody singly (one note at a time) rather than doubly, thus keeping the melody confined to a single row of keys (middle part of illustration). This is the so-called 'along-the-row' style of many later Irish players, especially those who played during the céilí dance era that followed the end of the house dance there.

Musical notation from the Carlos Minasi tutor of 1846 that illustrates octave scales for playing in the keys of C and G. This method became the most popular way of playing the instrument for house dances.

Boer and Irish players have refined the latter style into a cross-row approach that searches for the most efficient way to play any particular phrase, especially important with the more rapid tempos and/or increased use of ornamentation and chording in their respective modern musical settings (see bottom part of illustration, which shows one possible approach to playing a scale in D on an Anglo pitched in C and G).

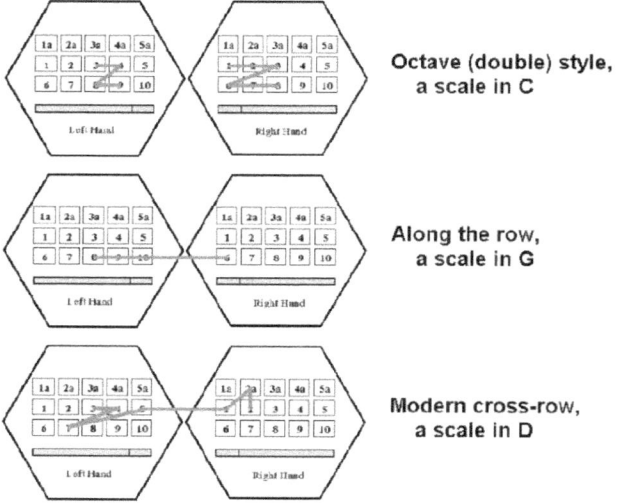

 Here is a link to an air recorded in the 1950s from the playing of legendary Clare player Stack Ryan that demonstrates the earlier octave style. Here he plays the air *Eamonn a' Chnoic*, which was recorded by Ciarán Mac Mathúna in the 1950s, who is the announcer in the track. The track is courtesy RTÉ, Ireland's Public Service Broadcaster. The first part of the tune is played both singly and in octaves, with the octaves adding extra strength to the parts that Ryan chooses to emphasize. The second part is played mostly in octaves.

Another characteristic of playing for house dances consisted of the great simplicity of the techniques employed. Where many modern concertina players in Ireland might add generous helpings of ornaments to such a tune, and where modern English or Boer players might be tempted to apply a thick layer of interesting chords, Stack Ryan in the above recording is monumental in his simplicity of approach; there is nary an ornament in the entire piece. This relative simplicity is to be found in the playing of nearly all concertina players of this time, and was brought about by the needs of dancers for a strong, easily heard beat. Consider the following four dance pieces, one from each of the four countries.

 Albert 'Dooley' Chapman (1892-1982) of Coborrah, New South Wales Australia, plays the *Starry Night Waltz* on a Stanley Anglo concertina. Track recorded by Bob Campbell in 1974.

 Scan Tester (1887-1972) of Horsted Keynes, Sussex England, plays *St Patrick's Day Jig* on a Jeffries Anglo concertina; recorded in the 1960s. Courtesy Vic Smith.

 Martin Howley (1902-1981), Fanore, County Clare Ireland, plays *Maggie in the Wood*, a polka, on a German concertina. Recording courtesy of Jim Carroll and Pat Mackenzie.

 Hans Bodenstein (1897-1978) and Die Vyf Vastrappers play an *Untitled Polka*. Bodenstein lived in Benoni, near Johannesburg South Africa. From a recording of the 1930s, courtesy of *Die Tradisionele Boeremusiekklub van S.A.*

The musicians who played the above four audio examples came from very varied locations and backgrounds, but they had one key thing in common: their general musical approach to a shared musical environment. They played simply and rhythmically, using melody notes that are often (although not always) doubled in octaves. During the ballroom dance era and concertina's heyday, the concertina player was often the only musician present in rural house dances that lasted from dusk until dawn. The dancers needed volume, a steady tempo, and a bit of lift, and because they paid the musicians, dancers tended to get what they asked for. Instead of emphasizing ornaments and fancy strokes, concertina players focused like a laser on a melody played simply and in octaves (for volume) and a steady, moderate tempo. Those who didn't were in for criticism from dancers.

Here is Dooley Chapman commenting on the lesser skills of many concertina players in his youth, including his brother Fred, who played along-the-row. Chapman was interviewed c.1981, and the recording is courtesy of Chris Sullivan.

In County Clare, Ireland, the late Tommy McCarthy (1939-2002) had a similar take on the needs of the dancers in country houses:

> *They'd dance better to a concertina than anything. 'Twas just the sound of it I think. It didn't matter how good you were, as long as you had the rhythm and they could get in t'ould batter. The technique in the music didn't mean a thing. Nice straight simple music and to be quite abrupt about it, you could be a great player and if your rhythm didn't suit them, they'd think you were no good. That was the situation on any instrument. If you hadn't that ould rhythm, that you could dance nice to, the tune you were playin' or the way you were playin' it didn't matter much. The grand notes you'd be puttin' in or the parts of the tune itself didn't mean anything because the dancers didn't take a bit of notice to it.* [1]

In Australia, 'Dooley' Chapman had a characteristically wry assessment of the demands of these dancers; interviewed c.1981. Recording courtesy of Chris Sullivan.

Octave playing developed partly because of the noise levels at house dances, partly because of the dancer's demand for steady rhythm, and partly because that style resoundingly fitted the jaunty, relaxed pace of ballroom dances. Sean O'Dwyer, of Dublin, whose mother Ella Mae O'Dwyer played for dances and in octaves (recordings of her are included below), put it this way:

> *The old style of concertina playing in this country was that of double-hand [octave] playing of the melody, especially for polka dances. One wonders was it a style which evolved from the lack of amplification? Did the player have to resort to this 'trick' to get himself heard above the din of the dancers?* * 2

As we shall see, there are many variants of this style, but all share a base platform where the fingers in each hand move in parallel with their counterparts on the other hand, resulting in two reeds being sounded for each note played. These two reeds yield a full, accordion-like sound that was quite penetrating in noisy rooms.

The octave style also had an advantage for longevity of play. In dances that often employed a solo concertina player from dusk to dawn, the double notes allowed the melody to sing through even if one tired finger of a fatigued player missed a note; its twin on the other side of the instrument would likely still find the right button.

Not all tunes were played entirely in octaves. In Ireland, double reels were typically played singly throughout the tune because of their rapid tempo, even by musicians who were otherwise octave players (note: Irish-style double reels are much less common, to completely absent, in the dance music of the other three study countries). In addition, melodies were typically played singly in difficult or ornamented passages. Finally, some musicians would play the notes of the lower octave (left hand) only on the first and third beat in common time, which tended to emphasize the rhythm even more. Such players often would add a third interval note to the remaining lower octave notes, which created a partial chord an octave below the (right hand) melody that added yet more emphasis to the beat.

English musician William Kimber (1872-1961) of Headington Quarry, Oxfordshire made particular use of this technique in playing for social dances, such as **Over the Hills to Glory**, a schottische that he recorded in 1936. The track is courtesy of the English Folk Dance and Song Society.

Regardless of the use of such rhythmic techniques, and the addition of partial chords, the two hands still trace a 'double Z' pattern on the keyboard, and his playing is essentially a variant of the octave style. Kimber's particular playing technique will be dissected in a bit more detail in the tutorial of Chapter 12.

Notes:

1. Tommy McCarthy, as interviewed in 1986, by Gearóid O hAllmhuráin. PhD thesis, 1990, pp.168-169.

2. Sean O'Dwyer, 'The concertina in traditional Irish music', Free Reed, The Concertina Newsletter, No.14 (1973), pp.13-17. Chapter 3. In their own words: playing for house dances

Chapter 3. In their own words: playing for house dances

Perhaps the best way to get a feel for the former world of house dances is to read and hear the accounts of eyewitnesses. In Ireland, concertina player Margaret Dooley (b. 1885) of east Clare recalled the house dances of her youth:

> *The young lads long ago, they had no place to go. They had nothing only goin' in there and collectin' in a neighbour's house for a dance. The concertina, 'twas in every house and the boys were able to play it as well as the girls. T'ould concertina shure! 'Twas easy to learn on it. In the neighbours' houses on the flag floor, they'd be dancin' wild with the nail boots and you'd hear them crackin' a fling before you'd come into the kitchen at all. 'Twas a nice way of putting down the time, but shure! 'tis all different now. Everywhere you'd go that time there was a concertina player. There was one nearly in every house.* * 1

The 'fling' Mrs Dooley mentions is the Irish term for a schottische, also called a 'Highland.' * 2

Mary Ann Carolan (1902-1985) grew up in The Hill of Rath, a country village near Drogheda, County Louth Ireland. In this audio clip from a 1986 RTÉ interview, she recounted that polka sets (polka quadrilles) were just the thing to enliven an evening at home, and then plays three polkas, *The Lass of Gowrie*, one that is untitled, and *Try and Help Him If You Can*. The recording is courtesy of RTÉ, Ireland's Public Service Broadcaster.

The Australian countryside in that country's colonial era was dotted with small, relatively isolated rural 'bush' settlements where dances in homes and barns provided an essential element of community. From an Australian parson's account of 1908:

Policemen and partners at a house dance in the West of Ireland, 1887. From The Graphic, London, February 19th, 1987

> *I wish I could do justice to a Bush social. I wish I could show you the great chaff-shed, its slab walls draped in art-muslin, and its beams decorated with green boughs, the pianist seated in the corner, supported by a violinist, in some cases a real musical genius, whose thirsty soul has proved his undoing. At some Bush dances the music is provided by a concertina, energetically played by a stalwart young Bushman, who sits on his heels in the corner in an attitude characteristically Australian. Outside the shed a temporary supper-room has been built with great pine-poles and tarpaulins, and long trestle-tables groan beneath delicacies brought from far and near. There are turkeys and chickens from every farm within miles, sucking-pigs, hams, tongues, fruit and cakes, trifles, and innumerable other delicacies. At midnight the whole company sits*

A wool shed dance in Australia, 1889. Note the solo concertina player, and the bales of wool used for seating. From the Illustrated Sydney News.

down to supper, and thereafter dancing is renewed and continued until daybreak makes it possible for the tired dancers to see to drive home, some of them a distance of fifteen miles or more. * 3

Because houses were typically small in rural areas at this time, instrumentation was limited to a concertina and maybe a fiddle. Clem O'Neal (1912-1980) came from Iron Bark (now Stuart Town) New South Wales, Australia, and was one of the last concertina players produced in his district. He described the house dances there as follows:

The dances were out in country places, mostly in the houses (which normally had) dirt floors or flagstone floors. Quite a lot of the houses were small. Some people danced inside the house and quite a lot danced outside the house. The concertina player moved about from room to room carrying the concertina . . . and so there were times when those outside couldn't hear him. The player just moved around in among them and some (players) actually waltzed in time with them to get through. * 4

Dances were often held outdoors in good weather, as in this account of a cross-roads dance in County Mayo Ireland, in 1904:

The scene is the King's highway in the ancient kingdom of Connaught; time, the dusky twilight of midsummer midnight ... The road just here runs through a vast expanse of bog, stretching away on either side to a far-away boundary of blue mountains, hardly to be distinguished now in the faint moonless light of this June midnight ...

The high-piled bonfire occupies half the road, and fragments are being blown and whirled about by the summer gale in a fashion that seems alarming. Standing about are some thirty or forty men and boys ... perhaps half that number of girls are crouching under the shelter of the boundary wall farthest from the fire. Their heads are bare, but they have shawls over their shoulders, and all, both men and women, are in everyday working clothes and hobnailed boots. The women in several instances have not even removed their aprons, as if any rearrangement of costume were considered unnecessary ...

Someone concealed from view is playing lively jig tunes on a concertina, and presently there is a movement in the little crowd; men select partners from among the ladies cowering under the wall, who doff their shawls, and the dance commences. It is formed of some ten or twelve couples; they mark well, with rough-shod feet, the rhythm of the tune on the hard road, and accurately observe intricate steps as they move in and out between other couples and turn their partners around, much in the fashion of a quadrille - all gone through with extreme gravity and decorum, till the dance is accomplished, and the fair sex retire once more into the shelter and obscurity of the wall. There ensues another interval, during which the men stand about as before.

The fire is occasionally replenished, and every few minutes the company break into a sort of subdued shouting, apparently for no particular cause; the concertina tunes are continuous, and are the liveliest feature of the gathering. * 5

Ella Mae O'Dwyer (1906-1992) of Athea, West Limerick Ireland, plays **Mrs O'Dwyers Fancy**, which is comprised of old quadrille tunes (polkas). The recording is courtesy of Neil Wayne of Free Reed Records, who recorded Mrs O'Dwyer in 1974.

Also outdoors, at a 'bucksail' dance in South Africa in 1897:

We went on by way of Enkeldoorn (in the old Transvaal Province, now Gauteng South Africa), where there is a Dutch community, and where a "bucksail" dance was being held that night.... For the uninitiated, I may explain that a bucksail dance is held in the open. The ground is flattened down and the big tent or bucksail, which is used to cover wagons, is spread over it to form a dancing floor. Partners are selected, and these are retained during the whole of the dance, which generally lasts from sunset to sunrise, with intervals for refreshments. The orchestra usually consists of a concertina and guitar or fiddle, but in default of these a mouth-organ or two does suffice. The dance was a very vigorous one. * 6

The Boer people had rustic farms scattered across the veldt. An English visitor recalled in 1900 a visit of some years previous:

And who has not heard of the Dutch dances at the Cape? ... They danced on the mud floor in the voorkammer - the living room of the house, into which the door opens from the outside - and the dust rose thicker and thicker until you could scarcely see across the other room. Then there was a pause, during which they watered the floor, and it, of course, became thick mud, and was ruination to the dresses. But the Boer girls generally change their frocks two or three times during the evening, in order to show off the extent of their wardrobe, and from their youth up are accustomed to dirt in the ballroom, so they do not take their soiled raiment much to heart. On they go, dancing merrily, often to the concertina where they can't get a piano, with their arms entwined around each other's necks in the Dutch fashion. * 7

Johannes Petrus 'Silver' de Lange (1904-1956) was born in Vrededorp, a village near Johannesburg, South Africa. He formed a dance band called *Die Vyf Dagbrekers* (The Five Daybreakers) in the early 1930s. The lively polka, **Warm Patat** (Hot Sweet Potato) is from a recording of that time, courtesy of *Die Tradisionele Boeremusiekklub van S.A.*

In rural England, a Northumberland vicar's wife invited local working-class parishioners over for a dance in 1877, providing a bit of culture contrast between the genteel lady, who was used to quadrilles played on a piano, and working class youth, who were used to playing polkas on a concertina and fiddle:

Our dance came off Wednesday with great success ... Our guests arrived at 7; we were forty-four altogether; our music was the only thing which was not altogether successful. The fiddler whom we had engaged had felt so bashful in coming to what he considered such a grand house that he had cheered his spirits by a little whiskey first, and the whiskey

A Boer family dancing in their kitchen. Drawn by John Guille Millais, 1895.

House Dance 31

seemed to have gone to his fingers and made his playing muddled. We varied his playing with quadrilles on the piano from me and polkas on the concertina from some of the young men.

You would have been surprised to see the number of dances they performed. They did everything that is danced in the ordinary ballroom, though their valsing [waltzing] did not come to much, besides they danced four or five kinds of country dances, schottische, reels and polkas. Some of them danced extremely well, and it was amusing to watch the difference in their dancing to that of people of our position. They put their whole energy into their dancing and thought of nothing else, conversation played no part in the proceeding, but the dancing was everything and had to be done as well as was possible. In fact, the faces of most of them were solemn all the time as if they were accomplishing an important task ... At 1:30, they all went home and left us very tired. * 8

A family band in Darlington, Durham England, ca.1910. Courtesy of The Beamish, The Living Museum of the North.

Dance musicians were typically semi-professionals and were paid for their work. They often traveled great distances to play at a dance. At the turn of the last century, in the tiny rural village of Duramama, near Bathurst in New South Wales, Australia, where concertina player Susan Colley (1881-1976) lived:

> *There was no public hall for the holding of dances and such-like functions. But dances were frequent. The younger folk, and some of the not-so-young, would congregate at the residence of a neighbour or acquaintance, coming by springcart (before the advent of a sulky), horseback or foot, and dance the whole night through to the music of a concertina or accordion. [They would] dance the Quadrilles, Lancers and Alberts, polkas, mazurkas, old time marches, etc., until after sun-up the next morning.* * 9

Mrs Colley recalled these dances, and the dress her mother made her for a rural ball, in this interview, recorded by Warren Fahey in 1973 when she was 92 years old.

You dance with it.' Ian Simpson dances with his wife Diane Simpson while he plays the concertina, c.1985. This was an old party trick at house dances in all countries where the instrument was played; Susan Colley remembers it in the above interview. Photo courtesy Peter Ellis.

Dooley Chapman recounted how his musical mentor Billy Chandler played for dances all over the region, using a bicycle for transport:

House Dance

I've seen him leave Coborrah there of an evening making to Lue to play for a dance ... Mudgee's fifty mile, and another twenty down to where he was playing for the dance ... [T]hat's a long way to ride, don't you reckon! ... Of course, Lue's not the only place, other places as well.

The dancers, they'd start at eight o'clock. They'd go all night, of course. I'd be playing, and I'd get a bit of a lunch at half past one, and I'd play on until four o'clock. Because the ladies, or the girls, weren't allowed to leave until daylight, the breaking day ...so they wouldn't get away with somebody. 10

Percy Yarnold (1907-1988) of Wingham, New South Wales Australia was a concertina player for the Keightley Dance Band during his youth. He described his payment (twelve shillings) for a typical bush dance, in a 1985 **interview** with John Meredith (track courtesy of the National Library of Australia).

An Australian woolshed dance.
From the Australian Town and Country Journal of December 24, 1870.
Note the solo fiddle player.

Notes:

1. Gearóid Ó hAllmhuráin, The Concertina in the Traditional Music of Clare, (PhD thesis, Queen's University Belfast, 1990).

2. Helen Brennan, 1999, The Story of Irish Dance, Brandon Books, Dingle Ireland, p.100.

3. C H S Matthews, A Parson in the Australian Bush (London: Edwin Arnold, 1908), pp.113-114.

4. Clem O'Neal, interviewed in Concertina Magazine, Australia, 1982.

5. Lady Onslow of Hengar, 1904, 'Midsummer Eve in Mayo', The Pall Mall Magazine, vol. 33 (1904), pp.429-430.

6. Gordon Le Seur, Cecil Rhodes, The Man and His Work (New York: McBride, Nast & Company, 1914), pp.157-158.

7. Beatrice M. Hicks, The Cape as I Found It (London: Elliot Stock, 1900), p.129.

8. Louise Creighton, writing in a letter (1877) quoted in James T Covert, A Victorian Marriage, (Continuum International Publishing Group, 2000), p.115.

9. Percy J Gresser, 1965, The Songs They Played - and the Dance Tunes They Played: unpublished notes, The Bush Music Club of Sydney, Australia.

10. Dooley Chapman, Your Good Self, CD, Chris Sullivan's Australian Folk Masters, CS-AFM-001, 2005.

Chapter 4. Nineteenth century social dances

Dance styles in England and Ireland before the arrival of ballroom dance

At the beginning of the nineteenth century, a few decades before the arrival of ballroom dance, social dance in England and Ireland consisted primarily of two principal forms: step-dances and country dances.

Although both were largely (although not completely) displaced by ballroom dances in most popular social situations by the end of the nineteenth century, both genres continued to be locally important in these two countries, and thus the dance music for these genres continued to be part of the repertoire of musicians who played at late nineteenth and early twentieth century house and barn dances.

Step dances

Various types of *step-dances* were performed to jigs, hornpipes and reels. These were typically danced solo, or by a pair or small group of dancers. Most of the movement occurred from the waist down, with emphasis being placed on intricate movements of the feet. Touching between partners was kept to a minimum.

In a late nineteenth century or early twentieth century Irish house dance, a solo or two-hand step dance or perhaps a four hand reel would typically be performed as an exhibition while the main body of dancers took a break from quadrilles, barn dances and waltzes.

Martin Howley (1902-1981) of Fanore, County Clare plays an *untitled jig* on his German concertina. The recording is courtesy of Jim Carroll.

Each of the three principal step-dance rhythms of Ireland were in all likelihood European imports, just as were the quadrilles, waltzes and polkas that were later so reviled as "foreign" by the Gaelic League and the clergy (see Chapter 6). The jig was in England by the sixteenth century, and arrived in Ireland in the seventeenth, according to Breandan Breathnach.*1 The hornpipe and the reel arrived in Ireland much later, by the end of the eighteenth century.*2

All of these arriving step dances had been integrated into Irish dance custom by the time of arrival of quadrilles in the early nineteenth century. As quadrilles then became more and more popular, their popularity came at the expense of these earlier step dances. However, arriving quadrille tunes were written in 6/8 and 2/4 time, which allowed local Irish step-dance tunes -jigs, hornpipes, and reels - to be substituted into the sets of quadrilles ("sets" in modern Irish usage). As Breathnach has observed of quadrilles, "Their sustained and widespread popularity was, without doubt, responsible for keeping alive a great deal of native dance music."*3

In England, step dances have long been performed by men in pubs, as Sussex resident Scan Tester recounted:

> *Course, they used to come in the pubs, you see, with their heavy boots on - the old pelted boots and all - and yorks and*

all on, and you see 'em out in the room that time of day doing the old stepdances, and they used to, if there was enough of 'em, they'd form a figure eight or form a four angles, you know, cross angles, and, you know, there was a lot of different ways they used to dance.

There used to be what we called a reel. It was ordinary four corners, four of them, and they used to step, and then the second part they change over and go in and form the figure-eight. And really, it was old people that done it, mind you. The young ones, they used to join in. Get two in a set, see, and learn 'em. 4

 Sussex native Scan Tester (1887-1972) plays a **Step Dance Tune**. The recording is courtesy of Vic Smith.

Dancing in the tap room of a Norfolk pub. From The Graphic, October 22, 1887, and from Reg Hall's I Never Played To Many Posh Dances (1990).

In colonial Australia - which was substantially populated by immigrants from England, Ireland, Wales and Scotland - jigs and reels were danced by these immigrants and their children. These dances, however, did not have particular staying power beyond the first or second generation. By the end of the nineteenth century it was not common, but still not unheard of, to see step dances occurring within typical Australian rural dances.

Tunes in single jig, single reel (rarely the double form of either) tempo, however, are prominently played in Australia figures of sets within quadrilles, just as they are in Ireland. The Irish also use hornpipes for some quadrille/set figures, which is uncommon in Australia.

George Bennett (1878-1966) of Gunnedah, NSW plays a step-dance jig, *George Redder's Step*, that was recorded in the early 1960s. The recording is courtesy of Rob Willis and the National Library of Australia.

Step dancing outside of a pub, Kent England; note the concertina player in the background. Scan Tester often played for step-dancing at these pubs during hop-picking season. The illustration is from Robert Machray, The Night Side of London, 1902.

Country Dance

Large group social dancing in Ireland and England in the early nineteenth century consisted primarily of the *country dance*, where relatively large groups of dancers formed long lines or circles and performed various geometric maneuvers. This form originated in rural England in the sixteenth century, and migrated to both Ireland and France. In France it became the *contredanse*, and was re-exported to northeastern America to become the contra dance. A variant in Ireland was called the *rinnce fada* (long dance), which was danced for King James at his arrival in Kinsale in 1689. Country dance was popular throughout the eighteenth century, and into the early nineteenth. Dancing masters taught both forms to eager pupils of all classes in rural Ireland.

Country dances typically employ rhythms in 2/4 and 4/4 time (single reels and marches) as well as jig time (6/8), although more exotic rhythms are also found (e.g., 3/2, 6/4, and 9/8). Typical and still-danced examples are the longways dances *Sir Roger de Coverley* (England) or the *Virginia Reel* (America), as well as the *Haymaker's Jig* (Ireland). These as well as a few other country dances migrated to Australia in colonial times, where they have survived and are danced to this day in the revived 'bush dance' scene.*5

By the 1820s, country dance began to decline in England, as the quadrille gained center stage. Country dance was still popular in Ireland by 1867, when Dundalk resident Kate Hughes recorded some 54 country dances in her dance book, along with a large number of ballroom dances: quadrilles (including Caledonian and Lancers sets), mazurka quadrilles, and waltz cotillons.

Remnant country (longways and figure) dances from Kerry, as well as newly composed ones, were introduced throughout Ireland in the early twentieth century as proper dance forms for *céili* evenings, in a bid by the Gaelic League to replace banned ballroom dance (see Chapter 6). Some of these dances, including the *Waves of Tory* and the *Siege of Ennis*, were brought to Australia as part of the folk revival of the 1970s.

Ballroom dance

The dancing scene in Europe was to change radically in the early nineteenth century with the arrival of the *ballroom dance*. First to arrive in Britain and Ireland were the *waltz* and the *quadrille*; they moved quickly from the balls in the big houses to rural house and crossroad dances, as well as to colonial areas such as Australia and South Africa. Later arrivals were the *mazurka, polka, schottische, galop, varsoviana* and the *barn dance*.

The emergence of these ballroom dances roughly coincided with the invention of the German concertina in 1834, and its Anglo-German cousin by about 1850. As was mentioned above, the earliest English-language tutor for the German concertina, published in London in 1846, contains marches, a waltz, and several schottisches. Most of these tunes were cribbed from a slightly earlier German language concertina tutor, which shows the strong central European cultural influence on song and dance of that era.

As the concertina's popularity mushroomed among working class musicians in English-language countries, it comprised a key platform on which music for ballroom dance was composed, at least in rural folk culture.

In the early twentieth century, new dance fashions from the United States and, somewhat later, from Latin America pushed the early ballroom dances out of the popular limelight. Jazz dances like the one-step, fox trot and the two step, and Latin dances like the tango and the cha cha, created the so-called *modern* ballroom dance era, which lasted well into the middle of the twentieth century before being largely displaced in turn by rock and roll era. In particular, some jazz tunes were very chromatic and thus were difficult to reproduce on German and Anglo-German concertinas as well as on button accordions. At this time, the saxophone, trumpet, trombone, guitar (and in the jazz age, the ukulele) took precedence over free reed instruments as the essential instruments for any small dance band.

The Anglo concertina largely faded into attics and pawn shops after World War I in England, Australia and in most parts of Ireland, although it played for the old dances slightly longer amongst the Boers of South Africa.

A standard reference for the following group of ballroom dances is the work of Australian Peter Ellis, whose books, *The Waltz, the Polka, and all Kinds of Dance Music* (2007) as well as *The Merrie Country Dance* (2005) were extensively consulted for the descriptions that follow. *6

The Waltz

The waltz originated in Germany and Austria in the eighteenth century, and was reportedly danced by Wellington and his officers after the battle of Waterloo in 1815. It arrived in England, Ireland and even Australia by the following year. *7 British military bands brought the waltz to the Cape Colony (modern South Africa), and it was entrenched there at least by 1822. *8

The close, body-to-body hold of the waltz and other round dances initially scandalized English society, who quickly acclimated to its charms. In Ireland, these dances were branded from the pulpit as immoral, and nationalist groups offered them as proof of the evils of foreign influence on pure Irish culture.

It caused a furor over its scandalously close clutch-hold between two partners, and for good reason. Whereas earlier dancing forms - both step and country dances - allowed only very limited touching between sexes who were usually at arms length, touching only at hands and elbows, the waltz put a man and a woman very close together, with his arm closely around her waist, for a significant part of the evening.

It is hardly surprising that the graceful waltz and its catchy, song-like three-beat music spread like wildfire across Europe, through England and Ireland, and to all of Europe's colonies, especially with young people. It spread first through upper class ballrooms, then rapidly migrated to the dances of working class and rural communities.

It was the first of what are known today variously as 'couple dances' or 'round dances;' these were later joined by galops, polkas, schottisches, mazurkas, varsovianas and the like. 'Couple' refers to that fact that one man and one woman dance together for the entire dance, like one person on four legs ... which only added to the scandal, as earlier country dances did not allow such close, lengthy contact between individuals.

'Round' dance refers to dances where the couple, and other couples, trace a circular pattern as they slowly make their way around the periphery of the dance floor, a bit like a skate around a skating rink. Unlike plain waltzes at modern popular venues, where the dancing is more or less free-form, each individual sequence-type old-time ballroom waltz (such as the *Veleta Waltz*, *Pride of Erin Waltz*, and *Parma Waltz*) had its own pattern of steps that each couple performed in synch with other couples, while all slowly traveled around the dance floor.

There were similar sequence dances in the other time signatures like progressive barn dance and Schottische tunes.

The waltz was easily the most popular of the round dances both with dancers and musicians, and every concertina player had a stock of them, ready for use. Here are three examples:

Ernie 'Son' James (1891-1981) was one of a number of fine concertina players to come from the Mudgee area of New South Wales, Australia. Here he plays his **Cornflower Waltz**, a tune which, according to folk music collector John Meredith, has been found nowhere else. Track courtesy the National Library of Australia.

Willie Palm, born in 1894 in Ficksburg in the Transvaal (now Gauteng), South Africa, was leader of the band *Die Vier Huguenote* in the 1930s, when this waltz recording, **Vergieet nie** (Never forget) was made. The track is courtesy of *Die Tradisionele Boeremusiekklub van S.A.*

Mary Ann Carolan (1902-1985) of The Hill of Rath, County Louth, Ireland, plays the **Veleta Waltz**, which was written in 1899 in England and introduced as a dance in 1900. It remains popular in Australia and amongst ballroom dance aficionados around the globe.

The Quadrille

The quadrille arrived in England and Ireland about 1816, having migrated from France, perhaps with returning officers of the

Napoleonic wars but also by way of the dance teachers who frequented the houses of the ever-fashionable landed gentry. Elizabeth Grant, a genteel Scottish lady, wrote of the winter of 1816-1817 that:

> *It was the first season of quadrilles, against the introduction of which there had been a great stand made by old fashioned respectables. Many resisted the new French figures altogether, and it was a pity to give up the merry country dance, in which the warfare between the two opinions resulted; but we were all the young people bit by quadrille mania, and I was one of the set that brought them first into notice.* * 9

The quadrille quickly moved from the palaces of the landed gentry to rural country houses, and to Britain's colonies. It arrived in Australia by the 1820s and caught on quickly with all parts of society. The quadrille had a remarkably long run in both Ireland and Australia, where it was popular for over a century (a century and a half in Australia) and was then revitalized in folk revivals of the late twentieth century.

The opening position of the quadrille, with four couples forming a square. From William De Garmo, The Dance of Society, 1875, New York.

Although it was danced by the well-to-do in Cape Town in the nineteenth century, it seems never to have made large inroads with rural Boer folk, and hence its music was not frequently recorded by musicians there.

Like the waltz, the quadrille is a partnered dance, but in this case four couples face each other in a square for a series of four to six *figures* that together form a *set*. For that reason it is sometimes known as a *square* dance, to separate it from contemporary *round* dances.

Indeed, the modern American square dance is a descendant, as is the *set* dance (for *set* of quadrilles) in Ireland. The *Plain Set* (*First Set* or *First Set of Quadrilles*), the *Lancers*, and the *Caledonians* are early sets that were introduced in the 1820s to 1840s, and they are danced to this day in Ireland and Australia.

A cross-roads set dance on a wooden platform, near Kenmare, County Kerry Ireland. From a 1948 tourist guidebook entitled 'Your Holiday in Ireland'.

What the dancers wanted was a good steady beat at a swingy march tempo, so 6/8 and 2/4 tunes predominated, although there were occasional figures in other time signatures, particularly waltz time. In the early days, higher class dances used printed scores of quadrille tunes composed for string orchestras and military bands. Themes from operettas were popular as well as arrangements of national songs from different countries.

As the dance migrated deeper into society, traditional musicians in Ireland, England and Australia began to substitute popular music hall and sentimental songs, military marches, single reels and American minstrel breakdowns. In Ireland, efforts were made in the early twentieth century to 'Irish-ize' the quadrilles, to use a phrase coined by Frank Roche in his 1928 collection of traditional Irish music, which contained a section of quadrille music.*10 'Irish-ization' included the substitution of Irish double reels, jigs and hornpipes for the earlier quadrille tunes, and was accompanied by a general quickening of tempo.

Here are two quadrille tunes in jig tempo by Mary Ann Carolan (1902-1985): ***The Perfect Cure* and *The Morning Glory***. Mrs Carolan played these tunes for quadrilles in her youth in County Louth. The recording is courtesy of RTÉ, Ireland's Public Service Broadcaster.

Dooley Chapman (1892-1982) of Coborrah, New South Wales Australia played this ***Lancers tune*** for a figure of the Lancers quadrille. The recording is courtesy of Chris Sullivan.

George Bennett (1878-1966) of Gunnedah, New South Wales plays another ***Lancers Quadrille*** tune, in single jig tempo. The recording is courtesy of Rob Willis and the National Library of Australia.

The Mazurka

The second type of round dance to emerge from central Europe, after the waltz, was the mazurka. It originated in Poland in the early nineteenth century, and found its way to the fashionable ballrooms of Europe. A number of composers have featured it in their work, including Chopin, who wrote mazurkas as early as 1825. Tchaikovsky used mazurkas in several of his ballet scores, and a number of well-known French and Czech composers were also enamored of it.

It is likely that it made its way to England and Ireland by the 1830s, although there is little documentation, and very few mazurkas are left in the traditional repertoires of either country. In Ireland, a very few have survived the early twentieth century purge of round dances, notably in Donegal, but none are known to have been recorded by early concertina players there.

Like the waltz, the mazurka is in triple meter (3/4) time, but with a bouncy rhythm created by the addition of dotted quavers (i.e. a dotted quaver followed by a-semi quaver), which typically provides a lively nuance. The mazurka usually carries an accent on the second or third beat rather than the first beat, as in the waltz.

Perhaps the most commonly known song with mazurka rhythm is *Clementine*, which exhibits these characteristics. The mazurka uses the same clutch-hold as the waltz, and as in the waltz a couple follows a circular pattern around the perimeter of the dance floor.

In Australia, the polka mazurka was a very popular colonial dance. The mazurka was typically a complicated dance of the dance-master's construction, whereas the polka mazurka was a simple sequenced routine that took on widely. According to Australian colonial dance authority Peter Ellis, the polka mazurka is a compound dance consisting of mazurka advances and polka step turns, but performed to mazurka music (it has no musical connection to the polka apart from perhaps an anacrusis combined with the dotted quaver that gives it spring).

Charlie Ordish (d.1966) of Corryong in northwestern Victoria, Australia plays an **untitled mazurka** for a polka mazurka dance. Track courtesy the National Library of Australia. *11

In South Africa, the mazurka arrived at least by 1848 and became a favorite dance, with its popularity extending to the present day. Many groups have recorded mazurkas; here are two from the classic era.

Stephen Emil (Faan) Harris (1886-1950) and *Die Vier Transvalers* play the **Kroomdrai Mazurka**. Harris, one of the great concertina players of his era, lived near Krugersdorp, near Johannesburg South Africa. This version is from a recording of the 1930s, courtesy of *Die Tradisionele Boeremusiekklub van S.A.*

Kerrie Bornman (1891-1968) was born near Vereeniging, perhaps twenty miles south of Johannesburg South Africa. Here he plays the **Pietersburg Mazurka**.

The Polka

The next of a string of round dances to migrate out of central Europe was the polka. The dance originated in Bohemia in 1834, the same year in which the German concertina was invented. The polka reached Prague in 1835, Vienna in 1839, and Paris in 1840. *12

It arrived in London in 1844, and by that time was migrating very rapidly. It reached the west of Ireland also in 1844, and arrived in both Australia and South Africa by 1845. Like the *Peppermint Twist* of more than a century later, the polka was a global popular hit, and it inspired worldwide polka mania in areas with European culture.

The characteristic dance rhythm of the polka includes a rise on the anacrusis leading into the bar with three short steps followed by a hop, as in *a-one-two-three-hop, a-one-two-three-hop*. Example popular songs with classic polka dance rhythm are *Little Brown Jug* and *Polly Wolly Doodle*.

Charlie Ordish (left, with mug) and two friends, one with concertina, at camp c.1915, probably on the Upper Murray River. With thanks to Peter Ellis.

In dancing the polka, the man rises on the 'a-' and the couple take three short steps followed by a spring-like hop. Classically, in Australia and South Africa, the spring lies in the ball of the foot and the ankle, although in America it is often danced with great bounding strides as exampled in the film *The King and I*. ✻13 The three-hop rhythm is important to the dance, as originally devised.

 Charlie Ordish (1886-1966) of Corryong, Victoria, Australia, plays a polka with a clear three-hop rhythm, *So Early in the Morning*, on a German concertina.

 Chris Chomse (1891-1978) of Lydenburg, about 150 miles northeast of Johannesburg, South Africa, and his band, *Die Lydenburg Vastrappers*, play the **Bosveld polka**, which has a distinctive three hop rhythm, in a recording of the 1930s. The recording is courtesy of *Die Tradisionele Boeremusiekklub van S.A.*

 In this recording, Willie Palm (b. 1894) of Ficksburg, South Africa and *Die Vier Hugenote* play the **Mampoer Polka**, recorded in the 1930s. The recording is courtesy of *Die Tradisionele Boeremusiekklub van S.A.*

Oxfordshire, England's William Kimber played a number of polkas; *Little Polly*, was a favorite of his. The recording, made in 1951, is courtesy of Topic Records.

The *Heel and Toe Polka* was a very popular round dance in late Victorian England, and there are numerous period references to it in working class haunts. Scan Tester recorded the tune several times. The Heel and Toe Polka was also popular in Australia where, in one variant, according to Ellis, a couple in a waltz hold use a heel and toe step followed by a circular polka half turn.*14 Other varieties of polka collected in Australia include the *Berlin Polka* (an early form, also collected in Donegal, Ireland*15), the *Princess Polka*, the *Nariel Three Hop Polka*, and the Kreuz Polka. Each has its own variation on the footwork and movements; all have classic three-hop rhythm.

Ernie James (1891-1981) of New South Wales, Australia plays the *Berlin Polka*. The recording is courtesy the National Library of Australia.

The polka arrived in Ireland, at least in Kerry, during the same year of 1844 that the polka arrived in England, as described in the following charming period account. A visitor to the Kerry seacoast wrote in her journal:

> *At the spring-tides here, a very fine cave can be entered from the land at low water, and one night we witnessed a novel* soiree dansante *in it ... The outer cave was the selected ball-room, and it was lighted up with torches made of tarred tog-wood stuck into the smooth sand, which threw forth a splendid light, making the shining sides of the caves, which were encrusted with myriads of tiny shell-fish, sparkle with a beautiful effect. The music certainly was not the most select; there was a piper and fiddler and some amateurs who tried alternately the cornet-a-piston and clarionet ... the music, indifferent as it was, and the merry voices and laughter of the gay dancers, and the murmuring of the billows, echoed by multiplied reverberations, made to my ears a most pleasing harmony. The polka had just been introduced into Kerry, and infinite were the pains taken by a laughing girl to teach the air to the fiddler. "Sure I'd learn it soon enough if I'd the notes," and quite satisfied with*

> *himself he played an improvised polka which sounded extremely like an old air the* Rakes of Mallow. *16

Irish polkas today are rhythmically quite different than those of the other three 'concertina countries,' and are used in a distinctly different dancing context. In the nineteenth century, the polka was a popular round dance in Ireland, and there were likely very many local tunes composed for it. These round dance versions survived only in the north of Ireland, with the *Kick Polka* in Fermanagh and the *Berlin Polky* in Donegal. *17

A recording made in the 1970s of Katey Hourican (c.1890-c.1990) of Lough Gowna, County Cavan, not far from the border with Northern Ireland, featured the song-tune polka **Spanish Lady**. Mrs Hourican played a German concertina in the old octave style, and the tune has the distinctive three-hop rhythm of early polkas in England, Australia and South Africa. The recording is courtesy of Comhaltas Ceoltóirí Éireann.

There are typical three hop polkas in the *Roche Collection of Traditional Irish Music* of 1929, in a section of dances of non-Irish origin, indicating that the ordinary polka was well known.

Elsewhere in Ireland, with the suppression of round dances in the early twentieth century (see Chapter 6), the polka was doomed to disappear, much like the mazurka, barn dance and schottische. However, set dancers began to incorporate polka tunes into their sets, as part of an effort to 'Irish-ize' the quadrille with local tunes and dance rhythms. Surviving polka sets were collected in southwestern Kerry and Cork, as well as a single locality in southwestern Limerick, all remote areas. *18

The shuffling steps of the quadrilles, however, were distinctly different than those of the polka, and typically used 'marchy' tunes like single reels and single jigs, at a significantly more rapid tempo. As a result the Irish polkas underwent a rhythmic transformation, largely losing their three-hop DNA in favor of a more *ONE-two-one-two* rhythm, with a first note slightly lengthened and the leading anacrusis of the three-hop polka deleted; this was a better fit with the shuffle steps and battering of the Irish sets/quadrilles, often known as 'Kerry polkas'.

One of many places in Munster where the polka sets were danced was Ardgroom, on the Beara Peninsula of Cork, near the Kerry border.

Ella Mae O'Dwyer (1906-1992) of Athea, West Limerick plays the *Ardgroom Set*, a polka set from that town. She and her husband owned a dance hall there where the sets were prominently danced. Set dancing, always of the local polka set, continued until the hall was closed in the 1950s.*19 (see more on the O'Dwyers in Chapter 8).

These polkas, as played by Mrs O'Dwyer for the sets, display a prominent *ONE-two-one-two* rhythm that is unlike the three-hop rhythm found in polkas as round dances, and is more like a single reel in feel. The recording is courtesy of Neil Wayne and Free Reed Records, who recorded Mrs O'Dwyer in 1974:

Bernard O'Sullivan (d. 2006) of Cooraclare, County Clare claimed that he learned most of his tunes from his mentor, the great Stack Ryan. ***Stack Ryan's Polka***, is played here in the old octave style, and like the previous tune from Mrs O'Dwyer, its rhythm has more of a single-reel rather than three-hop feel, indicating that Ryan (and O'Sullivan) likely played it for sets.

The surviving sets that were collected in County Clare by Larry Lynch*20 do not contain polkas. The recording is courtesy of Neil Wayne and Free Reed Records, who recorded O'Sullivan in 1974.

The assimilation of polka tunes into quadrilles clearly saved a large repertoire of Irish-composed polka tunes from oblivion. Whereas Irish music collectors largely turned up their collective noses at transcribing "foreign" schottisches, mazurkas, waltzes and the like - locally composed or not - Breandan Breathnach made a significant exception for polkas in his landmark *Ceol Rince na hÉireann*, and many of his polkas came from the Munster areas where the polka had been incorporated into sets.

Perhaps because polkas had become so similar to single reels in Irish music, he placed the two into a single category in Volume 2, and called that section of tunes *Polkas, Ríleanna Singil agus Eile* (Polkas, Single Reels and Others) without attempting to classify many in that category as one or the other.

The Schottische

The schottische, another of the folk round dances to come out of central Europe, closely followed the spread of the polka. The first tutor for the German concertina, attributed to Johann Gottlieb Höselbarth, was published in the late 1830s or early 1840s and contained a schottische. Although it is not known why a dance with a clearly German origin carries a Scottish name, it is thought that the Bavarians considered its rhythm to sound somewhat Scottish (something like a strathspey).

By about 1850 this dance and its rhythm had reached Britain, and it most likely reached both Australia and South Africa very soon thereafter. Like the polka, this dance soon developed many forms.

A schottische from Höselbarth's tutor of ca.1837-1840, entitled 'Anweisung das Accordion zu spielen'. The German concertina was known in Germany as a type of accordion until about 1846.

In the schottische, the couple usually assumes a waltz position. In its simplest and earliest version, according to a Mrs Nicholas Henderson of London in her mid-1850s dance manual:

> *'it [has] a very elegant and withal a particularly pleasing movement, for it is a combination of two movements, a polka movement and a circular hop movement; and the two combined make up a most agreeable variety not to be found either in the Polka, the Deux Temps or Redowa.'* * 21

The tempo is variously 2/4 or 4/4, and is marked by a clear lengthening of the notes on the first and third beat.

This dance did not ignite as large a craze as had the earlier polka and waltz, but nonetheless had great staying power in many countries. Its inclusion in the repertoire of an Italian barrel organ that plied the streets of London in the early 1860s provides a good measure of its popularity. Mayhew interviewed the barrel organ's owner, who said that:

Sheet music for an Australian schottische, 1886. Courtesy the National Library of Australia.

> *My organ play eight tunes. Two are from opera, one is a song, one a waltz, one is hornpipe, one is a polka, and the other two is dancing tunes. One is from 'H Lombardi,' of Verdi. All the organs play that piece ... The other opera piece is 'Il Trovatore'... The other piece is English piece, which we call the 'Liverpool Hornpipe'. There is two Liverpool Hornpipe. I know one these twenty years. Then come 'The Ratcatcher's Daughter'; he is a English song. It's get a little old: but when it's first come out the poor people do like it, but the gentlemens they like more the opera, you know. After that is what you call 'Minnie', another English song. He is middling popular. He is not one of the new tune, but they do like it. The next one is a Scotch contre-danse. It is good tunes, but I don't know the name of it. The next one is, I think, a polka; but I think he's made from part of 'Scotische'. There is two or three tunes belongs to the 'Scotische'. The next one is, I think, a valtz of Vienna [note: this is the varsoviana, introduced in 1853]. I don't know which one, but I say to the organ-man, 'I want a valtz of Vienna'; and he say, 'Which one?' because there is plenty of valtz of Vienna. Of course, there is nine of them. After the opera music, the valtz and the polka is the best music in the organ.* * 22

English schottisches played on the concertina have survived mainly through the playing of William Kimber (1872-1961) and Scan Tester (1887-1972), both of whom played for rural house and pub dances.

Kimber's **Moonlight Schottische**, was recorded in 1951 by Peter Kennedy and Maud Karpeles; the recording is courtesy of Topic Records.

Scan Tester knew a variety of *schottisches*, and the one included here was recorded in 1963. The recording is courtesy of Vic Smith and was included in Alan Day's *Anglo International* CD of 2005.

The schottische was danced all over Ireland. According to Helen Brennan:

> *In the north it is generally called the Highland, in Clare and Cavan it was known as the fling, in Cork as the Highland fling and in other areas some variant of 'seteesh' or 'satoosh'. In some areas it is danced to a particular tune and is known by this name. In south Connemara they use Johnny/Love won't you marry me? and it is there known simply as The Johnny.* ∗ 23

Relatively few schottische tunes survived in Ireland after the suppression of round dances. A few were published in Frank Roche's collection. Among older concertina players, especially the old octave-style players, the schottische figured significantly as part of their repertoire for the house dance.

In this example, Katey Hourican (c.1890 - c.1990) of Lough Gawna, County Cavan plays **The Moneymuck** fling (schottische). She was recorded in the 1970s and lived to the age of 103; the recording is courtesy of *Comhaltas Ceoltóirí Éireann*.

Mary Ann Carolan of County Louth knew several schottisches; here is **Lady Mary Ramsay**. The recording is courtesy of Jim Carroll and Jim MacArdle. This tune was originally a Scottish strathspey written by Nathaniel Gow and was published by Scott Skinner.

The schottische was particularly popular in colonial Australia, and there are a great number of recordings of music for this dance, both as a standard schottische as well as a Highland schottische. Here are three; each track is courtesy of the National Library of Australia.

Con Klippel (1909-1975) plays a schottische, ***Grandmother Klippel's***, associated with his grandmother. It is still played and danced to by his descendants in the Nariel Valley of Victoria. The recording is courtesy of his son, Keith Klippel.

George Bennett (1878-1966) plays an old schottische called ***Black Clouds***. The recording is courtesy of the National Library of Australia.

Clem O'Neal (1912-1980), from the old mining town of Iron Bark (now Stuart Town) New South Wales Australia, plays the ***North Wind*** schottische. The recording is courtesy of Bob Bolton and the Bush Music Club of Sydney.

In South Africa, the schottische was equally popular, and is known as the *settees*. It was present in the Cape Colony at least by 1849, when a Miss Woolf, "Professor of Dancing," taught it and a number of other round dances, including the waltz, polka, and Redowa at her studio in Cape Town.*24 Here are three schottisches, all from old 78rpm recordings of the 1930s. The rhythm in each is quite similar to the above European and Australian examples.

Kerrie Bornman (1891-1968) came from De Deur, south of Johannesburg. Here he plays a two-row *boereskonsertina* in a 1930s recording of schottische called ***Oom Tien*** (Uncle Ten). The recording is courtesy of *Die Tradisionele Boeremusiekklub van S.A.*.

Hans Bodenstein (1897-1978) of Benoni, a suburb of Johannesburg, and *Die Vier Vastrappers* play an ***Untitled settees***. The recording is courtesy of *Die Tradisionele Boeremusiekklub van S.A.*.

Silver de Lange (1904-1956) of Vrededorp, another Johannesburg suburb, and *Die Vyf Dagbrekers* play the ***Mielieblare settees*** (Maize Leaves Schottische).

The Barn Dance

The Barn Dance began as an American variation to the plain schottische that was originally called the 'Military Schottische'. It became popular in England and was typically danced to the tune *Dancing in the Barn*, and hence became more popularly known as the

'Barn Dance'. It was popular in all four of the study countries, and is danced to a schottische rhythm, usually a bit faster.

 Englishman William Kimber (1872-1961) plays a barn dance titled *Kitty Come* (the recording is courtesy of Topic Records).

 In Ireland, the *Stack of Barley* was a popular type of barn dance. This version is from the playing of Ella Mae O'Dwyer (1906-1992), courtesy of Neil Wayne and Free Reed Records.

 Hans Bodenstein (1897-1978) and *Die Vier Vastrappers* play a *Barndans met twee konsertinas* (Barn Dance with Two Concertinas). The recording is courtesy of *Die Tradisionele Boeremusiekklub van S.A.*

The Galop

The Galup. From a middle nineteenth century music cover.

The galop (or galup) was a popular final dance of an evening. A Hungarian dance, it was a forerunner to the polka. It was initiated in European ballrooms in 1822, and reached England about 1829. The music for a galop is typically played in rapid 2/4 time. A couple in waltz position executes gliding steps that mimic a galloping horse, and the dance could also include smooth but rapid whirling waltz turn steps.

It was one of the more exciting ballroom dances to execute, and yet one of the easiest to learn. The *William Tell Overture* of Rossini is a galop, as is Offenbach's *Can Can* and the old time American tune *Ta Ra Ra Boom De Ay*. In modern Australia, the galop is danced as a modified two-step.[25]

 Here, Con Klippel (1909-1975) of Nariel, Victoria plays the *Manchester Galop.* In this dance the galop steps and waltz turns are used, but to a tune with more of a schottische tempo. The recording is courtesy of Keith Klippel.

The Varsoviana

The varsoviana was originally a Scandinavian folk dance, but its ballroom adaptation was linked with Poland in 1850 as a show of support against Russian oppression; its title is said to be a corruption of the Polish words for 'woman of Warsaw'. It is a slow round dance in 3/4 time. A couple in waltz position executes dance elements taken from the waltz, mazurka and polka (or Redowa).

Mid-nineteenth century sheet music for 'The Celebrated Varsovienne'. Varsovienne is the French form of the word Varsoviana.

Popular throughout Europe, North America and in British colonies in the 1860s and 1870s, the dance had declined by the late nineteenth century except in colonial Australia, where it remained popular well into the twentieth century in rural areas like the Nariel valley of Victoria. John Meredith collected a large number of varsovianas in the Australian bush.

It does not appear to have been popular in twentieth century South Africa with the Boers, as evidenced by a dearth of recorded examples. The global tune *Happy Birthday* was reportedly adapted from an old varsoviana tune.

The quintessential varsoviana tune is globally known by traditional musicians to this day. In America its tune is known as *Put Your Little Foot*, in Ireland as *Shoe the Donkey* or *Father Halpin's Top Coat*; in Australia it is irreverently called **Kick Your Leg Up, Sal Brown** or, more politely, *Poor Babes in the Wood*.

Clem O'Neal (1912-1980) of New South Wales, Australia, plays this global tune in the old octave style in this recording, which is courtesy of Bob Bolton and the Bush Music Club of Sydney.

Australia is rich in varsoviana tunes, and the dance seems to have remained popular much longer in the bush dance music tradition.

This **Varsoviana** from George Bennett (1878-1966) shows similarities to the arch-typical original version. The recording is courtesy of the National Library of Australia.

Here is another example, the ***Turn Around and Then Stop*** varsoviana, from Charlie Ordish (d.1966) of Victoria. The recording is courtesy of the National Library of Australia.

The March

It may seem odd to think of the march as a dance type, but marches were part of many evenings of ballroom dance, at least when held in a woolshed, barn or hall large enough to accommodate one. Marches, of course, have military origins, and usually are written in 4/4, 2/2, or 6/8 time to accompany the footsteps of soldiers. In popular culture, march tunes have been used for street protests as well as for ceremony - for coronations and the like but also for processional Grand Marches at balls, even in rural areas.

The Grand March was used to promenade the dancers onto the dance floor, getting them in place for the first set of quadrilles. Such a promenade could be either short and functional at a barn dance or elegantly long at a fancy dress ball, with pairs of couples arm in arm executing figures in long columns around the dance floor. The latter type of Grand March can still be seen at the large masked ball held each year at the National Folk Festival in Canberra Australia.

Many popular songs were used as march tunes, such as the *Minstrel Boy* in Ireland, or *Golden Slippers* almost anywhere. In British colonial settings, such as in Australia, a string of national airs from various parts of the Empire might be used (for example, *Rule Britannia, Scotland the Brave, Men of Harlech*, etc).

Ella Mae O'Dwyer (1906-1992) of Athea, West Limerick, Ireland, plays an **Untitled March**. In Chapter 11, there is a recording of another of her marches, played by her son Sean O'Dwyer.

Mary Ann Carolan (1902-1985) of The Hill of Rath, County Louth, Ireland, plays **Napoleon's March**.

Fred Kilroy (ca.1910 - ca.1976) of Royton, Lancashire, England, plays *Blaze Away*, an American march tune written in 1901 that was popular both in England and in Australia, where it was used as a promenade tune. In Kilroy's Lancashire as well as in northern Ireland there is a long-standing tradition of concertina bands that play march tunes in street processions.

Notes:

1. Breandan Breathnach, Tús an Poirt in Éireann (The origin of the jig in Ireland), Irish Folk Music Studies, vol. 1 (1972-1973).

2. Helen Brennan, 1999, The Story of Irish Dance: Brandon, Dingle, County Kerry, Ireland, pp.22-23.

3. Breandan Breathnach, 1971, Folk Music and Dances of Ireland: Mercier Press, Dublin, p.47.

4. Scan Tester, as quoted in Reg Hall, 1990, I Never Played to Many Posh Dances: Musical Traditions supplement No. 2, p.77.

5. Peter Ellis, 2005, The Merrie Country Dance: Bendigo Dance and Music Club, Victoria Australia.

6. Peter Ellis, 2005, The Merrie Country Dance: Bendigo Dance and Music Club, Victoria Australia; and 2007, The Waltz, the Polka, and All Kinds of Dance Music, same publisher.

7. Peter Ellis, 2005, The Merrie Country Dance: Bendigo Dance and Music Club, Victoria Australia, p.B103, and Helen Brennan, 1999, The Story of Irish Dance: Brandon Press, Dingle Ireland, p.99.

8. Wilhelm Schultz, 2001, Die Ontstaan en Ontwikkeling van Boeremusiek (The Origin and Evolution of Boer music): A.V.A. Systems, Pretoria, p.107.

9. Elizabeth Grant and Andrew Todd, 1992, Memoirs of a Highland Lady: Canongate, U.S., p.47.

10. Frank Roche, 1929, The Roche Collection of Traditional Irish Music, republished in 1982 by Ossian Publications, Cork.

11. Peter Ellis, 2005, p.E35.

12. eg., see Wikipedia entry, Polka.

13. Peter Ellis, 2005, p.E34.

14. Peter Ellis, 2005, p.E23.

15. Grace Orphen, 1931, Dances of Donegal: London, D.M. Wilkie, pp.31.

16. Catherine O'Connell, Excursions in Ireland During 1844 and 1850, With a Visit to the Late Daniel O'Connell, M.P. (London: Richard Bentley Co., 1852) pp.47-48.

17. Helen Brennan, 1999, The Story of Irish Dance: Brandon, Dingle, County Kerry, Ireland, p.101.

18. Larry Lynch, 1991, Set Dances of Ireland, Traditions & Evolution: Séadna Books, San Francisco p.147.

19. Ibid., p.147.

20. Larry Lynch, 1989, Set Dances of Ireland: Tradition and Evolution: Séadna Books, San Francisco, p.324.

21. Henderson, Mrs Nicholas, Etiquette of the Ball-Room and Guide to all the New and Fashionable Dances. 3rd ed., London, n.d. (c.1854). Also, Henderson, Mrs Nicholas, 'Instructions for Dancing the Schottisch' on sheet music 'The Hungarian Schottische'. London, n.d. (mid-1850s?). With thanks to www.kickery.com

22. Henry Mayhew, 1861, London labour and the London poor: London, Griffin, Bohn and Co., p.178.

23. Helen Brennan, 1999, p.100.

24. Wilhelm Schultz, 2001, p.28.

25. Peter Ellis, 2005, p.E18.

Chapter 5. A global music

As we have seen in the preceding examples, each type of ballroom dance typically emerged from central Europe as a folk dance that migrated to high society European ballrooms from which it quickly spread throughout Europe. By the middle of the nineteenth century, music and dance instruction books accompanied new dances, allowing each new dance and its original accompanying tune to spread as quickly as a ship could sail or steam to Britain and its colonies. British military brass bands played a key role in popularizing the new dance music for illiterate street musicians; these bands would play both at the balls of the wealthy and in public parks.

The 'original' tunes for each new dance were usually based on the style of the tune of the original folk or national dance; many of these became globally known. The universal varsoviana tune highlighted at the end of Chapter 4, *Put Your Little Foot/Shoe the Donkey/Kick Your Leg Up Sal Brown,* is a good example of such a 'global' tune. In places like England and Ireland where the varsoviana dance faded with time, only this original version is still remembered in the folk tradition.

In Australia, where the dance lingered until the present day in the rural bush, there are many different versions of varsoviana tunes known among traditional musicians. This longevity of varsoviana dancing allowed time for local variations of the original tune to mutate, and for completely original versions to be composed. Some of these versions, like George Bennett's varsoviana in Chapter 4, above, are partly to largely similar to the original tune. Others, like Charlie Ordish's varsoviana tune (also in Chapter 4), seem completely new, and different.

Clem O'Neal described the process by which such tunes mutated in the Australian bush. According to O'Neal, the primary source of new tunes in his younger days was from people returning from trips, and the modifications of the 'folk' process started then:

> *The only way things was, was that someone would go away on a shearing trip and he'd remember part of a music, part of something. He'd have to keep it in his head; when he came back perhaps he'd remember only part of it. So to make up a dance tune, he'd probably remember parts of three bits of different things which someone had played in a town or somewhere or other, and he'd combine them together. Someone else would hear him play that, and eventually new tunes got created from one listening to the other and these seemed to go right up and down some twenty or thirty miles along the river.* [1]

There were many, many dance varieties of polkas and schottisches, and each had its own steps and its own signature tune. A modern day parallel would be the *Charleston*, or perhaps some of the rock and roll dances of the 1960s, when the *Twist*, the *Swim*, the *Frug*, and the *Monkey* were globally distributed and known to teenagers in much of the English-speaking world.

Today, nearly half a century later, it is sometimes difficult to remember the tune that fits the dance, or vice versa. Such is even more the case with those tunes that were played a century farther back in time. Polkas surviving in the Australian dance tradition include the *Berlin Polka*, the *Kreuz Polka*, the *Plain Polka*, the *Princess*

Polka, and the *Heel and Toe Polka*. Some of these polkas, like the *Heel and Toe*, were global dances with global tunes; Scan Tester played a variant of the *Heel and Toe* in Sussex, for example.

The global nature of much of this dance music is not always apparent today. Sussex musician Scan Tester (1887-1972), and Dooley Chapman (1892-1982) of New South Wales, were both rural working-class men who played professionally for dances. Both held high stature amongst traditional musicians in their day, but neither travelled outside of their home continent. In their youth there was little or no radio, and they were separated by twelve thousand miles of ocean. Nonetheless, both share an obscure polka tune to which neither could ascribe a title.

Here is Dooley Chapman's version of this **untitled polka**; the recording is courtesy of Chris Sullivan.

And here is Scan Tester's version of the same **untitled polka**; the recording was made by Reg Hall and is courtesy of Topic Records.

Most likely, this polka was once popular, perhaps with its own signature steps, but one that has faded a century later. It has affinities in its A part with the Irish song *Bog Down in the Valley*, and with the tune that accompanies the old Thomas Moore poem *Oft in the Stilly Night*, but it varies significantly in the B part relative to both of these.

Popular songs and music hall tunes

Popular and sentimental songs from both American and British music hall sources were heavily mined for waltz and quadrille tunes, many of which remained popular for many decades.

Break the News to Mother, a song in waltz tempo about a message from a dying soldier of the Spanish-American War, was played by George Bennett (1878-1966) in Australia. It was written in 1897 by Charles K Harris, a commercial New York songwriter and 'King of the Tear-Jerker', whose biggest hit was *After the Ball*, another concertina standard of the day. George Bennett was in his nineties when recorded by his family in the 1960s. The recording is courtesy of the National Library of Australia.

George Bennett also played *All Smiles Tonight*, which was written by American T B Ranson in 1879 and popularized in country and western recordings of the early twentieth century. *All Smiles Tonight* also made it into South Africa, where Boer concertina players know it as *Die Kalfie Wals* (The Calf Waltz). The recording is courtesy of the National Library of Australia.

In South Africa, Faan Harris (1886-1950) recorded the popular ***Wals van Tant Sannie*** (Aunt Sannie's Waltz) in the 1930s; it is a rename of the *Shannon Waltz*, an American tune first recorded in the 1920s by the East Texas Serenaders, and was taken from an itinerant fiddler known only as Mr Briggs. The recording of Harris and *Die Vier Transvalers* is courtesy of *Die Tradisionele Boeremusiekklub van S.A.*

Another yet more global nineteenth century song is the Irish-American sentimental song *Eileen Alannah*, composed in 1873 by American composer John Rogers Thomas. In South Africa, a beautiful recording of ***Eileen Alannah*** was made by Faan Harris and *Die Vier Transvalers* in the 1930s. The recording is courtesy of *Die Tradisionele Boeremusiekklub van S.A.*

This song was popularized by Irish tenor John McCormack, and the tune found its way into the 1929 *Roche Collection of Traditional Irish Music* as an old-time waltz. In Britain, it became the slow regimental march of the Royal Innskilling Fusiliers, now the Royal Irish Rangers, and was popularized in this century by accordionist Jimmy Shand. In Australia, it was a popular old-time waltz played by Con Klippel and others in the Nariel Valley, and found its way into the book of Nariel traditional dance music, *Music Makes Me Smile*.* 2

Another American hit tune that was popular with concertina players on several continents was *Two Little Girls in Blue*, written in 1893 by American composer Charles Graham and re-used for a 1921 Broadway musical comedy of that name, and here played by George Bennett. In Sussex, Scan Tester played the tune with his *Tester's Imperial Jazz Band*, and during the English Country Music surge of the 1970s it was again recorded by the English band *Flowers and Frolics*.

In Australia, ***Two Little Girls in Blue*** was part of George Bennett's repertoire: this recording of his version is courtesy of the National Library of Australia.

British Music Hall hits also had legs. The 1928 song, ***All By Yourself in the Moonlight***, was played by Clem O'Neal in Australia (the recording is courtesy of Sydney Bush Music Club and Bob Bolton). The tune was written by British songwriter Ralph Butler (1884-1969) under the pseudonym Jay Wallis.

Starry Night for a Ramble, which Australian Dooley Chapman played as the ***Starry Night Waltz***, also seems to have originated in the London halls, and is first known from a broadsheet published there in 1854.

Harry Thompson, a popular performer in the British Music Hall, with Anglo-German concertina, 1909. Thompson appeared under the stage name Harry Tomps and was the father of concertinist and Music Hall performer Peter Honri. From Percy Honri's Working the Halls, 1973.

Such tunes were despised by the Gaelic League, which had much loftier (and more nationalistic) cultural goals. A 1908 member had this to say of Ireland, the concertina and the Irish peasant:

> *They were at one time the most musical nation when a harp hung in every house, but now they had got down to the concertina and melodeon, and even to the mouth organ. They had thrown away the music of their great composers for the abortions and abominations of the English music halls, which if they had any sense at all had an immoral sense that any man would be ashamed of.* [3]

Old time concertina players appear to have had less shame than many.

The minstrel shows

Perhaps the most widespread source of new tunes in the nineteenth century global repertoire were the American minstrel shows. The shows themselves took Europe by storm in the mid-nineteenth century, as well as far-flung colonies like Australia, New Zealand and South Africa.

The German concertina and the American banjo were featured instruments. Each evening's entertainment was comprised of lively dances and sentimental songs laced with raucous racially-charged humor, organized in what later became known as a variety show format.

The shows were performed at first by traveling American troupes but later by homegrown British, Irish, Australian, New Zealand, and even Boer 'Christy minstrel bands'.

A blackface minstrel show in London, late nineteenth century. Such shows were rowdy, musically varied, and hugely popular for decades around the globe.

*Soldiers in a 'Christy minstrel' group, Opunake New Zealand, 1876.
Note the 'end men' in garish garb; these were the jokesters of the show.
Also note the central placement of the musician with the German concertina.*

Some of the tunes played by concertina players in this archive have titles that clearly identify them as minstrel tunes.

Dooley Chapman (1892-1982) of Coborrah, New South Wales Australia, played **Old Dan Tucker**, a comic minstrel tune with words reportedly written by early minstrel leader Dan Emmett (the recording is courtesy of Chris Sullivan).

An instant hit after its introduction in 1843 by Emmett's Virginia Minstrels, it tells the story of a black man who finds himself in a strange town, fighting and getting drunk. The tune that Dooley Chapman plays has morphed a bit since leaving America, but was commonly played in Australia; George Bennett played a similar tune called *Old Man Tucker*.

The origin of other minstrel tunes has been hidden by the addition of new titles at some point in their history. Such seems also to be the case with present-day Clare concertina player Chris Droney's version of *The Blue Gentian Waltz*, which he played on a Free Reed records release of 1974, *The Flowing Tide*. This waltz seems to have been learned from Chris Droney's father, Jim Droney, whose music is featured in Chapter 9 of this archive. *The Blue Gentian* is the name of an Irish wildflower, but that may not have been the first title of this waltz.

The tune is nearly identical in its 'A' part to a tune very popular in Australia among traditional musicians, ***Why Did My Master Sell Me***. This version is from Jim Harrison (1911-c.2000) of Khancoban, New South Wales, on concertina, playing with Neville Simpson on accordion. It was recorded in 1982; courtesy of the National Library of Australia.

The tune was tune was originally a popular American abolitionist tune about the evils of slavery, which was appropriated as a tear-jerker by the minstrel shows and as a hymn-tune by the Salvationists. The original song was written at least by 1852, because Catherine Booth (Herbert Booth's mother) wrote about hearing it sung in the streets of London that year.

> *Oh! I have lost my Dinah, away down Carolina,*
> *O, tell me where to find her, Alas! she's gone away.*
> *My master he does scourge me, and oft to work does urge me,*
> *And Dinah's freedom forg'd he, upon our wedding day.*
> *Chorus:*
> *O, why did my master sell me? Why did master sell me?*
> *Why did master sell me, Upon my wedding day?* * 4

A number of traditional musicians in Australia were recorded playing this song, and it became a popular waltz tune.

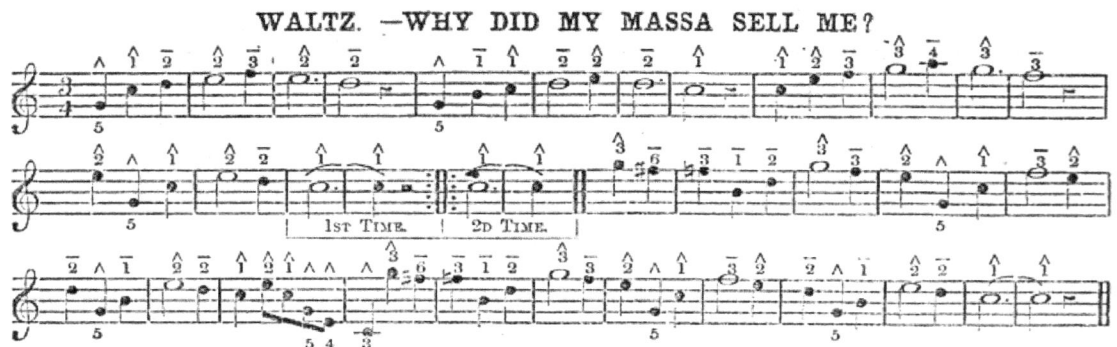

Sheet music for Why Did My Massa Sell Me?, an American abolitionist song, from Dance Music for the Concertina, published in Glasgow in 1864. The song was spread by the minstrel shows and found its way to some far corners of the world.

The most universally known of the minstrel tunes among concertina players were those of Stephen Foster. Some of the song tunes spread by the minstrel shows (which are included in dozens of nineteenth century concertina tutors and tune books published in Britain and the USA) include *The Old Folks at Home*, *Camptown Races*, *Oh Susannah!*, *Beautiful Dreamer*, *Old Black Joe*, and *Jeannie with the Light Brown Hair*. It is perhaps safe to say that nearly all concertina players in late nineteenth century England, Australia and Ireland could play, hum or sing many if not all of these tunes. Susan Colley (1881-1976), a singer and concertina player of rural Duramana New South Wales, could sing all of these as well as other minstrel favorites like *Nellie Grey, Lily Dale, Massa's in de Cold Cold Ground, Old Kentucky Home*, and *I'se Going Back to Dixie.* * 5

In England, good social dance tunes were always in high demand for Morris dancing, and minstrel shows provided a wealth of possibilities. In Lancashire, the village of Royton's Morris team used Stephen Foster's minstrel tune *Oh Susannah*.

Ellis Marshall (1906-1993) and fellow concertina player Norman Coleman, along with some drummers, played for the Royton men's Morris team at an exhibition dance at the St Paul's Working Men's Institute in 1979, using a medley of tunes they had played in previous decades with the side. The medley included bits of Foster's **Oh, Susannah**, as well as the traditional English single reel **Brighton Camp** (aka *The Girl I Left Behind Me*), as well as a **Cross-Morris** dance tune. The recording is courtesy of Ellis's grandson, Tony Marshall.

At nearby Manley, concertina player Caleb Walker also used *Oh, Susannah!* for the local Morris, although he called it *Banjo on My Knee*: "It's a good tune - nearly all those American tunes fit - you could pick half a dozen out that'd fit it a treat." * 6

In Headington Quarry, Oxfordshire, William Kimber (1872-1961) played **Getting Upstairs** for the Headington Quarry side. It was recorded by Kimber in 1935, and is courtesy of the English Folk Dance and Song Society.

American Joe Blackburn wrote this tune for blackface minstrelsy in the 1830s and published it under the title *Such a Getting Upstairs*.* 7 It is not clear that folk music and dance collector Cecil Sharp realized that *Getting Upstairs* was a former minstrel tune when he noted the tune and accompanying dance, and included it in his 1919 collection of classic English Morris dances.

Notes:

1. Clem O'Neal, interviewed in *Concertina Magazine*, Australia, 1982.

2. Peter Ellis and Harry Gardiner, 1998, *Music Makes Me Smile: a Tribute to Con Klippel and the Music of the Nariel Valley*: Carrawobbity Press, Albion Park NSW, 228p.

3. *The Anglo-Celt* (Cavan), April 18, 1908.

4. From an 1850s broadsheet, for sale on an internet site.

5. Percy J Gresser, 1965, *The Songs They Sang - and - the Dance Tunes They Played*. Copies of Gresser's extensive manuscript and list of songs recorded from Mrs Colley were sent to the archives of the Bush Music Club of Sydney, as well as to the Wild Colonial Days Society of New South Wales. I am grateful to Bob Bolton for a copy of this work.

6. Derek Schofield, 'Concertina Caleb', (1970s).

7. Rhett Krause, 'Morris Dancing and America Prior to 1913', *American Morris Newsletter* 25, no.4, (2005).

Chapter 6. A harvest lost: the banning of house dancing in early twentieth century Ireland

In preceding chapters some mention has been made of the contrast between the repertoire of music as it was played by Irish concertina players in the house dance era, and music as it is played by young Irish concertina players today.

In this chapter we will examine the changes that happened to Irish music in the early twentieth century, and why the modern Irish traditional repertoire is so different not only from that of the Irish concertina players of the house dance era, but from the repertoire of traditional musicians in all other countries where the concertina was played in its heyday.

If we look at the sum total of the recorded legacy of three Irish women who played the concertina in the house dance era and compare it with the recorded legacy to date of three modern Irish women who play the concertina, a stark contrast emerges. The graphs on the next page show a count of tunes by dance type for these three old time players:

Mary Ann Carolan (1902-1985), who played for house dances in The Hill of Rath in rural County Louth in the second decade of the twentieth century, and then stopped playing for over sixty years; Ella Mae O'Dwyer (1906-1992), who played for house dances in her youth and later for dances at her family's dance hall in rural Ardgroom, County Cork in the early twentieth century; and Katey Hourican (ca.1890-ca.1990) of Lough Gowna, County Cavan, of whom little is known, but who was of the same generation as the previous two women.* 1

Together, these women left recordings of 57 tunes, all made in the middle to late twentieth century. As young women, they played in the last decades of the house dance era, well before the House Dance Act of 1935. All played the German concertina.

A second part of the graph shows a count of tune types by dance for the current repertoire of three well known modern Irish women who play the concertina. Claire Keville, of Claran, County Galway; Edel Fox of Miltown Malbay, County Clare; and Dympna O'Sullivan of Lissycasey, County Clare were all born in the late twentieth century, nearly a century after the earlier three women listed above. All play the Anglo concertina. Each has issued either one or two CDs in the first decade of the twenty-first century. A total of 120 recorded tunes were counted from these recordings.* 2

Of course, neither graph captures the entirety of the repertoires of any of these six women, but perhaps it captures the general essence of the music they mostly preferred/prefer to play.

THE CHANGING IRISH REPERTOIRE

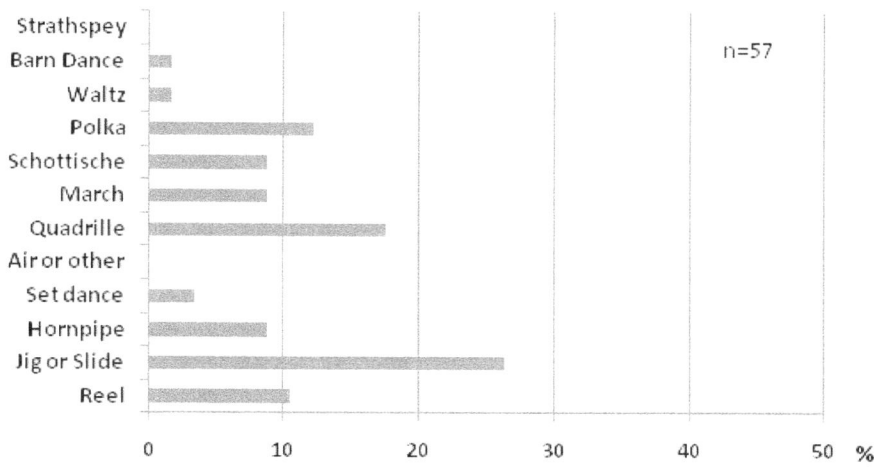

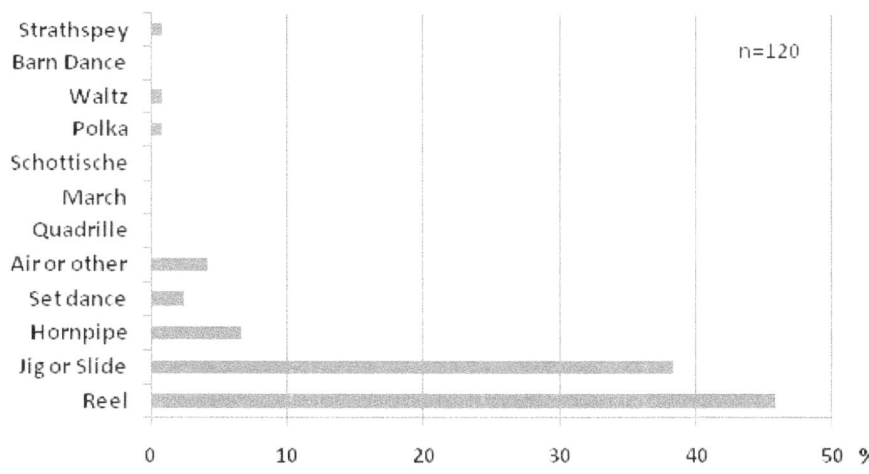

Top: the recorded repertoire of three women concertina players of the house dance era, by dance type: Mary Ann Carolan, Ella Mae O'Dwyer, and Katey Hourican. *Bottom:* the recorded repertoire (CDs to date) for three modern day women concertina players. Dance types are shown by percentage. The chart shows that the house dance favorites (schottisches, quadrilles, polkas, waltzes) of the early players are absent in the repertoires of modern players, to an extent not seen in the traditional music of the other three countries studied.

The differences are very clear. Over the past 80 years or more there has been a great narrowing of focus in the repertoire of Irish musicians - especially concertina players. This change in repertoire favors the step dance music of largely pre-Famine origin (primarily reels and jigs) to the near-exclusion of the many dances of the late nineteenth and early twentieth century house dance era: quadrille tunes, schottisches/flings, polkas, mazurkas, marches, waltzes and barn dances.

But is it traditional music? A concertina and a banjo playing for round dances, England 1890s.

This abrupt change in repertoire has occurred among musicians all over Ireland, including the Gaeltacht of the west, leaving a gap in the modern Irish repertoire relative to that of the other countries in this study, where the repertoire of 'traditional' dance music played today in Australia, England and South Africa is not particularly different in its mix of dance types than that once played by Carolan, O'Dwyer and Hourican.

The story of what happened to early ballroom dance music in Ireland, after a half century of suppression and banishment by clerical, patriotic and government groups, is an important one, not just historically and sociologically, but because of the strong impact it had on concertina playing, both on the repertoire played and on the playing styles employed.

It is safe to say that when house dances were banned in Ireland, the concertina nearly died out too - along with most locally composed Irish ballroom dance tunes. If we rejoice in the great nineteenth century collections of Irish music (O'Neill's work has been called *A Harvest Saved* ✳ 3) then we must also consider the harvest of locally composed square and round dance music that was lost, never to be recorded by collectors and their recording machines.

Gaelic heritage under threat, late nineteenth century

After the national tragedy of the Great Famine in the 1840s, the pace of Anglicization of language in Ireland - the growth in the use of the English language over the native Irish tongue - increased dramatically. Whereas Ireland before the famine was mostly Irish-speaking in all areas except for Dublin and its surrounding environs, by 1870 it was predominantly Irish speaking only in the western half of the country.* 4

By the early twentieth century the only remnant Irish-speaking areas were in small enclaves, mostly in western Kerry, Galway, Donegal, and Mayo. These areas constitute the *Gaeltacht,* which has a similar outline today. The change was enormous, not only for the language, but also for the culture that went with it, including music and dance.

The great Chicago collector Francis O'Neill began his collecting of Irish music as he lamented the loss of the Gaelic songs sung by his mother in his youth, before the Famine. He noted that 'Where a generation ago a wealth of folk music was the common possession of the peasantry, now scarcely a fraction of it is remembered'.* 5

O'Neill built his music collection from the memories of immigrant pipers and fiddlers in Chicago, the last remnants of the old pre-Famine Irish patronage system with its wandering professional musicians. They left during and after the Famine, as there was little money left in rural areas for such luxuries as professional musicians.

The German concertina came to Ireland during this time of great cultural change, and because it was inexpensive and easy to learn it helped fill the gap left by departing professional musicians. This instrument, along with the button accordion and the mouth harp, accompanied an invasion of ballroom dances from central Europe: a popular craze, that had global dimensions.

The 1867 dance book of Dundalk resident Kate Hughes contains instructions for eight sets of quadrilles and eight set dances 'of quadrille type', including Caledonians, Lancers, mazurka quadrilles, and waltz cotillons. There were also instructions for some 54 English-style country dances. The dance book only contains instructions for only two reels.* 6

As Breandan Breathnach noted, 'Before the end of the last [nineteenth] century the sets and half sets had pervaded the country and had completely ousted the old solo dances, jigs, reels and hornpipes, and the group dances based on them...'*7

And then there were the round dances. As Helen Brennan notes:

> *Apart from the sets, the most popular new dances in the nineteenth century were the ballroom dances such as the schottische, the barndance, the military two-step and the waltz, which became the dance practice of all classes of [Irish] society. When they reached the areas where traditional dance was strong, they were absorbed into the repertoire and subtly changed by the effects of Irish 'stepping' and local musical taste.**8

Not only did the concertina accompany these imported ballroom dances in their conquest of Irish culture, it was also used to play music from the ever-popular minstrel shows and music halls, along with the banjo. Traditionalists and Irish nationalists connected these two instruments and the global music and dance styles that they promoted with the wave of Anglicization that was sweeping away the old Gaelic language from the countryside. In response to this shockingly rapid Anglicization and consequent loss of culture, Douglas Hyde and Eoin MacNeill founded the Gaelic League in 1893. Its goal, as related by historian Donal McCartney, was:

An Irish dancing class in New York, 1905. The dancers are learning the 'Irish quadrille', at a time when the quadrille was being banned as 'foreign' back in Ireland. From the American Memory collection, Library of Congress.

> [T]o keep Irish alive where it was still spoken, and later, to restore Irish as the spoken language of the country. By giving up our native language and customs, said Hyde, we had thrown away the best claim which we had upon the world's recognition of us as a separate nation. Therefore the task facing the present generation of Irishmen was the re-creation of a separate cultural Irish nation, and this could only be done by what Hyde called de-

Anglicization - refusing to imitate the English in their language, literature, music, games, dress and ideas. * 9

Both the nationalists and the more culturally-oriented members of the Gaelic League took square aim at the concertina and banjo, as well as the "foreign" dance music that was played on them. As this nationalistic observer wrote in 1894:

Since the Union, Ireland has shuffled off her ancient language, with its thousand years of history and its striking imaginative literature, with almost indecent haste. She has neglected the priceless treasure of her ancient national music, and her western peasantry sing the music hall songs of London. The Irish harp and the Irish pipes have given way to the banjo and the concertina. The people have even in thousands of cases changed their names, lest any trace of their Celtic nationality should cling to them. * 10

A group of farmers and townspeople from Athea, Co Limerick, celebrating the potato harvest, 1911. Several on the right are preparing boxty for the party, and a concertinist (May Nan Stevens) is ready to play for the dance that would accompany the celebration. With thanks to the National Folklore Collection, University College Dublin, and to Sean O'Dwyer and Nora Hurley.

A decade later in 1906 music collector Francis O'Neill returned for the first time to the Ireland of his youth, noting that:

A six week's trip through Munster and Leinster ... after an absence of forty years, disclosed nothing which afforded much evidence of a musical regeneration. Not a piper or a fiddler was encountered at the five fairs attended, and but one ballad singer. The competitors at the Feis at Cork and at Dublin were amateurs, except one or two fluters. Their very best performers on any instrument at either Feis are easily outclassed (by émigrés) here in Chicago. * 11

The pipers and fiddlers had largely emigrated, but the music scene was not as depleted as O'Neill let on. Ireland was at this time at the very peak of both the concertina's heyday and the ballroom dances' popularity.

It was a time, as many people have reported, that nearly every cottage had a concertina or an accordion. And as Helen Brennan noted (above), ballroom dance was at the peak of its popularity in all parts of the country.

O'Neill observed little 'music' in Ireland on his 1906 trip, mainly because he did not think of the ubiquitous ballroom-style popular music and dance that surrounded him as at all 'Irish.' He and those in the like-minded Gaelic League considered ballroom dances, and the concertina and banjo, as abominations, and the ruin of Gaelic Ireland.

Country people, including those in the Gaeltacht, saw this somewhat differently, and voted with their feet. Witness the recollections of Patrick Flynn, of rural Loughrea in County Galway:

> *My first dance was at a wedding in 1909. It was in a big barn with a good concrete floor and two oil lamps gave light. There was one melodeon and three men and a girl played it in turn. The rule seemed to be a different dance after the last one. They danced Quadrilles or as it was called, the Plain set and the Reel set. The Lancers, which seemed to require more skill, was danced once or twice. After each set, a polka was danced and partners were changed. Then a Fling [schottische], danced in pairs, the Military Two-Step, sets again, and then the Valeta Waltz. There was no M.C. [Master of Ceremonies]. The music seemed to regulate what the next dance would be. When there was a lull, somebody called for a song ...*
>
> *Dances were mostly held in farm kitchens ... Waltz, Polka, and Lancers were the thing. Reel sets were for the lesser breeds, without the law.* * 12

In the above account, two very new dances (the 1900 *Valeta Waltz* and the 1904 *Military Two-Step*) show that Irish dancers were, like their counterparts elsewhere, eager to keep up with the latest fashions. European ballroom dances had by that time been fully integrated into house dances, and were comfortably danced alongside older forms of step-dancing; all were part of an evening's fun.

A Ballivor, County Meath woman remembered the dances of her youth, at this same time in the first decade of the twentieth century:

> *The actual dances were chiefly sets [quadrilles] or more usually half-sets except there was a lot of room and a big crowd. Now and then there was a set of Lancers and now and then some of the men did a step dance - jig, reel, or hornpipe - and I remember some of the old people - a man and two women - doing a three-hand reel. I remember a man who lived near us who had worked for some time in the "North" (south Armagh) and he always did a special dance across a long straw on the floor. There was also a dance called by us a "Seteesh" [schottische]. Also, the Waltz was coming in and one or two could do the Military Two-Step. There were always songs between dances at any dance.* [13]

The war of the clergy

The dominance of these ballroom dance styles over older, pre-Famine reels and jigs had caused resentment by moralists and Gaelic nationalists for decades. A key element of moral concern was the clutch-hold of the waltz and other round and square dances, which contrasted so vividly with the relative lack of touch between sexes in the older forms of Irish step dance. Many although not all village priests took direct action against this perceived moral problem, as in the following descriptions, the first from 1912:

> *The heart and spirit gave way in a sort of terrorism before the priest. In his day of dominance, he did much to make Irish local life a dreary desert. He made war on the favourite cross-roads dances - with exceptions here and there - and on other gatherings where young men and women congregated in the company of their older relations and friends.* [14]

> *Wooden road-side [dancing] platforms were set on fire by curates; surer still, the priests drove their cars backwards and forwards over the timber platforms; concertinas were*

> *sent flying into hill streams and those who played music at dances were branded as outcasts.* *15

In 1924, the Bishop of Galway railed about house dances, where imported 'foreign' dances were featured, and about the young women who flocked to them, often staying out very late:

> *The dances indulged in were not the clean, healthy, national Irish dances. They were, on the contrary, importations from the vilest dens of London, Paris and New York, direct and unmistakable incitements to evil thought and evil desires.* *16

> *Fathers of this parish, if your girls do not obey you, if they are not in at the hour appointed, lay the lash upon their backs. That was the good old system and that should be the system to-day.* *17

Lenten pastoral sermons in 1925 took up the call, recognizing a distinction between Irish dances and 'degenerate' foreign dances:

> *It is no small commendation of Irish dances that they cannot be danced for long hours. That however, is not their chief merit, and while it is no part of our business to condemn any decent dance, Irish dances are not to be put out of the place that is their due, in any educational establishment under our care. They may not be in the fashion in London or Paris. They should be in fashion in Ireland. Irish dances do not make degenerates.* *18

The Gaelic League and the government abolish the house dance

At first, the new Gaelic League was primarily an Irish language organization, but it soon turned its attention to dance as a result of developments in its London branch. The largely middle class, white-collar membership there had little idea of what constituted Irish dancing, and apparently had little first-hand knowledge of the house dance culture in the Gaeltacht.

When a Scottish dance group performed at the League's first ever *céilí* in 1897, it caused a bit of cultural envy within the League. A

Kerryman living in London stepped forward to teach League members some long dances and eight hand reels that he had known in Kerry. When the London branch brought the dances to the Dublin branch in 1901, a hot debate ensued on whether those Kerry dances were really 'Irish' dances, and also whether or not the ballroom-style round and square dances should be banned as non-Irish. An acid-tongued Mayo dancer wrote in 1904:

> *Those figure dances were brought to Dublin from London and the city of Limerick and foisted on the Gaelic League as genuinely Irish by some enterprising individuals who saw ... the opportunity of making money ... The apostles of the figure dances urge them as substitutes and antidotes for the round and square dances. But in this way they are perfectly wrong. Their figure dances are jumbles of the quadrilles, the polka, the lancers - the very ones they want to avoid.* * 19

The end result of a very lengthy and acrimonious debate was that a Commission for Irish Dancing was formed in 1927 to regulate dance throughout Ireland. It held competitions and formulated dance books of approved dances, and these completely excluded the waltzes, schottisches, polkas and set dances of the country people. Instead, people were urged to support the new *céilí* dances, which included both eight hand reels and the line and circle country dances that either descended from Kerry remnants or were newly minted (*The Waves of Tory, The Siege of Ennis,* etc.).

Music collector Frank Roche, who alone among Irish music collectors of that era made room for some of the old ballroom dances in his collections of Irish music, observed in 1927:

> *It was unfortunate that in the general scheme to recreate an Irish Ireland, the work of preserving or reviving our old national dances should have largely fallen to the lot of those who were but poorly equipped for the task. For the most part they were lacking in insight and a due appreciation of the pure old style, and had, as it appears, but a slender knowledge of the old repertoire ...*
>
> *The spectacular and difficult dances for the few were cultivated to the neglect of the simple ones for the many, leaving the social side untouched except to criticise or condemn ... The ballroom dances in vogue at the time were*

> *the quadrilles or sets, lancers, valse, polka, schottische or barn dance, two step and mazurka. These were all banned and nothing put in their place but for a couple of long dances. An exception should have been made, one would imagine, in favour of the popular old Sets (that had been Irish-ized), if only on account of the fine old tunes with which they were associated, but they were decried amongst the rest.*

The League banned ballroom dances at their events, and after the foundation of the Irish Dancing Commission in 1927 they acted as an empowered national organization. Then the young Irish Government put its mark on the contentious issue.

The Public Dance Hall Act of 1935 was the final blow to the old house dances, and in particular to round dances. It decreed that "no place shall be used for public dancing unless a public dancing license is in force in respect of such a place." The late, renowned fiddle and concertina player Junior Crehan, of Ballymakea, Mullach, County Clare describes the background of the law and its effect:

> *The Dance Hall Act was passed in 1935 and the clergy and the politicians abolished the country house dances. They believed that there was immoral conduct carried out at the country houses and that there was no sanitary arrangements. That was their excuse. You had to pay three pence tax to the shilling going into the hall which meant money to the government ... They didn't care if you made your water down the chimney, as long as they collected their money. That put an end to the country house.* * 20

> *So, they barred the country house dance, and the priests was erecting parish halls. All they wanted was to make money - and they got 3d. into every shilling tax out of the tickets to pay the government for tax. So the country house dance was knocked out then, and 'twas fox-trots, and big old bands coming down, and our type, we'd be in a foreign country then. We couldn't put up with it at all, the noise and the microphones, and jazz and so on ... the music nearly died out altogether - Irish music. Then the emigration started, a lot of the lads I used to play with went off to England and America, and there was no-one but myself - Scully was dead - and I used to go down the road, and I*

> *used, honest to God, I used to nearly cry. Nowhere to go, no-one to meet, no sets in the houses, nothing left but the hall ...* * 21

The triple pincer effect of the Church, the Gaelic League, and the Irish Government soon finished off the house dance and in particular ballroom dance, at least for the time being. Not approved for use in national competitions that underpinned modern Irish culture, and banned from the dance halls that were now largely Church or state-run, the old dances fell away. Breandán Breathnach had this to say:

> *It is ironic that the sets and half sets should have been outlawed in that fashion. They were the only form of dancing practiced by the people of the Gaeltacht; in providing a function for traditional musicians they had helped greatly in preserving the traditional music, and there can be little doubt that in movements, and structure the Irish or céilí dances owed a lot to their inspiration.* * 22

Effects upon Irish concertina repertoire and styles

With no more house dances and thus no reason to play the tunes for those house dances, and no interest from official Irish dance and music organizations in collecting or recording that music, a vast repertoire of tunes that had either been imported and modified or had been newly composed in Ireland fell away.

It is for this reason that the concertina repertoires of the old women of the house dance era and of the young women of today are so different; the dance tunes of nineteenth century Ireland were cast away and discarded by the bigotry of moral and cultural authorities. The new *céilí* dances in the public halls used the officially blessed reels, jigs and hornpipes. Once the country house dances were banned, there was no more demand for polkas, mazurkas, schottisches, quick-steps, varsovianas, and the like.

Music collectors turned their back on these dance tunes. Francis O'Neill despised them and transcribed none. Even Breathnach, in his definitive and relatively recent collection of Irish music, could only bring himself to include polkas, largely because they had been incorporated (albeit in a rhythmically modified form) along with

Irish double reels into the sets, which were revived by various organizations during the 1970s and 1980s.

Other than a few handfuls of schottisches, barn dances, and mazurkas transcribed by Roche in 1927, and a few recordings of aging musicians made by Ciarán Mac Mathúna of RTÉ and others, the Irish ballroom dance repertoire - much of it comprised of modifications on imported tunes as well as completely locally-composed tunes - was largely lost. In the Australian, South African, North American and British traditional music repertoire, there are thousands of such tunes nestled away in collections, and they are regarded as part of each country's cultural heritage. Not so in Ireland, where round dances even today are often considered as foreign.

Attitudes are slowly changing, however. There has been a great resurgence of set dancing in Ireland, albeit to 'Irish-ized' music, and many of these dance evenings now include a schottische, a *Shoe the Donkey* varsoviana, or a *Stack of Barley* barndance.*23

Set dancers, it seems, are keenly aware of history and sympathetic to these lost dance forms. Schottisches/flings, polkas, barn dance and quadrille tunes are now allowed in Irish music competitions of the *Comhaltas Ceoltóiri Éireann*, and that organization has preserved old field recordings of schottisches, polkas and waltzes in its audio archive.

Topic Records produced a recording of 'Irish country-house music' in 2001 that gathered early twentieth century recordings of Irish musicians, especially emigrés in America, who continued to play ballroom dance music after the ban in Ireland.*24

But for the most part, the currently played traditional repertoire in Ireland that stems from the house dance period is very lean, indeed. From the beginning of the *céilí* dances, Irish concertina players have concentrated on learning reels and jigs to the exclusion of almost everything else.

An adjacent chart compares the same group of three women whose repertoire, recorded in their senior years, firmly reflects the house dance era (Carolan, O'Dwyer and Hourican) versus a four men (and one woman) of the same general range of birth years who chose in their later years to play a repertoire that reflected the *céilí* dance era that replaced it.

A Changing Irish Repertoire

Group 1: Three musicians with a house dance repertoire

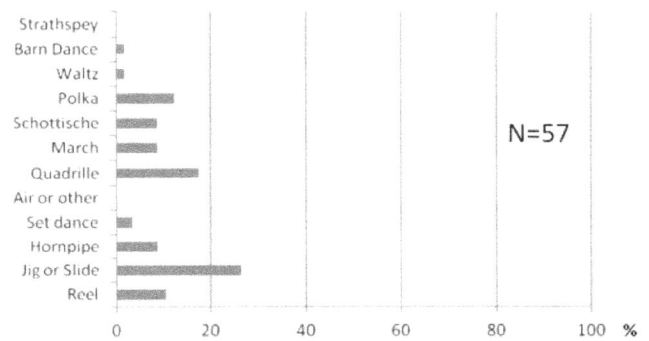

Group 2: Five musicians with a ceili dance repertoire

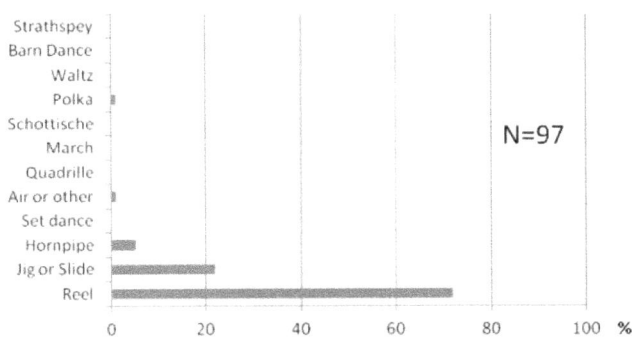

A comparison of dance types in the repertoire of two groups of contemporaneous Irish concertina players. Tune counts (shown in percentages of total) include those of all known recordings for each individual, and include a total of 57 separate tunes from group 1, and 97 from group 2. The second group has narrowed its focus greatly on reels and jigs. **Group 1:** *Mary Ann Carolan, Ella Mae O'Dwyer; Katey Hourican, who played a house dance repertoire.* **Group 2:** *William Mullaly; Patrick Flanagan; Tom Barry; Elizabeth Crotty; Michael Doyle, whose playing reflected the céilí dance repertoire.*

Their music and this chart are explored in Chapter 8. Women players in Ireland tended to play in the home rather than in pubs, and were thus less exposed to changing fashions of music. The one woman in the second group, Elizabeth Crotty, played often in her family's pub, and also was an officer in *Comhaltas Ceoltóiri Éireann*, where the renewed *céilí* dance repertoire was preferred.

Beyond repertoire, the ways in which the concertina was played also changed dramatically as a result of the banning of the house dance. After the Public Dance Hall Act, dances moved from small neighborhood houses to large parish and community halls. Whereas a solo concertina or fiddle player had long been thought adequate for a house dance, groups of musicians were needed to fill the larger volume of space in public dance halls.

These new *céilí* bands had a varied instrumentation of fiddles, flutes, pianos, drums, and accordions playing together, and most of these musicians preferred the 'fiddle' keys of G, D, and A to the old key of C (and G) used by the those who played German concertinas. Playing in the keys of D and A requires a third row of buttons on a concertina, and most German concertinas only had two rows. Many if not most concertina players gave up playing at this time, due to the double whammy of changing repertoire and changing keys.

By the 1950s, the few remaining Irish concertina players, by then mostly men concentrated in County Clare, had moved from the old octave style of playing to a single-note, along-the-row style, the better to keep up with reel tempo for the new Irish dance repertoire, and the better to play in the keys of G, D and A.

Reels in Ireland had always been played mostly singly (one note at a time) and along-the-row, largely because of their rapid tempo.

With the advent of the *céilí* dances, these more rapid reels and jigs dominated the repertoire, and a new generation of concertina players began to adjust its playing style accordingly, playing almost everything in that manner. By far, most of the concertina players who were recorded during the 1970s played in this new manner, for example Tommy McCarthy, Bernard O'Sullivan, John Kelly, Solus Lillus, and Packie Russell.

The Green Isle Céili Band, 1950s. Donnie Connor, first president of the Tulla Comhaltas, is seated at right, holding a German concertina. Céili dances with large bands replaced the earlier house dances that typically had solo musicians. Relatively few céili band musicians played the German concertina. Photo courtesy of Tulla Comhaltas.

Solus Lillis, a blacksmith from Clonreddan, near Cooraclare in West Clare, recalled the older generation - the house dance generation - as follows:

> *I started to play when I was no more than eight or nine years old or less, maybe. My mother used to play. A lot of old people used to play, you know. They sounded a lot of bass keys down below on the left hand side of the concertina. A lot of unnecessary noise I used to call it. They had more or less only the bones of the tune, a lot of them; the old women especially. 'Twas nearly all women who played*

around here. They never played for tape recorders or anything like that. * 25

The 'unnecessary' bass notes that Lillis refers to are the lower notes on the C row, used when playing in octaves in the key of C, in the older style of the house dance era. "The bare bones" he mentions refers to the practice of dance musicians to play simply, for the step of the dancers.

During the revival of Irish music of the latter half of the twentieth century, playing styles changed again when concertinas began to be played for judges at competitions as well as for listeners in pub sessions. Inevitably, concertina players began to play in a more ornamented style and at a more rapid tempo, the better to hold the attention of a static listener.

The result today is a highly ornate style, played singly, within a reel-rich repertoire that bears little resemblance to that of the Irish musicians of the house dance era. This is not to criticize the modern style, as it has won thousands of converts to Irish traditional music and to the concertina, and there is much to commend in its beauty and gracefulness. It seems a pity, however, that so few in Ireland play tunes of the house dance repertoire and in the old style today.

In the other three countries, all of which were spared the early twentieth century cultural warfare that plagued Irish music and dance, the ballroom dance repertoire has remained largely intact amongst modern day 'traditional' musicians, although of course the general, worldwide collapse of most forms of European social *dance* in the present era is well known.

In England, it could be said that ballroom dance music was ignored by folk music authorities until an 'English Country Music' movement began in the 1970s, turning a spotlight on surviving rural musicians there who still played many ballroom dance tunes alongside tunes of the older step-dance and country dance genres, in country pubs.

In South Africa, another small movement has begun within the *Tradisionele Boeremusiekklub* to preserve the old style of playing the two-row German *boerekonsertina*, in octaves with associated chords. New German-style instruments are now being produced there in order to help that movement to grow.

In Australia, collecting efforts of both traditional music and dance began in the 1950s, and as a result old time music and dance were passed on to a newer (albeit less numerous) generation before the last of the old guard had passed away. As we shall see in Chapter 11, there are still a few players in rural Australia and South Africa who both play for ballroom dance and still play in the old octave playing style.

Notes:

1. Data sources: private tapes and RTE recordings for Mary Ann Carolan, recordings from the Comhaltas Ceoltóirí Éireann archive and from Neil Wayne of O'Dwyer, and Comhaltas Ceoltóirí Éireann recordings of Hourican.

2. As of writing, there are two published CDs featuring Edel Fox, two of Claire Keville, and on for Dympna O'Sullivan.

3. Nicholas Carolan, 1997, *A Harvest Saved: Francis O'Neill and Irish Music in Chicago.* Ossian Publications, Cork, 79pp.

4. E G Ravenstein, 'On the Celtic Languages of the British Isles: A Statistical Survey', *Journal of the Statistical Society of London*, vol.42, no.3 (1879), p.584. Citation found in Wikipedia, *History of the Irish Language*. Note: A good map-based summary of the famine and its cultural aftermath in Ireland may be found at http://www.irelandstory.com

5. Francis O'Neill, *Irish Folk Music, a Fascinating Hobby* (1910; repr. Darby, Pennsylvania: Norwood Editions, 1972), p.288.

6. Frank Maginnis, Joan Flett and Chirs Brady, *Kate Hughes' Dancing Book, Dundalk, 1867* (online at www.chrisbrady.itgo.com/dance/dundalk, 2002).

7. Breandán Breathnach, Dancing in Ireland: Dal gCais, 1983, p.27.

8. Helen Brennan, 1999, p.28.

9. Donal McCartney, 'From Parnell to Pearse', *The Course of Irish History* (Cork: Mercier Press, 1967), pp.295-296.

10. Anonymous, 'The revival of Irish Literature, and other addresses, 1894', *The Quarterly Review*, 190 (London: John Murray, 1899), p.17.

11. Francis O'Neill, *Irish Folk Music, a Fascinating Hobby*, (1910, repr. Norwood Editions 1972), p.288.

12. Helen Brennan, 1999, p.109.

13. Helen Brennan, op.cit., p.105.

14. W P Ryan, 1912, *The Pope's Green Island*: London, J Nisbet. Quoted in Helen Brennan, op.cit.

15. Bryan MacMahon, 1954, *The Vanishing Ireland*: Dublin, O'Brien Press, p.212.

16. Irish Catholic Directory, 1925, p.563. Quoted in Breandán Breathnach, The Church and Dancing in Ireland: *Dal gCais*, 1982, pp.59-71.

17. Ibid, p.568.

18. Breandán Breathnach, The Church and Dancing in Ireland: *Dal gCais*, 1982, pp.59-71.

19. Anonymous 'Gaedeal,' writing in *The Western People*, Mayo, 27 August and 4 September 1904. As quoted in Helen Brennan, op.cit., p.32.

20. Junior Crehan, as quoted in Larry Lynch, 1991, p.43.

21. Recorded conversation between Junior Crehan and Barry Taylor, Ballymackea, County Clare, 8 July 1976.

22. Breandán Breathnach, 1983, Dancing in Ireland: *Dal gCais*, 1983, p.27.

23. See for example Bill Lynch's online *Set Dancing News*, www.setdancingnews.net

24. Reg Hall, ed., *Round the House and Mind the Dresser: Irish Country-House Dance Music*: Topic Records, London, CD TSCD606, with liner notes by Reg Hall.

25. Ibid., p.175.

Chapter 7. Australia

Of the four countries where house dance music of the concertina's heyday has been recorded, Australia is the country with the most complete record. Where most of the Anglo concertina music of the instrument's heyday was to be only meagerly recorded in England and Ireland (and completely unrecorded in the United States and New Zealand), there is a rich though little-known body of recordings from a number of Colonial-era musicians Down Under.

With the first appearance of the global folk revival in the 1950s, music and dance collectors (first among them John Meredith) fanned out across the bush with tape recorders, a process that has continued to the present. As a result, Australia has a rich array of recordings of aging concertina players from the instrument's heyday, almost all of whom were active players for country house and wool-shed dances in their country's late Colonial and early Commonwealth era.

In addition, Australia had little of the ambivalence toward popular ballroom dance music exhibited by many in traditional music circles in England, and none of the outright hostility to it seen in Ireland. Here, these round dances and quadrilles have been considered a very important part of the Australian national cultural heritage. Finally, Australia is the country where the dances themselves are most likely to be encountered today in a form not too unlike that of the ballroom dance era.

Colonial Australia was a very sparsely populated country in the late nineteenth century, when dances provided a very special type of social 'glue' to small rural communities.

A good example is provided by a report of a dance in the small village of Newcastle (now called Toodyay), in the Avon Valley of Western Australia, perhaps fifty miles northeast of Perth, in 1875:

The Colemane brothers circa 1890, including Alfred Colemane (ca.1837-1912) on German concertina. They played for dances in Cootamundra, New South Wales. From the Bush Music Club's 'Singabout Magazine', 1966, with thanks to Bob Bolton.

> *The Settler's Ball which took place at Leeder's Hotel on Wednesday the 1st September was a complete success in every way, nearly eighty persons being present on the occasion. The music, consisting of harmonium, violin, and concertina was good; the refreshments which were of the best and most liberally applied, were excellent; and dancing, which commenced about nine o'clock, was kept up with unflagging spirit, until daylight on Thursday morning.* * 1

A 1908 non-fictional account by an Anglican parson paints a detailed picture of a 'bush dance':

> *I wish I could do justice to a Bush social. I wish I could show you the great chaff-shed, its slab walls draped in art-muslin, and its beams decorated with green boughs, the pianist seated in the corner, supported by a violinist, in some cases a real musical genius, whose thirsty soul has proved his undoing.*

> *At some Bush dances the music is provided by a concertina, energetically played by a stalwart young Bushman, who sits on his heels in the corner in an attitude characteristically Australian. Outside the shed a temporary supper-room has been built with great pine-poles and tarpaulins, and long trestle-tables groan beneath delicacies brought from far and near.*
>
> *There are turkeys and chickens from every farm within miles, suckling-pigs, hams, tongues, fruit and cakes, trifles, and innumerable other delicacies. At midnight the whole company sits down to supper, and thereafter dancing is renewed and continued until daybreak makes it possible for the tired dancers to see to drive home, some of them a distance of fifteen miles or more.* * 2

Albert George 'Dooley' Chapman (1892-1982), of Coborrah, New South Wales, played the concertina for rural dances in a wide part of his district during the first two decades of the twentieth century. He recalled one reason for such all-night dances:

> *The dancers, they'd start at eight o'clock. They'd go all night, of course. I'd be playing, and I'd get a bit of a lunch at half past one, and I'd play on until four o'clock. Because the ladies, or the girls, weren't allowed to leave until daylight, the breaking day ... so they wouldn't get away with somebody.* * 3

A perhaps more pertinent reason for such all-night dances involved the dangers of nighttime travel in the bush, including encountering flooded rivers and open mining shafts, among other things.

The era of informal house and woolshed dances (now termed 'bush' dances, although that is a modern term that would have been relatively unfamiliar back then when they were typically called 'balls') lasted well into the early twentieth century in many rural areas, and because of the numerous field recordings of surviving players from that era we have a very good idea of how the tunes were played.

Stylistically, these Australian concertinists were nearly all octave players who played sparsely, with few if any ornaments - not unlike early players in Ireland and England. This is not surprising, as they all shared a common purpose: playing for house (and barn and woolshed) dances. Dancers needed volume and a rhythmic beat, and the musicians needed to have stamina for playing, often solo, for all night dances. Some players used a frequent pulsation of partial chords in the manner of a William Kimber, and many others had the sparse, rhythmic but much less chorded style of Scan Tester or Katey Hourican.

It is likely that these styles for playing the concertina were developed independently and locally, and did not arrive with immigrant players from Ireland or England, because the ballroom dances, their accompanying repertoire of music, and the concertina arrived in all of these countries simultaneously. Players in isolated rural areas devised their own ways of dealing with the demands of house dances, and seem to have all gravitated naturally to the use of octaves to produce volume. Earlier immigrants did bring step dances (jigs, reels and hornpipes) and country dances with them, in the early Colonial period, but they arrived playing these tunes on fiddles and flutes.

Anglo-German concertina player with two fretless banjo players, Australia, ca.1870. With thanks to Peter Cuffley and Peter Ellis

By the time that the concertina arrived in the 1850s, and as it became established in the 1860s, quadrilles and round dances were all the popular rage not only in the colony but in the 'mother countries' of England, Scotland, Wales and Ireland, and it is this nineteenth century ballroom dance repertoire that is most remembered by the concertina players who survived into the middle of the twentieth century.

Bush dances were essentially gone from most areas by the 1930s, and field collection of bush music began in the 1950s. Of particular importance to the concertina enthusiast is the work of John Meredith, who in the process of compiling his two-volume treatise on the *Folk Songs of Australia*, published in 1967 and 1987, encountered and recorded the music of a number of rural concertina players, as well as the music of descendants of former concertina players, many of whom had moved on to the accordion. Meredith, along with later folk music collectors like Rob Willis, Warren Fahey and Peter Ellis, recorded perhaps a dozen or more surviving concertina players from the heyday of the instrument.

John Meredith (with accordion) and Peter Ellis (with concertina) on a folk music collecting trip in Western Australia, 1991. Photo courtesy of Peter Ellis.

The collection of the colonial era *dances*- both the global ballroom dances and their local variants - arguably began with the efforts of Shirley Andrews, of Melbourne. She began her research into early Australian dance in the 1950s and quickly learned that the common assumption that dancing in Australia was based upon earlier dances brought from the British Isles was incorrect, and that Australia, like England, Ireland and South Africa, had followed the latest fashions in overseas ballroom dances throughout the late nineteenth century. In 1962, her work was greatly aided by the discovery of the Klippel family and others in the Nariel Valley of Victoria who were still dancing many of the ballroom dances of the late colonial era in their community dance hall (Con Klippel is one of the recorded players below).*4

By the 1970s, traditional-style bush dances were being resurrected at festivals all over Australia, with the help of a number of bush music and dance societies, among them the Sydney Bush Music Club, the Bush Dance and Music Club of Bendigo Victoria, the Victorian Folk Music Club of Melbourne, and the Wongawilli Colonial Dance Club in Illawarra, New South Wales. A key annual event is the National Folk Festival held in Canberra A.C.T., which started as a venue for bush dances.

A significant number of concertina players are active with these societies and festivals, and a number of these musicians continue to play in the traditional octave style - many more than in England and Ireland, even though overall numbers of concertina players are much lower than in those other countries. At the same time, however, trends are moving away from such players.

The old community dance hall in Nariel, northeastern Victoria

One such trend is the tendency of festivals like the National to expand in the direction of a wide variety of concert performers for listening audiences (a traditional concertina performer recently described them as "bums on seats") rather than the participatory dances of the recent past, where the musicians and the dancers shared a symbiotic bond. As will be demonstrated in Chapter 8 below, playing for listening ultimately changes the music that is played.

Additionally, younger concertina players in Australia are increasingly coming under the spell of imported modern, highly ornamented styles of playing from Ireland that are also mainly aimed at listeners rather than dancers, and which favor a repertoire that is largely alien to the round and square ballroom dances that both countries once shared. At the end of the day, the survival of older styles of Anglo playing in Australia seems to depend upon the survival of old time dances.

Dooley Chapman

Albert George 'Dooley' Chapman (1892-1982) was born in Coborrah, New South Wales, and in later years he lived in Dunedoo, a larger farming town nearby. Chapman played the concertina for rural dances in a wide part of his district in the first two decades of the twentieth century.

Dooley Chapman in his kitchen. Photo courtesy of Chris Sullivan.

When in his eighties, Chapman met folk revival concertina players Tom Bromley, Mark Rummery and Chris Sullivan. They recorded him in a studio in 1981, a year before he died. These recordings were issued as a CD, *Your Good Self*, that is the best and most easily accessible of the recordings of Australia's old players. The biographical notes that follow were summarized and modified from Chris Sullivan's liner notes to that CD, as well as from an earlier biographical sketch by him in *Concertina Magazine*.*5 The quotes below from Dooley Chapman are from the above-mentioned recorded interviews.

Although of English descent, Chapman's parents were both born in New South Wales; his mother was from Coborrah. His was a musical family; his father and an uncle played violin, and his brothers and sisters played violin, concertina, and piano. Chapman began playing concertina at the age of ten, and began playing for local house parties and dances. In his younger years, Chapman was a farmer, but he later built concrete silos and sheep dips for a living.

As bush dances were dying out in the 1920s, Chapman extended his playing days by teaming up with his sister Grace on piano. He played for dances as late as World War II; such dances returned briefly as feelings of Australian patriotism rose during the war.

Chapman's repertoire reflects the key dances of his era: round dances such as waltzes, polkas, mazurkas, schottisches, breakdowns, and varsovianas; as well as quadrilles such as the Lancers and the Alberts. He also played the odd jig for step dancers, although the ballroom dance styles were more central to his experience.*6

Although he lived in an out-of-the-way rural area in a time before radio and television, Chapman's repertoire reflects a global tune resource, just as does the repertoire of all recorded early Australian players. *Old Dan Tucker* came from the minstrel shows, his *Varsoviana* from continental Europe. The *Alberts Quadrille* and the *Highland Schottische* had English and Scottish origins. He played a breakdown to the tune of *Ring the Bell Watchman*, an American song of Civil War vintage that was also in Susan Colley's repertoire. Other tunes appear to be of local origin.

Chapman's musical mentor was his cousin Billy Chandler (ca.1870-1905), who played a Bb/F concertina made by John Stanley of Bathurst. Billy Chandler played for dances all over the region, using a bicycle for transport, as Chapman recalled:

> *I've seen him leave Coborrah there of an evening making to Lue to play for a dance... Mudgee's fifty mile, and another twenty down to where he was playing for the dance. [T]hat's a long way to ride, don't you reckon!... Of course, Lue's not the only place, other places as well.*

Chapman (and apparently Chandler) played in an octave style, moving the melody in cross-row fashion across the two home rows. In this interview, Chapman was quick to point out that not all concertina players were that well trained in his day (the recording is courtesy of Chris Sullivan).

> *[My] brother Fred always said that I played the same as Billy Chandler... See, Fred played more up and down straight on the keys [in other words, along the row], see that's a bit different. Well, they didn't all play the same.*

Of such less-skilled players, and of those with little experience at playing for dancers, Chapman pointed out that:

> *They weren't as good as the best of them, that's for sure. See, the time wouldn't be there. No, no. See the waltz and the schottische, all them was all to the step. What you'd find even in many players, you put them out to play for the dancers and see where they are. See the waltz, the schottische and the varsoviana and that. See if they're on to the step. Well, what are they doing?* ✻ 7

The tunes had to be accurately played, as well; this was a dancing crowd with high standards. In this interview, Chapman makes this point clear (the recording is courtesy of Chris Sullivan):

> *When I was playing, if only I missed a note, by God, you'd see them [the dancers] look 'round, if you only missed one note! They'd had it ... which didn't happen too often then, I can assure you.*

The following four recordings of Chapman's playing were made by Chris Sullivan and colleagues in 1981, who kindly made them available to this collection; all are from the CD *Your Good Self*.

A quadrille tune, the **Lancers Tune**, is played in an octave style in the key of C, and the melody weaves back and forth between the C row and the G row. In general, lower passages are played on the C row, and higher passages on the G row.

An oddity of Chapman's playing, as well as several other Australian players, is the use of an F# in a key that is in C, and thus should have no sharps. This gives the tune an odd modal sound. It happens because the cross-row transition from the C row to the G row in the playing of the C scale should happen between the solfège *fa*, F (on the C row) and the *sol*, G (on the G row. See discussion, Chapter 12). In Chapman's case, he sometimes places that cross-row transition between *mi*, E (on the C row) and *fa*, F# (on the G row, where the F is sharped). The practice seems intentional, as a full look at his music suggests.

The American minstrel tune *Old Dan Tucker* was popularized by Dan Emmett and the Virginia Minstrels in 1843, who spread the tune worldwide. Played as a breakdown in its original form (a tune in common time where the emphasis falls on the second and fourth beat), it has clearly made a number of melodic and rhythmic changes before coming to Chapman.

It is played in the key of C in a similar two-row octave manner, starting on the G row. In it, Chapman again uses an F# in the A part that is not in keeping with the rest of that passage, which is clearly in the key of C.

 Dooley Chapman's *Ring the Bell, Watchman* was written by Henry C Work in 1865 as a victory song at the end of the American Civil War. It was spread by minstrel groups, and became a very popular song in Australia; it was universally known and played by old time concertina players there, and remains popular today (a version of it played by New South Wales musician George Bennett is included below).

The cover to an 1868 Australian version of the song shows how quickly tunes like this moved across the oceans into the popular music repertoire. Its melody was later attached to an Australian verse, becoming *Click Goes the Shears*, an iconic Australian folk song. That verse was later popularized by American Burl Ives in the 1950s, a recording that became popular across Australia.

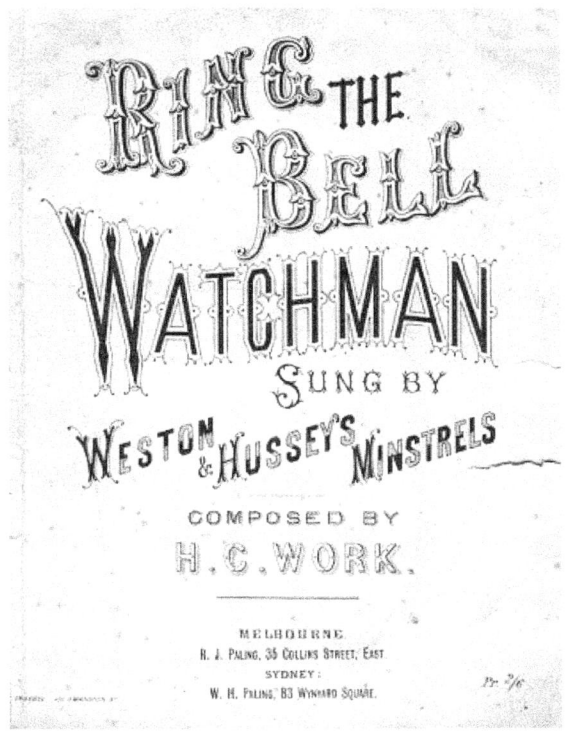

A version of Ring the Bell Watchman published in Melbourne, 1868.
From the National Library of Australia.

An *Untitled Polka* by Chapman (termed *Dooley's Polka* in the following transcription) has affinities in its A part with the Irish song *Bog Down in the Valley*, and with the old song *Oft in the Stilly Night*, composed by Thomas Moore, but varies significantly in the B part relative to both of these. It was played with piano accompaniment.

Chapman said in an interview that playing with a piano accompaniment provided by his daughter extended his playing years for dancing significantly; the piano added more respectability to the music at a time when the solo concertina began to be seen as a bit old-fashioned and rural. It is a simple tune, played mostly in octaves, and the entire tune is played on the C row.

The *Starry Night Waltz* is a local version of *Starry Night for a Ramble*, which seems to have been a song from the London music halls, with the earliest known broadsheet of it published there in about 1854. It was popular in Australia from the goldfield days, and like the previous song it is widely known to the present day. Chapman's A part of the tune is modified slightly from the commonly known version.

John Meredith collected this tune from a number of sources during his research in the 1950s and 1980s. This recording of Chapman was made by Bob Campbell in 1974, and was kindly made available by Alan Musgrove.

George Bennett

George Bennett (1878-1966) and his brother Jim Bennett (1881-1978) lived in the Gunnedah area of New South Wales, a small village in an agricultural area about 300 miles NNW of Sydney. John Meredith and Rob Willis found them in 1992 while searching for owners of rare old Stanley concertinas; George Bennett's son Ken (b. 1908, now deceased) owned and still played his father's Stanley concertina at the time of that visit. The biographical details of George and his family written here are paraphrased from descriptions prepared by Rob Willis, a folklore collector for the National Library of Australia.

George Bennett (1878-1966) in his years as a champion axeman, in the late 1890s. Photo courtesy of the National Library of Australia.

George Bennett was a timber worker who cut pine logs for the local mill. As the photograph shows, he was a champion axeman, and he won the woodchop event at the Gunnedah show six years in a row. Jim and George also sheared sheep in this wool-producing region. At one stage, George worked at the Gunnedah coal mine, which had opened in the late 1870s. In a tragic accident, he lost a leg while working the coal cutting machine. Undeterred, and turning his woodworking skills to use, he began designing and making wooden legs.

Both George and his brother Jim Bennett (1881-1978) played both button accordion and concertina for local dances, and both were singers. In the early to middle 1960s, when George was in his mid-eighties, his family recorded him on a small reel to reel tape recorder. Willis and Meredith learned of these recordings of George and Jim when they first visited George's son Ken in 1992, by which time the two brothers were deceased.

Attempts to make a copy of the tapes at that time failed, as Ken's house had no electricity. Rob Willis returned in 2001 with John Harpley, and the two managed to copy and preserve the recordings. They are now housed at the National Library of Australia, which has made them available for this archive.

By the time of the Meredith and Willis visit in 1992, the bellows on George's Stanley concertina had deteriorated, and had been replaced by the bellows of an old German concertina (sometimes known in Australia, somewhat derisively, as a "chinese lantern concertina."). The adjacent photograph shows Ken playing that instrument at the time of the 1992 visit.

George Bennett's playing on this tape made in the 1960s is lively and vigorous despite his advanced age. He appears to be pacing through his repertoire, tune by tune, in order to please his family members, who wished to preserve his music.

Ken Bennett, Gunnedah Australia, 1992. He is holding his father, George Bennett's Stanley concertina, with its modified bellows.

There are a number of songs as well as song tunes, as well as a large variety of dance tunes from the late nineteenth and very early twentieth century: waltzes, schottisches, polkas, a galop, jigs, breakdowns, quadrilles, and varsovianas...a trove of about sixty separate tunes and songs. Because of their quality and abundance, as well as importance, some eighteen dance and song tunes, and one song, are included in this archive.

Dick Cribb is a single reel, or perhaps more correctly, a breakdown, so classified because of the great emphasis on the second and fourth beat (off-beat) in Bennett's version of the tune. Its origin is unknown, but seems to show minstrel influence in its off-beat breakdown rhythm, which is not particularly common among Australian players. Bennett plays the tune in Bb on his Bb/F Stanley concertina.

A search on present day persons named Dick Cribb in Australia turned up one, in nearby Queensland, who is active in an environmental group called 'Men of the Trees;' perhaps an ancestor was a timber colleague of Bennett's? At very least, the unusual surname Cribb is found in Bennett's general region.

Bennett plays *Dick Cribb* all in octaves in the classic traditional style, mostly on the Bb row but with a cross-row transition to the F row in the higher pitched beginning of the B part. The off-beat breakdown rhythm is produced in an unusual manner, by adding partial chords to the right hand side on the offbeat; most players restrict such chords to the left hand. This higher pitched offbeat rhythm is somewhat reminiscent to the sound of a clawhammer banjo, hence the suggestion of minstrel influence.

Waltzes.

[I'll Be] All Smiles Tonight is one of a large number of waltzes in Bennett's repertoire. It is an American sentimental song, written by T B Ransom in 1879 but was resurrected by generations of bluegrass and country and western singers, including the Blue Ridge Highballers in 1926, the Carter family, Mac Wiseman, Johnny Cash, and even the Chieftains. Bennett plays it in the key of F, entirely on the F row, and mostly in octaves with some left hand partial chords.

Break the News to Mother is an American sentimental song written by Charles K Harris, the "King of the Tear-Jerker," who wrote the global hit waltz and song *After the Ball [Is Over]* in 1892. *Break the News to Mother* was originally written in 1891 about a dying firefighter, but was not successful. It was re-written in 1897 about a dying soldier of the Spanish-American soldier, and became an instant hit. Bennett plays this tune on a German concertina that is pitched in GD. He plays it in the key of D, mostly on the G row.

The Gundawindi Waltz (probably named for Goondawindi, Queensland) appears to be of Australian origin. He plays it on his G/D German concertina, in the key of D, in a similar manner to the above waltz.

My Pretty Girl is another waltz (and likely was a sentimental song) played in Bb on his Bb/F Stanley Anglo, in a cross-row style that weaves from the Bb to the F row and back again. It is largely in octaves with occasional partial chords.

Darling Wait 'Til Morn, another sentimental waltz tune, is played in the key of F.

Two Little Girls in Blue was composed in 1893 by Charles Graham, an American composer, and was popularized by the minstrel shows. It later was used in a Broadway play of that name written by Paul Lannin and Vincent Youmans, with lyrics by Ira Gershwin, that premiered in 1921. Its title song became a global hit as both a song and a waltz tune. Bennett plays it in the keys and manner of the above three waltzes.

Other dance tunes.

George Bennett played several step dance tunes, all jigs. *George Redder's Step* is an unusual, rather slow jig played in F, in a cross-row octave manner, with the lower segments of the A part played on the Bb row. Partial chords are used sparingly and full chords are inserted at ends of phrases.

What'll They Do if the Billy Boils Over is a version of the Irish jig *St Patrick's Day*, and is played in Bb.

The Rakes of Mallow is of probable Irish origin, and is one of those global tunes that is seemingly known by everyone who plays traditional dance music. It is a single reel, usually played for a quadrille. Bennett plays it in Bb in octaves, with chords at ends of phrases. The A part is played wholly on the Bb row, and the B part is played in a cross-row manner.

Bennett played a number of polkas, among them the following two.

My Mother Said I Never Should [Play With Gypsies in the Wood] is an old children's rhyme, probably of English origin, from an earlier, less politically correct era. It is set to a three-hop polka in Bb, played entirely on the Bb row, and in octaves.

Turn That Old Man Around is a polka of unknown, perhaps local origin, played in a cross-row manner in the key of F.

Bennett plays the old schottische *Black Cloud* in F, mostly in octaves and across the rows. It was likely once a song tune, with the words of the first line as 'Don't you hear the black clouds rising over yonder'.

His untitled *Old Time Schottische* is played in F, modulating to Bb in the B part.

He played a jig for a figure of *The Lancers* quadrille; it is in the key of Bb, modulating to F in the B part.

House Dance

The *Varsoviana* was a popular dance in late Colonial Australia, and a great number of tunes have survived for it. Many are variants of the globally known standard tune, as is this one. He plays it in F, mostly on the F row.

Almost everyone, it seems, knew *Ring the Bell, Watchman*; here is Dooley Chapman's version. George Bennett played his in F, in octaves, and in a cross-row manner between the two rows. Chapman played it all on the middle row (the C row on his C/G Anglo).

Although not a concertina tune, Bennett's song *The Capture of the Kelly Gang* relates an event that had connections with the concertina, and is a superb Australian folk ballad.

In Australia, Ned Kelly (1854-1880) remains a controversial person, and one's opinion of him depends largely on whether one supports law and order and frontier justice, or sympathizes with working class persons (especially Irish immigrants) who found the British constabulary to be overbearing and arrogant in their work.

Kelly was born in Victoria to Irish parents, and fell into trouble with the law early, becoming an outlaw after he and his gang killed three policemen at Stringybark Creek in 1878. As a result they were outlawed by act of the Victorian parliament, which was basically a 'wanted, dead or alive' decree. Later that same year, he and his gang raided the National Bank at Euroa on December 10, and the Jerilderie bank on February 8, 1879.

Still on the run months later, the Kelly gang arrived in the small town of Glenrowan, Victoria on June 27th, which set into motion a classic set of events that ended the careers of all in the gang. They took about seventy hostages at the Glenrowan Inn, then ordered the town's railroad tracks pulled up, as they knew the police were on the way via the train and they wished to derail it.

In the hotel were the Kelly gang members - Ned, brother Dan, Joe Byrne, and Steve Hart - along with a captured constable named O'Sullivan and all the hostages. All were tensely waiting for events to unfold, according to the following account by Constable O'Sullivan:

Between 12 and 1 o'clock on Sunday morning one of Mrs Jones sons sang the Kelly song for the amusement of the gang, and his mother occasionally asked him to sing out louder. Most of the prisoners were cleared out of the front parlour, and the gang had a dance. They danced a set of quadrilles, and Mr David Mortimer, brother-in-law of the schoolmaster, furnished the music with a concertina. Ned Kelly had the girl Jones for a partner, Dan had Mrs Jones, and Byrne and Hart danced with male prisoners. Thinking they heard a noise outside, the gang broke away from the dance abruptly, and Dan went outside. It was at this time that I secured the key of the door ... when I heard the special arrive (the train with the police), I ... unlocked the door and bounded away. 8

A period illustration of the quadrilles danced by the Kelly gang as they awaited the police at the Glenrowan hotel. Note the solo concertina player at left.
Picture courtesy of the National Library of Australia

The town's schoolmaster, a hostage who had earlier been released by the gang, alerted the police train to the danger imposed by the destroyed rails. All was now in place for the climactic shootout. Each of the four men was equipped with homemade body armor made of steel plate, but only Ned was outside when the shooting began. Dismounting his horse when a bolt in his armor failed, he was shot in the arm and legs, which were unprotected.

The other three members died in the hotel, which was set ablaze by the police. Byrne bled to death as he poured himself a final glass of whiskey at the bar, and Dan Kelly and Steve Hart reportedly committed suicide. Ned Kelly stood trial and was hanged in 1880, later to become an Australian folk hero. His skeletal remains were recently identified from DNA evidence, after they had long been lost; plans to reinter the remains at Glenrowan are in the works.

Bennett believed that Kelly was a hero, as the first stanza of his ballad suggests:

Ye sons of Australia, forget not the brave,
But bring wild flowers and strew o'er their graves,
Those four daring outlaws whose race it has run,
And place on their tombs the brave laurels they've won.

Con Klippel

Conrad Charles 'Con' Klippel III (1909-1975) was born in Berringama, Victoria, not far from the Nariel Valley along the road from Corryong to Tallangatta; his story is told in a collection of dance music of that district, *Music Makes Me Smile*, compiled by Peter Ellis and Harry Gardner. Con's grandfather, also Conrad Charles Klippel (b.1838), immigrated to Australia in 1854 from Essen Germany, and followed the gold rush to Ballarat and later Yackandandah. He played an early flutina that is still in the possession of family members today. Con's father, also Conrad Klippel (II), worked as a bullock driver and played concertina on those wagon trips, as well as for local dances.

Con Klippel with two-row Anglo-German concertina, ca.1970. With thanks to Peter Ellis and Keith Klippel.

Con Klippel, the grandson of the German immigrant, worked in many jobs, some related to farming, the others involving insurance sales and managing a fleet of school buses. He mostly played accordion, but also played concertina and a variety of other instruments, and along with Shirley Andrews and other musicians and dancers of the Nariel area, was instrumental in reviving old time music and dance in the Nariel Valley in the 1960s and 1970s. He died on stage in 1975 while playing his concertina for a dance.

Klippel's Old-Time Dance Band, Nariel Victoria, 1973. Left to right; Sid Simpson, Charlie Fardon (MC), Betty Coulston, Keith Klippel, Neville Simpson, Con Klippel, George Klippel. With thanks to Peter Ellis.

 In this recording made in 1969 he describes the dances that were performed on one of the early meetings with Shirley Andrews and other members of the Folklore Society of Victoria (based in urban Melbourne) in the early 1960s, when they visited Nariel and became awestruck that so many of the old dances had survived out in the bush (despite the fact that such dances were still being held at other country districts in Victoria, in addition to Nariel. * 9)

The list of still-active dance types performed on one of those occasions, as listed by Klippel in this recording, is very long and rich.

This and other recordings of him are included here courtesy of his son, Keith Klippel. Keith Klippel, a third-generation concertina player and fourth-generation free-reed player, continues the tradition by playing accordion and concertina for local dances in Nariel. A tune from Keith is included in Chapter 11.

The *Manchester Galop* was brought to Australia from Germany by Klippel's immigrant grandfather, according to family history. The galop is a vigorous dance, and for that reason was often the last dance of the evening. This dance however is usually done less vigorously in Australia, more like a two-step or a schottische. It is played by Con Klippel in the key of C, entirely on the C row, in octaves on his two row Lachenal Anglo CG concertina. Con Klippel was fond of swinging his concertina around in a windmill pattern while playing this tune.

Conrad Klippel's Manchester Galop. Transcribed for C/G Anglo by Dan Worrall.

Grandmother Klippel's Schottische is another of the tunes associated with the Klippel family. It is also played in the key of C, in octaves, and entirely on the C row, with additions of phrase-ending C chords.

Arthur Byatt's Schottische is named for a Thougla (Nariel area) musician. It is played in the key of C, and like the previous tune is played entirely on the C row.

The Mill Belongs to Sandy is a single reel typically used in quadrilles. It is derived from a children's rhyme that is also known in England, Ireland, and America. Like Con's other tunes, it is played in octaves all on the C row.

Me Smokey Smokey is a song tune that was composed by Con Klippel, and again is played in C, in octaves, and on the C row. From this limited collection of concertina recordings, one can gather that Con was always a one-row player on his Anglo. This probably developed from his main instrument, the one row button accordion. Both instruments define the popular melodies and dance tunes of the Nariel Valley.

Jim Harrison

Jim Harrison of Khancoban, New South Wales, with his concertina, 1986. Photograph by John Meredith; from the archives of the National Library of Australia.

Jim Harrison (1911-ca. 2000) was born in Khancoban, New South Wales, just to the northeast of the Nariel Valley, and just slightly across the state boundary from Victoria. He was a dairy farmer, and trapped rabbits for extra income. He married in 1934, and had four children. Harrison learned the violin in school, but later played mouth organ, piano, button accordion, concertina, and mandolin. He remembers that the first tune he played on the violin was *Ring the Bell, Watchman*, which we have seen above in the playing of Chapman and Bennett.

Harrison played for dances in the Khancoban School with his friend Rob Scammell; both played accordion and concertina. Sometimes they ventured into Nariel valley, as well as the district around Corryong, to play for dances. In the 1960s, he joined with his friend Con Klippel in the Klippel family's band and dance activities in the Nariel

Valley. Peter Ellis relates that he "was a showman on the concertina, and could play a cossack-type dance (frog dance) on his haunches whilst playing, and in fact one night pulled the instrument in half." *10 He also enjoyed swinging the concertina around, windmill fashion, for the effect on the instrument's tone.

Harrison's repertoire was rich in waltzes, polkas, mazurkas, varsovianas, and set dance tunes, as well as songs. He played mostly button accordion player in his later years, but in a field-recording made by Peter Ellis and Ian Simpson in 1982, he played the German concertina of his youth. By this time, he was many years out of practice, and what is preserved is in no way a recording of him at his best. The National Library of Australia has made these recordings available for this collection.

In his later years, Harrison was considerably more practiced at playing the button accordion; the switch to accordion had been the end of many a concertina player of his era.

One of his dance tunes, *Princess Polka*, provides a good example of his playing technique. Like other Australian players, Harrison plays in octaves. The tune is in C, and the A part is played entirely on the C row. Harrison freely dropped octave notes when difficulties - either in the form of extra low notes or notes with fast transitions - were met, as in measures one, three, and five. The B part moves back and forth from the C to the G row. Like Chapman, Harrison frequently used a dissonant F#, even though the tune itself is in C.

Princess Polka

Australia
Polka

As Played by Jim Harrison
Transcribed for CG Anglo by Dan Worrall

An *Untitled schottische* is played in the key of C, in octaves and all on the C row.

The Mill Belongs to Sandy is a single reel which Harrison plays in the same fashion: in the key of C, in octaves and all on the C row.

In *Why Did My Master Sell Me* he plays with Neville Simpson of the Nariel area. This particular tune is an old American abolitionist tune, spread by the minstrels by at least the early 1850s. This tune is very commonly known and played in present day Australia.

Charlie Ordish

Charlie Ordish (1886-1966) was another of the early-twentieth-century Nariel Valley concertina players, and a good friend of Con Klippel's and Jim Harrison's. He was born in Corryong, the youngest of nine children. During his twenties and thirties, Ordish was a wagon driver who drove a team of nine horses on the two-day run from Corryong to Tallangatta, New South Wales.

As his grandson Ray Simpson has noted:

> [H]e played music as the horses walked the track as they knew where they were going; he played the mouth organ, banjo mandolin, tin whistle, concertina, accordion, mandolin, violin (and the piano at home). He whistled his dance tunes while he worked. He would stop along the way at camp fires belonging to other travelers or bullock teams and play music and sometimes at people's houses for birthdays and other such family celebrations. The homestead kitchen or the local school would have the furniture removed and dance was soon under way... As time went on and the automobile put his wagon team out of business he turned his hand to carpentry, a trade his father (an English ship's carpenter) passed on to him. He would spend weeks at a country town or homestead and build sheds, houses and do renovations for people during the day and of course play music at night. *11

Charlie Ordish, with German concertina, at a Nariel Valley music gathering in the 1960s. With thanks to Peter Ellis and Dave de Santi.

Charlie Ordish played a German concertina. According to Peter Ellis (who learned the story from Shirley Andrews), Ordish and his friend Jim Harrison 'took great delight in swinging their concertinas in big loops overhead while playing, and Charlie would get niggly if there were too many musicians onstage to cramp his style. He would then stand on a chair to perform. *12

Charlie's grandsons Ian Simpson and Ray Simpson are concertina players in Victoria, and their playing is featured in Chapter 11; Ian builds Anglo concertinas in the district of Nariel.

Ordish was recorded informally with Jim Harrison and Con Klippel in the 1960s; the recording is in the Norm O'Connor collection at the National Library of Australia, and the Library kindly made them available for this archive.

So Early in the Morning is a popular Australian polka of probably American origin, and Charlie plays it on his CG German concertina. It is played in the key of C, entirely on the C row, as are all his recorded pieces. He appears to have been strongly influenced by the one-row C accordions used in the Nariel area.

The Irish jig *St Patrick's Day in the Morning* is also played in the key of C, and all on the C row. It is played at a sprightly pace, and only about half in octaves as a result, and with a few end-of-phrase chords. He only plays the A part. A recording of the same tune by Englishman Scan Tester is included in Chapter 9, below.

An *Untitled Polka Mazurka* is played at a slower tempo, all in octaves on the C row, and in the key of C. Several polka mazurkas were played by the Nariel band through the years, and this one is similar to the one they called *Little Children*. 13

A varsoviana used in the Nariel band called *Turn Around and Then Stop*, is played in the key of C, again all on the C row in octaves.

Fred Holland

Fred Holland (1869- 1958) was a stockman, sheep shearer and gold miner. He was one of the earliest-born concertina players recorded anywhere, and a renowned musician who influenced many younger musicians in his family and surrounding area. Born near Mudgee, New South Wales, he spent all of his life in that district. He played for school and country dances, often playing with concertina players Walter Allen and Alec Orth. He played a Stanley concertina that was made in Bathurst. Holland is noted for his versions of the *Mudgee Waltz* and the *Mudgee Schottische*.* 14

Fred Holland, of Mudgee New South Wales, with his John Stanley concertina, 1957. He is demonstrating the old practice of waving the concertina for emphasis during the playing of dance tunes. Photograph by John Meredith, in the archives of the National Library of Australia.

According to John Meredith, Holland lived in a particularly inaccessible valley set in steep hills, an area still without electricity in the 1950s. He was recorded at the very advanced age of 88 and with a concertina that is clearly in need of a tune. These field recordings hardly do Holland's playing justice, but they are all we have of this well-known and respected musician. They have been made available by the National Library of Australia.

The existing recordings, made by Meredith in 1957, record a sparse playing style with few ornaments, accented mainly by frequent octave notes and only an occasional chord. The first two tunes below are pitched in the key of Ab on the recordings. This seems to be an artifact of the tape recordings - some sort of pitch wobble caused by the current inverter that was used to power the tape recorder, from the battery of a Land Rover (Meredith later began using a tuning fork at the beginning of recordings, to avoid such problems). Holland's house had no electricity at the time of Meredith's visit. It is likely that his concertina was pitched either in Bb/F or C/G.

 In the transcription the *Mudgee Schottische* is transposed to the key of C, which fits the pitch of concertinas owned by most players today. The tune is played mostly on the C row, with occasional brief ventures onto the G row. Holland played nearly entirely in octaves, like most other old-time players in Australia who were recorded. It should be noted that the entire A part is reasonably easily played on the G row, an octave up, but clearly that was not Holland's preference.

 An *Untitled Schottische* is played similarly in the key of Ab on the tape recording (again, probably actually Bb or C).

 *Write Me a Letter Home* was one of the popular hits of 1866, and was written by the American poet and lyricist William Shakespeare Hays. Many of Hays' songs and tunes were spread by the minstrel shows, and he claimed to be the author of *Dixie* (a claim in dispute, as most consider it the work of Dan Emmett). *Write Me a Letter Home* is played by Holland in the key of C# on the tape, clearly the problem of the wobbling pitch of the tape recorder used.

Clem O'Neal

Clem O'Neal (1912-1980) came from Iron Bark, now called Stuart Town, a New South Wales mining town that lay in a particularly concertina-rich district; his town is about thirty miles west-southwest of Mudgee (the home of Fred Holland), fifty miles south of Cobborah (Dooley Chapman), forty miles northwest of Duramana (Susan Colley), and forty miles southwest of Gulgong (Walter Allen). Later in life he moved to Sydney, where he became aware of the folk music revival in the 1970s as a result of the LP record *Bush Traditions* produced by Warren Fahey.

O'Neal made a number of concertina and button accordion recordings for members of a concertina session that took place in the Wentworth Park Hotel in Sydney at that time. He later recalled that until those

Clem O'Neal, at an Irish session in Sydney, 1977. O'Neal emerged into the Australian folk revival scene in the 1970s unaware that other Australian concertina players still existed. When Dave de Hugard, an Australian-style Anglo player took him to this Irish session, he said that he liked it but that he "never heard anything like that where I am from." With thanks to Dave de Hugard.

events he had not seen another concertina player for forty years, and that he was the last player who had learned 'by ear' in his district. A brief biography of him appeared in *Concertina Magazine* in 1982, from which the following is excerpted.* 15

Both O'Neal's father and grandfather were also born in Iron Bark; his great-grandfather seems to have come to Australia after the Wicklow rebellion in Ireland, in 1828. Clem O'Neal learned the concertina at the age of ten, after an unsuccessful stint on the violin. His first instrument was a 20-keyed German concertina, but he later played Lachenal Anglo-German concertinas.

According to O'Neal, the primary source of new tunes in his younger days was from people returning from trips, and the modifications of the 'folk' process started then:

The only way things was, was that someone would go away on a shearing trip and he'd remember part of a music [tune], part of something. He'd have to keep it in his head; when he came back perhaps he'd remember only part of it. So to make up a dance tune, he'd probably remember parts of three bits of different things which someone had played in a town or somewhere or other, and he'd combine them together. Someone else would hear him play that, and eventually new tunes got created from one listening to the other and these seemed to go right up and down some twenty or thirty miles along the river.

O'Neal's tunes were nearly all ballroom dance tunes: polkas, waltzes, schottisches, mazurkas, and such. He recalled that:

The dances were out in country places, mostly in the houses (which normally had) dirt floors or flagstone floors. Quite a lot of the houses were small. Some people danced inside the house and quite a lot danced outside the house. The concertina player moved about from room to room carrying the concertina ... and so there were times when those outside couldn't hear him. The player just moved around in among them and some (players) actually waltzed in time with them to get through.

O'Neal was recorded by Dave de Hugard in 1977, and three tunes included here are from that session: The *Boston Two-step*, an untitled *Schottische*, and a sentimental waltz, *Only a Bird in a Gilded Cage*. O'Neal also recorded many tunes himself, as gifts to his friends in the Sydney Bush Music Club, who were always eager to hear tunes from a surviving player of the house dance era. The remainder of the tunes here are from those homemade cassette tapes, and were made available by Bob Bolton and the Sydney Bush Music Club.

Clem O'Neal had a number of schottisches; here are three.

The **Untitled Schottische** is played on a CG Anglo, in the key of C, and like the above varsoviana, it is played entirely on the C row. He was mostly a single-row player, and lamented the fact that he did not learn how to cross-row like other Australian players. He tended to play octave notes rather sparingly, as accents, and added the odd chord at ends of phrases.

Tom Mitch's Schottische* and the *North Wind Schottische are recorded on a cassette player that is off-pitch (one semitone sharp); he appears to be playing both of them in G, all on the G row of a GD concertina. The *North Wind* was a globally popular tune, and was recorded by American accordionist Myron Floren, among others.

All By Yourself in the Moonlight is a barndance tune (schottische rhythm) played on a G/D concertina, in the G row in G (the cassette tape is one semitone sharp). It is a British music hall song, written by Ralph Butler (his pseudonym was Jay Wallis) in about 1928. Peter Ellis considers it one of the best barndance tunes, because it helps emphasize for dancers the pause and kick at the end of each relevant bar in the song.

Here is the first verse: *There ain't no sense sitting on the fence, all by yourself in the moonlight.*
There ain't no thrill by the watermill, all by yourself in the moonlight.
There ain't no fun sitting beneath the trees,
giving yourself a hug,
giving yourself a squeeze.
It's insane swinging down the lane, all by yourself in the moonlight.

Varsoviana (Kick Your Leg Up, Sal Brown) was a nearly universally known tune in O'Neal's younger days, and is still known among musicians and dancers in England, Ireland, and the United States (a version by George Bennett is included above). O'Neal plays it completely on the C row of a C/G concertina, partly in octaves (note: the cassette recording is about 30 cents sharp).

Varsoviana

Australia
Varsoviana (dance)

As played by Clem O'Neal
Transcribed for CG Anglo by Dan Worrall

A Bird in a Gilded Cage is an American popular song composed by Harry von Tilzer (music) and Arthur Lamb (lyrics), and was one of the hits of 1900. It bemoaned the fate of a girl who married for money. Von Tilzer reportedly asked Lamb to change a few of the original stanzas to make it clear that the woman was married, and not a prostitute. Clem plays it on a C/G concertina in the key of C, all on the C row.

The Boston Two-Step, despite its title, is an English dance composed by Tom Walton in 1908. Clem O'Neal's version is fairly close to the dance's signature tune. A variant of the two-step, it is danced to this day in Ireland and Australia.

Susan Colley

Susan Colley (ca.1884-1976) came from Duramana, a pioneer village about fifteen miles north of Bathurst in New South Wales. Colley was born Susan Pateman. Her father was a bullock driver and farmer, who lived on ninety acres near Duramana.

Most of what we know of her playing is from recordings of her songs made by Percy Gresser of Bathurst along with members of the Bush Music Club of Sydney in 1965, copies of which are housed at the National Library of Australia; as well as field recordings made by Warren Fahey in 1973. Gresser noted of her family that 'One family in particular, the Pateman family, and close neighbours of my people, were outstanding as concertina players. Not one of them ever had a lesson in music and one of the girls, Lottie, was an exceptional player.'

Susan Colley, holding her grandchild and standing next to her daughters. Photo courtesy of Warren Fahey.

Duramana's heyday as a pastoral village was in the late nineteenth century. Gresser described the village's dances:

> *There was no public hall for the holding of dances and suchlike functions. But dances were frequent. The younger folk, and some not so young, would congregate at the residence of a neighbour or acquaintance, coming by springcart (before the advent of the sulky), horseback or foot, and dance the whole night through to the music of a concertina or accordian. (They would) dance the Quadrilles, Lancers and Alberts, polkas, mazurkas, old time waltzes, etc., until after sun-up next morning. More than one residence was built so that a partition between a couple of rooms could be readily removed in order to have sufficient space for the holding of a dance.*

Gresser meticulously recorded the words of scores of songs from Susan Colley; many of them she had learned from her father, and he from his father. Gresser recalls that:

> Mrs Colley also informed me that one of her earliest recollections was hearing her father singing 'Bonnie Moon' as he would be riding home from work through the bush during moonlight nights. After Mrs Colley was married her home was situated for a number of years in a valley surrounded by hills, and she told me that she and her sister, Clara, would, on a summer's night, get a concertina each, seat themselves outside the house and play together hour after hour in order to hear the music echoing around the hills.* 16

The wide variety of songs in her repertoire shows the global resources available to the working-class resident of even the smallest out-of-the way Australian hamlet at the turn of the last century. A large number were from the American minstrel shows, like *Massa's in de Cold Cold Ground*, *Old Black Joe*, *I'se Gwine to Dixie*; *Nellie Grey*, and *Lillie Dale*. Many were Irish sentimental favorites of the late nineteenth century, like *Kathleen Mavourneen*, *Mother Machree*, *Endearing Young Charms*, and *The Rose of Tralee*; some were American and English popular song tunes, like *Two Little Girls in Blue*, and *Wait 'Til the Clouds Roll By*.

Others came out of the early American country music repertoire, such as *I'll Be All Smiles Tonight*, and some dated back to the California gold rush days, like *Clementine*. A fair number of songs were Australian in origin, like *The Wild Colonial Boy*, and *Botany Bay*. Few were anything that a folk collector of Child's Ballads would find interesting, but these were the tunes passed from person to person in the Australian Bush.

Susan Colley's repertoire of dance tunes primarily consisted of waltzes, mazurkas, polkas, and varsovianas, as well as tunes for set dances - quadrilles like the *Lancers* and the *Alberts*. As befits that of most Australian players, her style was melodic and sparsely (if at all) ornamented by grace notes; she played for the dance. She used frequent octave notes for emphasis and volume, and in doing this she often substituted a note a third up from the lower octave, which gave a harmony to her playing. She did not often use full chords.

Susan Colley was recorded by Warren Fahey in 1973, when she was living in an old age home in Bathurst. She was 92 years old at that time. Warren has kindly made several recordings available to this archive. In the first, she describes the old dances to Fahey.

Her *Varsoviana t*une is a distant variant of the one played by Clem O'Neal in the previous section. Its apparent key on the recording is E, but it is likely that the tape is sharp and that she played it in D on a G/D instrument. It is played all on the D row, largely with octaves and with many partial chords.

The Wild Colonial Boy, is a traditional Australian ballad about an Irish rebel who became a bushranger. Like Bennett's song about Ned Kelly in a previous section, this ballad sympathizes with the Irish-Australian outlaw.

Ernie James

Ernie James (1892-1981) lived in the Mudgee area of New South Wales, like Fred Holland. He was a nephew of Walter Allen of nearby Gulgong New South Wales, as well as a friend of Fred Holland and Orley Benson (an accordion player also living in Mudgee). Benson told stories of James and Allen:

> [They] would play for a dance, one on the concertina, and the other on a fiddle, and how, such was their versatility, after each dance they would exchange instruments and play on ... Walter Allen, who lived in a little galvanised iron cottage, would, during a heat wave, put his precious concertina into a sack and lower it halfway down the well to keep it cool and preserve the tone ... On a Saturday morning Walter Allen would bring his concertina into Mudgee and visit his old

Ernie James (right), at Home Rule, New South Wales, in 1957. Photo by John Meredith, courtesy the National Library of Australia

friend Stan Gudgeon who had a sports store in Church Street. When he began to play crowds would assemble in the street until the traffic was brought to a standstill. * 17

James was recorded in 1974 by Bruce Kurtz and his father, Reg Kurtz. The tapes were given to John Meredith and are housed at the National Library of Australia. Bruce Kurtz and the National Library have made them available for this collection.

Ernie James played an old German concertina, and knew a variety of dance tunes and old songs.

The Berlin Polka is one of many dance variants of the polka. In Australia, a version of this dance was collected by Shirley Andrews in Nariel, but to a different tune and dance than that played by Ernie James here. James version is played for a 'Kreuz' form of that polka, and is a fine tune. The tape appears to be about a semitone sharp. If that is correct, James plays it in the key of G on a C/G Anglo concertina. He played much of the tune in octaves. James was a skilled cross row player, and such playing is evident in all of his recorded tunes.

The Bullfrog Hop is a form of two-step played in jig tempo, and is played by James in the key of G, largely in octaves. Frank Bourke (1923-1989) of Binnaway, New South Wales claimed to have written the tune, and it worked its way into the local dance repertoire.

An **Untitled Schottische** is played in G on a C/G concertina, largely in octaves and in a cross-row manner.

The Cornflower Waltz was written by American Charles Coote around 1879. It is played on a G/D German concertina, in the key of D. Like all of James's tunes, it is played in cross-row manner and largely in octaves, with a few phrase-ending chords.

Percy Yarnold

Percy Alexander Yarnold (b.1907) came from Wingham, New South Wales, about 200km north-northeast of Sydney. According to John Meredith, who interviewed him in 1985, he 'came from a family in which everyone played a musical instrument. [Besides the concertina] Percy could also play the button accordion, piano accordion, and electronic organ.

A member of Keightley's Dance Band, Percy used to receive 12 shillings for a whole night's playing'.
* 18

All of Yarnold's recordings were made by Meredith in that 1985 visit, and are included here courtesy of the National Library of Australia.

Percy Yarnold in 1985, playing his German concertina. Photo by John Meredith, courtesy the National Library of Australia.

Claude Keightley was a bullock driver and Anglo concertina player; Yarnold began playing with him in 1917. In the first track, Yarnold describes playing with Keightley, and then plays *Keightley's Schottische.* He played a baritone C/G German concertina that had two sets of reeds and sounds like a button accordion as a result. Yarnold plays this piece in C, modulating to G on the B part. A skilled cross-row player, he played this tune on both rows.

Here Yarnold discusses the dances that they played for.

Early in the Morning is a widely known Australian polka. It is played in the key of C, and nearly entirely in octaves. It is played mostly on the C row, except for a few high notes on the B part.

The Woolly Tail Foxtrot is played in C, in octaves, and in a cross-row fashion. The foxtrot was introduced in the 1920s, one of a number of progressive (sequence) dances of that era.

Notes:

1. 'Newcastle', *The Western Australian Times*, (Perth), September 10, 1875.

2. C H S Matthews, *A Parson in the Australian Bush* (London: Edwin Arnold, 1908), pp.113-114.

3. Dooley Chapman, *Your Good Self*, CD, Chris Sullivan's Australian Folk Masters, CS-AFM-001, 2005,

4. see Lucy Stockdale, Obituary, Shirley Andrews, OAM: at the online website *Australian Folk Songs*, www.folkstream.com.

5. Dooley Chapman, *Your Good Self*, CD, Chris Sullivan's Australian Folk Masters, CS-AFM-001, 2005, Also see Chris Sullivan, 1983, Albert 'Dooley' Chapman, Australian Concertina Player: *Concertina Magazine*, Number 3, pp.7-11.

6. Dooley Chapman, *Your Good Self*, CD, (2005).

7. Ibid.

8. 'The Kelly Gang', *Marlborough Express* (New Zealand), July 21, 1880, p.2.

9. Peter Ellis, personal communication, 2011.

10. Peter Ellis and Harry Gardner, *Music Makes Me Smile*, (1998), p.12. The biographical sketch of Harrison is drawn completely from this source, pp.28-29.11. Ray Simpson, in a personal note to Peter Ellis, 2009.

12. Peter Ellis and Harry Gardner, 1998, *Music Makes Me Smile*: Carrawobitty Press, Albion Park, NSW, p.12.

13. Peter Ellis and Harry Gardner, 1998, p.126.

14. John Meredith, *Folk Songs of Australia*, (1967), pp.227-232. Also Bruce Kurtz, 1985, Fred Holland, Concertina Player from the Past: *Concertina Magazine*, No. 11. pp.7-9.

15. 'Clem O'Neal, Anglo Player', Richard Evans, ed., *Concertina Magazine*, Winter 1982, pp.7-10.

16. Percy J Gresser, 1965, *The Songs They Sang - and - the Dance Tunes They Played*: Copies of Gresser's extensive manuscript and songs recorded from Mrs. Colley were sent to the archives of the Bush Music Club of Sydney, as well as to the Wild Colonial Days Society of New South Wales. I am grateful to Bob Bolton for a copy of this work.

17. Ibid., pp.51-52.

18. John Meredith, 1995, *Real Folk*: The National Library of Australia, Canberra, p.19.

Chapter 8. Ireland

When most people are asked today about classic recordings of Irish concertina players, they think of such superb Clare players as Tommy McCarthy, Paddy Murphy, Chris Droney, Bernard O'Sullivan, Packie Russell, John Kelly and others, many of whom were visited by Neil Wayne and John Tams in the 1970s, resulting in an epic set of classic concertina recordings. These players, however, are the next generation on from the musicians discussed in this section.

Patrick Flanagan, for example, taught Packie Russell and his brothers to play music. Stack Ryan taught Tommy McCarthy and Bernard O'Sullivan to play, and Chris Droney learned from his father, Jim Droney. The players of the older generation - those active before 1920 or so - have much to teach us about the changing face of traditional music in Ireland during the early to middle twentieth century.

As we saw in Chapter 6, ballroom-style round dances and quadrilles were scorned as 'foreign' and house dances were effectively banned by Irish clerical and nationalist leaders in the early twentieth century, during the country's struggle for independence and its early years as an independent State. Just as the Gaelic League sought to reinstitute the Gaelic language, that organization and others sought to promote more purely Irish music and dance, and this goal had widespread public support.

Eighteenth century reels were brought back from a general decline and put to use in the figure dances of the Gaelic League. The *céilí* dances required a new Irish repertoire, long on reels, jigs and hornpipes, with effectively none of the old schottisches, barn dances, mazurkas and varsovianas, and a greatly reduced numbers of polkas and waltzes.

With the beginning of these 'more-Irish' *céilí* dances and the departure of the old house dance repertoire, usage of concertinas was to fall precipitously; the new parish dance halls required bands, not solo concertina or fiddle players as in the old house dances. Some players simply stopped playing as the older dance styles receded, and many others fully embraced a new Irish repertoire.

As a result, recordings of concertina players of the house dance era in Ireland, when ballroom-style dances were king, are scarce indeed, despite the incontrovertible evidence that such dancing in country houses was the most popular form of entertainment in the late nineteenth century, from the Gaeltacht to the Pale.

The concertina players represented in this archive lived through this tumultuous period of cultural change, and may be separated into two general groups.

A first group contains musicians whose recordings reflect the classic house dance repertoire, where an evening's fun would contain primarily round dances and quadrilles as well as some reels and jigs. All but one of the musicians in this first group are women. Two of them (Mary Ann Carolan and Ella Mae O'Dwyer) more or less stopped playing as the house dance era declined, and were recorded late in life; of a third (Katey Hourican) less is known.

There is little doubt that the cessation of playing allowed those women to retain their early repertoire in a way that active, continued playing in an era of rapid changes in repertoire – from *céilí* dances to pub sessions to folk revival - would not. A fourth, Terry Teahan, emigrated to the United States in the late 1920s. After finding his footing in the New World, he resumed playing about 15 years later, playing for the set and round dances that had by that time been discouraged and banned back in Ireland.

A second group of musicians, although of the same generation, left behind recordings that are almost entirely in the style of the *céilí* dance era, consisting nearly entirely of reels and jigs, with lesser numbers of airs and hornpipes. All but one of these musicians were men.

Some had actively supported their country's struggle for independence (Michael Doyle of Clare, for example, was a member of the early IRA), and the effort to regenerate a more Irish music and dance requested by the Gaelic League and later Comhaltas Ceoltóirí Éireann came naturally to them.

The one woman among this group, Elizabeth Crotty, was an officer of the CCÉ and its first president for life, and no matter what types of dances had been popular in her youth, her apparent choice was to play an 'Irish' repertoire.

Other members of this second group include William Mullaly of Westmeath, who recorded in the 1920s, as well as Patrick Flanagan and Tom Barry of Clare.

A Changing Irish Repertoire

Group 1: Three musicians with a house dance repertoire

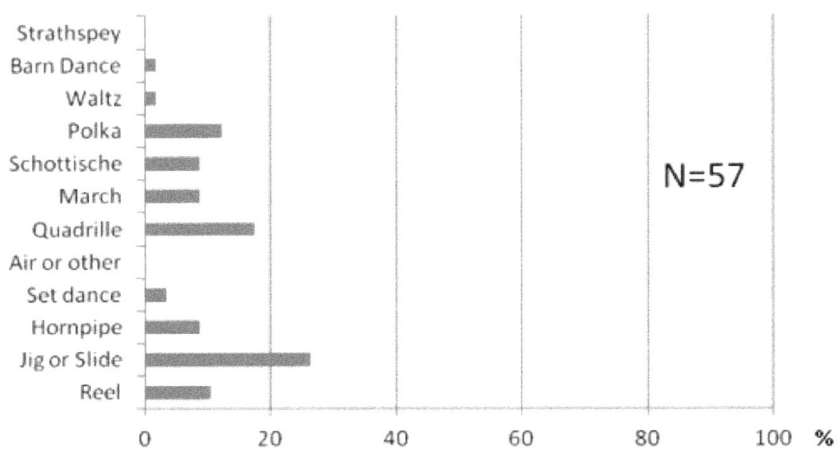

Group 2: Five musicians with a ceili dance repertoire

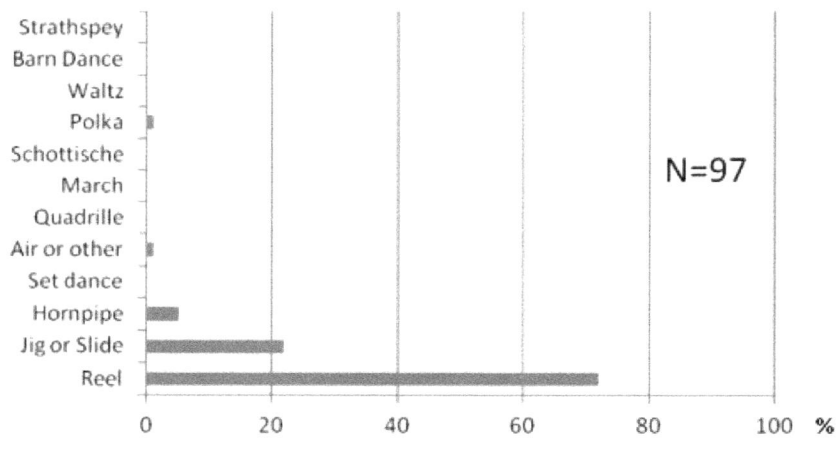

A comparison of dance types in the repertoire of group 1 (house dance repertoire) with group 2 (céilí dance repertoire). Tune counts (shown in percentages of total) include those of all known recordings for each individual, and include a total of 57 separate tunes from group 1 and 97 from group 2. The second group has narrowed its focus greatly on reels and jigs. **Group 1:** *Mary Ann Carolan, Ella Mae O'Dwyer; Katey Hourican.* **Group 2:** *William Mullaly; Patrick Flanagan; Tom Barry; Elizabeth Crotty; Michael Doyle.*

The differences of the tune choices of the individuals in these two groups is striking.

In the chart, the known repertoire of the three women of group 1, consisting of some 57 tunes, is classified by dance type and compared to those of the second group, with some 97 known recorded tunes. The much narrower repertoire of the latter group, dominated by reels, is clear. In the *céilí* dance era, the reel was king in Irish music, and still is today.

The mix of ballroom dance styles in the music of the former group, however, closely resembles that used by concertina players of similar vintage recorded in Australia, England and South Africa, with the exception of double reels and hornpipes. Yet the individuals in both groups belong to the same generation; all were born between 1885 and 1906.

A third group of three musicians in this archive left behind so few recorded tunes that their position with respect to the great change in repertoire is not fully known. A recording made by Ciarán Mac Mathúna of RTÉ in 1956 of Clare musician Jim Droney includes only a reel and a jig, but the repertoire of his son Chris, who learned most of his early music from his father, is rich in polkas, waltzes, and marches, as well as reels and jigs; all were used in old-time house dances.

Stack Ryan, also of Clare, is a legendary player of the house dance era, but the only publicly available tune of his that remains is an air. However, the tunes he passed on to those pupils who learned from him, in particular Bernard O'Sullivan, included numerous polkas, waltzes and marches from the old house dance repertoire.

Martin Howley of remote Fanore, County Clare, was a traditional singer who lived a quiet rural life and left only a very few concertina tunes, among them an archaic jig played on an equally archaic German concertina. It is impossible to know or even guess the range of his repertoire.

Group 1: Musicians of the house dance repertoire

It should be no surprise that the rare recordings of the house dance generation are mainly of women. Women live a bit longer than men, and thus there was a greater probability that a woman of this earlier era would live long enough to be recorded.

More significant is the fact that Irish women in the early twentieth century did not get out much, and did their playing largely at home. The late Tommy McCarthy once commented:

> *'Twas very much a woman's affair too. Of course women used to be indoors a lot in those days. They usedn't to go to pubs and all that. The husband used to be out of course in those days. The woman used to be always inside looking after the children, baking bread or something and they had t'ould concertina and they'd be playing away. Around Sheane alone ... every woman used to play one nearly. There was a Mrs O'Brian and my mother. Mrs Crotty wasn't far away in Gower.* [1]

Mary Ann Carolan played music for house dances until about 1920 when she married a farmer from another town, where music and dance were relatively absent in her immediate environment.

She returned to the concertina perhaps fifty to sixty years later, in Rip van Winkle fashion, when she was given a concertina by a relative. Memories of a long-ago time flooded back into her fingers, with a repertoire little altered by decades of playing newer tunes.

Another woman with a multi-decade interruption in her playing career was Margaret Dooley of Knockjames, a townland near Tulla in East Clare. Born in 1884, she was interviewed by Gearóid Ó hAllmhuráin in 1985 at the age of 101 years.

She played for house dances in her youth, like the one that she spoke of in the quote that began Chapter 6. She reportedly stopped playing in the second decade of the twentieth century, which coincidentally was the time of the anti-foreign music crusades and the beginning of the end of house dances. She did not play again until 98 years of age when given a concertina by a relative in America.

Her resurrected repertoire was very like that of Carolan, O'Dwyer, and Hourican: polkas, flings/schottisches, and mazurkas mixed in with jigs, reels and hornpipes. Like them, she played in a simple fashion, mostly in the key of C, with a rhythm designed for the needs of dancers. According to Ó hAllmhuráin, she knew that 'traditional' music had changed enormously since her youth.

Certainly she knew that it had grown more complex, saying:

> *Maybe the music of today is better, but the music we had in our time was all right too. They were well able to dance to it, anyway. There was no* meas *in you if you weren't able to play for a set. But 'tis different now. Even the sets are different now. There isn't as much hardship in them as long ago. (Ó hAllmhuráin, 1986, p.351).*

As was mentioned above, Solus Lillis, a blacksmith from Clonreddan, near Cooraclare in West Clare recounted the earlier style of his mother's concertina playing. She played in octaves and without much ornamentation, for her own amusement and for informal house dances:

> *I started to play when I was no more than eight or nine years old or less, maybe. My mother used to play. A lot of old people used to play, you know. They sounded a lot of base keys down below on the left hand side of the concertina. A lot of unnecessary noise I used to call it. They had more or less only the bones of the tune, a lot of them; the old women especially. 'Twas nearly all women who played around here. They never played for tape recorders or anything like that.* [2]

Fiddle and concertina player John Kelly (1912-1989), of Rehy West, in southwestern County Clare, learned to play the concertina from his mother, Eliza Keane, who played the German concertina. An aunt, uncle, and grandmother also played, so his roots in the genre were very deep indeed. [3]

Kelly's real learning on the instrument, however, was from a woman named Mary Houlihan, who had mastered the octave style, or "double style" as he called it:

> *She was supposed to have been the queen of them. It was like going to high school. When I graduated from home I went to her and got a good bit of instruction from her. She learnt the double style of playing from a man by the name of Patrick Murphy from Frure. I heard afterwards that his father was a tailor and he came back there [Loop Head] during the War of Independence. I don't know whether Murphy was on the run or whether he was working back there. But 'twas he showed her the double style of goin' across the keys, and she had it very good. She had a beautiful concertina, wherever in the name of God she got it, I don't know. There was a great sound in it ... 'Twas a high class German concertina.* * 4

What Kelly meant by saying "across the keys" is the practice, within the octave 'double' technique, of playing the lower parts of a tune on the C row and the higher parts on the G row rather than attempting to keep the entire tune on the C row, as an along-the-row player would.

The earlier days of ballroom dance styles at house dances were recalled by the late Tommy McCarthy (1939-2002), who recalled of his youth in Clare that:

> *There was a lot of Kerry music played around here ... I'm talkin' ... over fifty or sixty or maybe seventy years ago and I think they fell into a lot of polka playin'. Even in the country house dances a lot of polkas used to be played. Then of course Clare people used to go across to Kerry and brought polkas back with them. For the older sets the polka was easier than the reels. You could be playin' an ould polka away for half an hour - not that there was anything wrong with it, but 't was easier on the musician and handier.* * 5

Polkas, and all the other dances of the ballroom genre, were easier to play than reels even when played rapidly because most of them had been composed on the concertinas and accordions.

Mary Ann Carolan

Mary Ann Carolan (1902-1985) was born in Tenure, a small village a few miles northwest of Drogheda, County Louth, in eastern Ireland. Her father, Pat Usher (b. 1866), was also a concertina player, and her brother Pat played the fiddle. Mrs Carolan is best known as a traditional singer, and she sang ballads and old songs from her native County Louth on a 1982 Topic recording, *Songs from the Irish Tradition*.

A few tracks of her concertina playing were recorded by RTÉ in a 1985 interview, and at about the same time she was recorded by a young Drogheda concertina player, Jim MacArdle. Many years later, MacArdle and some of his friends released a CD of County Louth traditional music that included some tunes and songs that he had collected from her.
* 6

Music and dance were a common occurrence at her childhood home in Tenure. As she put it in a 1985 RTÉ interview:

I used to play for the half sets in the house, at home ... we used to have a little bit of fun on a Sunday night. A big swing-around and polka... Around where I lived, at home, we just had the sets. We called them the half set, and we'd have a whole set when we had the number [of dancers].

Mary Ann Carolan (1902-1985) holding her German concertina at the Drogheda Folk Festival, c.1977. Photograph by Joe Dowdall, courtesy of the Irish Traditional Music Archive.

As a young woman she married a farmer from the nearby town, The Hill of Rath, not far from Drogheda. Leaving her musical home behind, she applied herself to raising a family, and did not play the concertina again until late in her life, when one of her family members gave her one at about the same time as she became known outside of her area for her traditional singing.

Her song repertoire contains a strong Scottish influence, as well as a number of songs written by an earlier Drogheda songwriter named John Shiels. She also had some American minstrel songs, one in particular being *Young Bob Ridley* that exists today in America only in archived nineteenth century broadsheets, but that lived on in the rural County Louth singing tradition.

Her concertina repertoire strongly reflects the house dance tradition. This mixture of quadrilles, waltzes, polkas, and marches indicate a thriving ballroom dance component to the house dances in her home. At the same time, she recorded several reels and jigs that reflected a strong traditional component to her repertoire, just as existed in her repertoire of songs. She tended to play reels singly rather than in octaves, very probably because of their rapid tempo.

She recorded a number of what she called 'quadrille tunes', among them a medley of slides, **The Perfect Cure** and **The Morning Glory**, as well as a medley of polkas for the sets, **The Lass Of Gowrie**, **Untitled**, and **Try And Help Him If You Can**. The slides are played all on the C row and mostly in octaves on her C/G German concertina, as is the polka *The Lass of Gowrie*.

But the next two polkas in the medley of polkas, although in also the key of C and mostly played in octaves, spread to both rows of the concertina - especially the last tune, which is higher-pitched and is played mainly on the G row. Both medleys were recorded in 1985 and released in the program *The Long Note*, and appear courtesy of RTÉ, Ireland's Public Service Broadcaster.

The following six recordings were made of Carolan's playing in the 1980s, by Jim MacArdle of Tallanstown, County Louth, who has kindly made them available.

A schottische/fling, **Lady Mary Ramsay**, is also played in octaves, and all on the C row. Like some of her traditional songs, it shows a Scottish influence in her repertoire.

She recorded several marches, of which one, **Napoleon's March**, is included here. Marches were commonly used as 'curtain raisers' in old time house dances to begin to form up sets for quadrilles. Like the above tunes, it is played in C on the C row, in octaves.

 The *Veleta Waltz* was a ballroom sequence dance that was introduced in 1900, shortly before Mrs Carolan was born. The tune she plays for it is in C, played all on the C row.

 *Bonnie Kate* is an example of one of her reels, which she plays mostly singly (one note at a time rather than in octaves), because of the rapid tempo. Playing reels singly is typical of all recorded old-time players in Ireland.

 *Quadrille #3* is a single reel used for sets. She plays it mostly singly. The A part is in C and played all on the C row, and the B part is in G and played on the G row.

 *You're Welcome Home Prince Charlie* is an example of one of Carolan's jigs. Like most of her other tunes, it is played on the C row, in C, and in mostly in octaves.

Mrs Carolan played a C/G German concertina that had double banks of reeds tuned an octave apart, which meant that when playing in octaves she was sounding four reeds for each melody note, which gave a full, accordion-like sound.

In a 1985 RTÉ interview she makes it quite clear that volume (one of the benefits of octave playing) was an important part of her dance music. When asked about the demise of the concertina in the middle and late twentieth century, Carolan said, "It has died out. There are better instruments - louder. Louder instruments."

As music moved from house dances to the new public halls, the concertina faded before the much louder accordion.

Ella Mae O'Dwyer

Ella Mae O'Dwyer (1906-1992) from Athea, County Limerick was born as Ella Mae Quille in 1906. She emigrated to America as a young woman, and there met and married Liam O'Dwyer, in Detroit Michigan. After the birth of their first child, they returned to Ireland in 1934, and settled near Ardgroom, a tiny village on the Beara Peninsula near the Cork and Kerry border.

Her son Riobard O'Dwyer recounts their life in Ardgroom, playing for dances:

My father built a dance hall... The band consisted of my father playing the accordion and my mother playing the fiddle and concertina. There were no microphones in those days. The music consisted mostly of old-time waltzes, sets (traditional Irish dancing), barn dances, the Stack of Barley, and two-steps.

I was at the door, at the age of 6, collecting the 4 pences (approx. 4 cents later). One night a man from Kerry, seeing that I was so small, passed me in without paying. He went over to the right and sat down. Off I went after him looking for my four pence. I stayed at him for about 20 minutes until I got the four pence off him ... but by then about half the hall had got in for nothing! When I was 8 years old, I went up on the stage playing the accordion with my mother, and my father went on the door collecting the four pences.

Ella Mae O'Dwyer

Bit by bit the remaining members of the family joined in the band: Norelene on piano, Liam on the piano accordion and drums, Maura on piano and cordovox, and Sean on drum and vocals, and guitar and trumpet in the 1960s ... *7

For a good while, the Parish Priest (to put it mildly) was not favourably disposed towards the dances as he looked on them as "occasions of sin". He would ask people in Confession if they were dancing in our hall the Sunday night before. On occasions he would walk into the hall, spread out his hands in a gesture that would say "All out" to those who would go out for him. At the time many people used be walking up and down the road in front of the hall afraid to go in. It wasn't until my father, cycling to Castletownbere one day, stopped the Parish Priest on the road and said to him: "May God forgive you, Father. You are taking the bread and butter out of the mouths of my children", that this nonsense stopped.

Despite what was done to them as regards the dance hall in the early years, my father and mother, who were deeply religious, kept the Faith and attended Mass regularly... 'Tis strange how the ways of the world change. The dance hall, which in early years had come under considerable opposition from the then Parish Priest, came in handy in 1994/1995, as Masses were held there while the Ardgroom Church was being renovated. * 8

The O'Dwyer's former dance hall is the building with the rounded tin roof, which is behind the O'Dwyer family home in Ardgroom (2011).

Mary O'Sullivan, who lives in Ardgroom, recalled the dancing of sets there well into the 1940s:

> *In 1945-1946 I went to the dance in Ardgroom at O'Dwyer's Hall where they danced the set....The O'Dwyer family played in Ardgroom hall. Ella Mae played the concertina; her son Riobard, the accordion; her son Liam, the drums, and her daughter Norelene, the piano....we only had to say 'we'll dance a set' because there was only one set in the locality. There was a Sunday night dance always, never during the week. The next generation hadn't an interest in it and they went on to modern dancing.* 9

The sets in Ardgroom, as Riobard remembered, were danced to "all polkas, sometimes jigs."

In 1974, Mrs O'Dwyer was recorded by Neil Wayne and John Tams on their recording trip to the west of Ireland. She was the oldest and also the only woman of their sources on that trip, and stands out in that group with her use of the German concertina.

The following three tunes were recorded at that time and appeared in the CD *Irish Traditional Concertina Styles* (re-released in 2007). They appear here courtesy of Neil Wayne and Free Reed Records.

Dancing the Ardgroom Set in the O'Dwyers' dance hall, 1960s. Courtesy Sean O'Dwyer.

Mrs O'Dwyer's Fancy is a set of polkas that were used in the set dances at Ardgroom. She plays this tune in the key of F on her Bb/F concertina. She starts the tune on the lower row (F), then moves up to the upper (Bb) row, and then weaves the tune back and forth the two rows. Every convenient note is played in octaves; only the quicker or inconvenient parts are played singly.

 That driving, heavily cross-row octave style is also evident in **The Ardgroom Set,** which also consists of polkas (known as *Johnny Leary's Polka* and *Tournmore*, or *Wallace's Cross*, according to Gearóid Ó hAllmhuráin).

 **The Stack of Barley**, a hornpipe presented as a barn dance in her 1974 recording, is played very rapidly, and for the most part, singly.

Mrs O'Dwyer was also recorded by Séamus MacMathúna in the 1970s. The following two tunes are from that session, and appear courtesy of RTÉ, Ireland's Public Service Broadcaster.

 **Old Set Tunes** include a set of slides. They are played largely singly with octaves and drone notes interjected occasionally.

 An **Untitled march** is played partly in octaves, and partly singly, as fits each phrase.

Few today in Ireland have heard the sound of the old German concertina live; modern players typically use high quality English-made (or German or North American) Anglo concertinas. In 2013, the author hosted a small musical project where an old-style German concertina that had belonged to Ella Mae O'Dwyer was passed around during a six-month period to six modern-day Clare women musicians, to hear them take the old instrument through its paces. The resulting CD was published in 2014 by Oidreacht an Chláir, Miltown Malbay, and was entitled *Tripping to the Well: Six Clare Women & Mrs. O'Dwyer's Old German Concertina*. The women included Angela Crotty, Ann Kirrane, Mary MacNamara, Jacqueline McCarthy, Josephine Marsh, and the late Dympna O'Sullivan. All came from rich traditional musical backgrounds.

A peculiar result of this exercise was a slowing down of tempos amongst most of the recorded pieces relative to modern practice, due in no small part to the limitations imposed by a less-efficient instrument. Notably, the women mostly chose old pieces – waltzes, polkas, jigs, schottisches and hornpipes more than reels – learned from a parent or other older relative, as if the German concertina called for tunes from an older era.

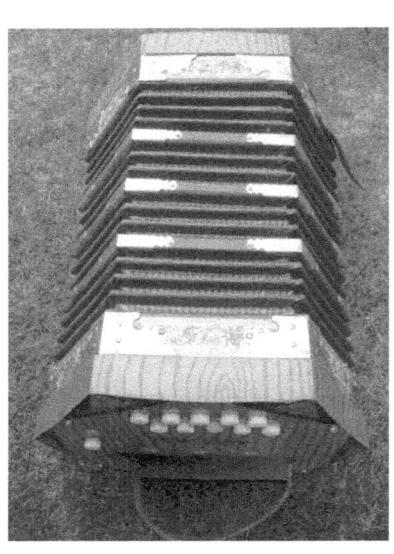

Ella Mae O'Dwyer's Ceilí Band concertina, made in Germany. It is double reeded, with two sets of reeds tuned an octave apart. With thanks to Maura and Sean O'Dwyer.

Katey Hourican

Katey Hourican lived in Lough Gowna, County Cavan. Very little is known about her, except that she was recorded by a T Smith at some time in the 1970s, when she was in her eighties, and that her daughter lived in Lough Gowna. She lived to the age of 103 years. She is said to have had a lovely singing voice, but that by the time she was recorded, most of her songs were forgotten.

Mrs Hourican recorded 11 tunes. Of them, five were flings (schottisches), two were polkas, two were jigs, and two were reels. Her repertoire reflects the house dance days, and her playing style is not unlike that of Mary Ann Carolan or of Ella Mae O'Dwyer. Her tunes appear here courtesy of Comhaltas Ceoltóirí Éireann.

She plays a German concertina keyed in C/G. **Spanish Lady**, a song/polka, is played in G, using octaves nearly throughout; she plays across the two rows.

An **Untitled polka** is similarly played, with a few bass chord notes occasionally injected amongst the low octave notes of the left hand.

Like Carolan and O'Dwyer, she plays with a drive and sparseness that suggests a history of playing for dances.

Two flings (schottisches), **Moneymuck** [*sic*] and *Mammy Will you Buy Me a Bow Wow*, are played at a relaxed tempo, with lower octaves and partial bass chords added intermittently to enhance the beat. The latter tune is a version of *The Keel Row*, as the tune is generally known. O'Dwyer's title for it is a mnemonic device that recalls the first notes of the tune.

A reel, **The Merry Blacksmith**, is played mostly singly, along the G row, in the A part, with left hand octave notes added occasionally for emphasis. The B part is played mostly in octaves.

Terry 'Cuz' Teahan

Not all recordings of Irish musicians of the house dance era are of women. Terry Teahan (1905-1989) was born in Castleisland, County Kerry, the son of a farmer. He wrote a short sketch of his life in a 1980 book of his music entitled *The Road to Glountane*, written with Josh Dunson and published in Chicago; all the quotes from him below are taken from that resource.

Terry 'Cuz' Teahan, as seen in the insert of the 1977 Topic LP Old Time Irish Music in America. Photo by Mick Moloney.

Although mainly remembered as a button accordion player, the German concertina was his first instrument, and he continued to play it throughout his life. He was eight when he started playing the concertina, getting a first lesson from the great Sliabh Luachra fiddler Padraig O'Keefe, who at that time also played the concertina. At the age of ten, Teahan first received his own concertina. After that instrument was accidentally dropped into a stream by a girl to whom he had lent it, he played the concertina at a neighbor's farm instead. For a while he stopped playing, and by the time he was 15 or 16, he became actively involved in crossroads dancing:

> *We danced at Barrack's Cross in them days. There were two or three who used to play there. At that time I didn't play. I used to sit around and dance. They had a 'kept' concertina, made up of everyone chipping in to buy it. There was a slight argument, and they asked me to hold the concertina instead of the woman who usually did. I kept it outside in a wooden box, wrapped in paper.*

There were also house dances, which he recalled in some detail:

> *In the winter they would start in the evening about six o'clock, and you'd be out of anyone's house by eleven. In the kitchen they would sit around a great big fire, and if the*

crowd wasn't too big there would be eight people playing cards at the table. There would be the man and the woman who owned the home and the neighboring men. The neighboring women hardly went out at night. It would be most every night. You would always know where it would be, meeting each other going along the boreen ...

Usually there would be four fellows standing in one line to finish and then four others to get started. Usually you never had the same kind of dancing. If one crowd danced The High Caul Cap, *that tune would be played all the way through. And the next crowd would dance* Hurry the Jug, *and that tune would be played all the way through. Another crowd might dance* The Jenny Lind *which was five complete figures...*

He mentions that at this time, any dances held at schools would be the new ceili dances, for example *The Siege of Ennis, The Waves of Tory, The Walls of Limerick* and the like. But at the house and crossroad dances where he played and danced, quadrilles consisting of sets of polkas and slides were the thing.

An IRA ambush of British soldiers in Castleisland in 1921, where a number on both sides were killed only hours before a general truce was called, left a deep impression on Teahan. He wrote a tune about the skirmish, and stopped playing for nearly twenty years, until about 1940. Teahan emigrated to Chicago Illinois in 1928, and lived there for the next six decades until his death in 1989.

In the 1940s he began playing for Irish dances in Chicago, playing into the early 1960s. He recalled that these dances included set dances, the Stack of Barley, the Highland fling, the varsoviana, and the barn dance: all staples of the old house dances in Ireland that continued to thrive among immigrants. After another playing hiatus, he began playing again in the 1970s, during the revival of Irish music in America.

Although mostly a button accordion player, he also played the fiddle and the concertina. Two recordings included here were recorded in the 1970s and are taken from a Topic LP of 1977 entitled *Old Time Irish Music in America* produced by Mick Moloney. They are included with permission of Topic Records Ltd.

His recorded repertoire on that LP consists of four polkas, seven slides, one barn dance, two flings/schottisches, three hornpipes, a waltz and an air: a mix of tunes not unlike that of the three women discussed above. Three of these recordings were on a concertina.

Teahan played a German concertina not unlike those owned by Carolan, O'Dwyer and Hourican. *Sword Dance* is a slide, played in the key of C mostly on the C row. Perhaps because of years of playing singly on the button accordion, Teahan played most of his tunes singly on the German concertina, but with rhythmic pulses of lower octave notes as an accompaniment.

Poll Ha'Penny is a fling/ schottische, also played in C and entirely on the C row.

In the liner notes of the 1977 LP, Mick Moloney observed of Teahan's playing and that of Gene Kelly (another accordionist on that LP):

> *Both play their music with a relatively more sparing use of ornamentation than is common among modern accordion and concertina players. Their playing awakens echoes of a bygone era, a time of house visiting and crossroads dancing. Neither is greatly concerned with technical perfection but rather with the spirit and lift of the music.*

The following two musicians, Stack Ryan and Jim Droney, left behind few recordings, but a fair amount is known from them by way of their pupils (in the case of Stack Ryan) and descendants (in the case of Jim Droney). On that basis, they are here tentatively grouped with the house dance players. Finally, the late Martin Howley, a traditional singer who also played concertina, left only a few recordings of concertina tunes; these are jigs and a polka. It is difficult to even guess the broad thrust of his repertoire, and he is included in this section by default.

Stack Ryan

Mick 'Stack' Ryan is a legendary name in Clare concertina playing, of whom very little has been written. He lived in Leitrim, not far from Kilmihil in west central County Clare. He is known today by way of his pupils, who became outstanding concertina players in their own right: Tommy McCarthy, Solus Lillis, Sonny Murray, and Bernard O'Sullivan. All lived near Ryan, and visited him to learn tunes.

According to the late Tommy McCarthy, Ryan played for country house dances and played a "Kerry" repertoire of slides and polkas ... the old house dance repertoire. McCarthy was interviewed by Gearóid Ó hAllmhuráin in 1986:

Stack Ryan as a young man. Photo courtesy Neil Wayne and Free Reed records.

I started maybe when I was eleven or twelve; not much more, anyway. I used to go to Stack Ryan. Mick was his proper name. He's dead and gone a good many years. Myself and Solus Lillis went to Stack together. We used to sit there in the corner of the old farmhouse at night. He'd play bits for us. The three of us were playing the same concertina. He'd give it to me and I'd try a bit, and then I'd give it to Solus. When he'd have learned us a bit of a tune, maybe the first part of something, he had a habit of sayin', "I must go out now and look at the cows."

He'd disappear outside you know and myself and Solus would be gigglin' inside and plain' any old thing at all you know and we'd be playin' it and one of us would say, "Is that good enough?" "Ah, 'tis good enough." Next thing Stack would call in, he'd open the door and he'd come in and say, "You played a wrong note there, I was listenin' to you outside." ...'Twas good fun.

He was a real lovely man you know. If he was around today I don't know how you would describe him.... He was a farmer and never went very far away, only around the country house dances. He had great ould tunes. He used to play a lot of slides and Kerry music. Bernard O'Sullivan back here in West Clare would be maybe the only one who continued on the way he used to play.

House Dance

> *The music played by Stack Ryan and his equals would not be anywhere near as intricate as it is now, but 'twas correct music and nice for dancin'.* * 10

Ryan was recorded by Ciarán Mac Mathúna of RTÉ in the 1950s. Only one tune of these recordings is publically available, although there may be more in the vaults of RTÉ in Dublin.

This recording is the air ***Eamonn a' Chnoic***, which appears in this archive courtesy RTÉ, Ireland's Public Service Broadcaster. Ryan plays it on an Anglo concertina pitched in C/G, and the tune is remarkable for its abundant simplicity and quiet dignity. It is played part singly, and part in octaves, without a single ornament. It is remarkable to consider the difference in how that tune might be played by concertina players of today, with ornaments hung on every bough.

As Tommy McCarthy mentioned (above), the player of modern times who best carried on the legacy of Stack Ryan was the late Bernard O'Sullivan (d. 2006) of Cooraclare, County Clare. Of his own playing, O'Sulllivan commented to Muiris O Rócháin that:

> *These are the notes as Stack had them fifty years ago or more. I was only twenty when I heard him; my fingers were more supple then. I was twenty and he was sixty at the time I was picking up the tunes from him. Stack had a very large and varied repertoire, obtained locally and from travelling pipers, and also later form the gramophone.* * 11

Three tunes from Bernard O'Sullivan, all of them thought to be connected with Stack Ryan, are included in this archive. They are from the 1974 CD entitled *Tommy McMahon & Bernard O'Sullivan, Irish Traditional Music of County Clare* (re-released in 2007), and are included here courtesy of Neil Wayne and Free Reed Records. Two of the tracks are polkas, and one a waltz; all feature octave style playing.

The late Bernard O'Sullivan with his grandson, 2006. Photo courtesy of Shay Fogarty.

Stack Ryan's Polka is played in C, with all four of its parts played exclusively on the C row. Octaves are used extensively throughout the piece, in some places used sparingly for rhythmic emphasis, and in other places used on nearly every note.

 Another polka, *I have a Bonnet Trimmed with Blue*, is played with O'Sullivan's friend and neighbor, the younger player Tommy McMahon. A transcription of their playing of it is included below. It is played in the key of G on a C/G concertina, and is played nearly completely in octaves in a cross-row style. The first four notes, in a low part of the scale, are played on the C row, and the next four notes, which rise in pitch, are played on the G row; the rest of the tune bounces back and forth from one row to the other.

Two-row octave playing is a powerful technique, not only for volume but for its ease of playing and the accuracy it imparts; one can play in this manner with great intuitive confidence, and it is perfect for dancing. Stylistically, O'Sullivan's playing (and presumably that of his mentor Ryan) is very, very close to Australian player Dooley Chapman; both have a sparse, extensively octave two row style, and beyond the obvious issue of repertoire it would be difficult to separate them in an audio line-up.

The second tune of that medley, *The Rakes of Mallow*, is variously referred to as a polka or a single reel.

I Have a Bonnet Trimmed With Blue

Ireland
Polka

As Played by Bernard O'Sullvan and Tommy McMahon
Transcribed for CG Anglo by Dan Worrall

A waltz medley, *My Heart Is in the Highlands*, and *The Dew Drop*, is also played by O'Sullivan in tandem with Tommy McMahon. These tunes are played on Bb/F instruments, with the first tune in the key of Bb, and the second in F. Highlands starts singly, with the left hand octaves added only for occasional emphasis, but the B part is played solidly in octaves, as is the entire second tune.

All three of these tracks from Bernard O'Sullivan and Tommy McMahon are clean, simple and graceful expressions of the old octave style once so prevalent in Irish playing.

Jim Droney

Jim Droney was born around 1886, and had a farm in Bell Harbour, in the Burren region of northern County Clare, which is still the home of the Droney family. He was one of the last native Irish speakers in Clare, and a fine musician. Jim Droney owned a Lachenal concertina for which he had sold a bullock in the 1930s, paying four pounds and ten shillings for it by mail order from London. His own father, Michael Droney also farmed in Bell Harbour, and also played the concertina. * 12

The Bell Harbour Ceilidhe Band, 1946. Chris Droney holds an accordion, and his father, Jim Droney plays the concertina. From Joseph Green, 'A Conversation with Chris Droney' in 'Concertina and Squeezebox', 1995.

Jim Droney had five sons, and although several could play concertina, it was his son Chris Droney (b. 1925) who excelled, carefully learning much of the repertoire of his father. He was interviewed by American concertina player Joseph Green, in 1994:

> My father was a great concertina player. He had the right old style altogether. He played it, oh, when we were only that big he was playing it. I had four brothers - I had no sisters - four brothers. And he used to be showing us a tune,

you know, showing us how to play a tune, but my four brothers didn't bother much. I was the only one who started playing. * 12

Chris Droney recalled the local house dances of his father's day:

They had no radio, no television, nothing in them times, do you see? What they used to do, they'd visit each other. Visit the houses in the locality. And they'd no transport, nothing. But wherever you went, you'd walk. So it meant that in a village, if there was five or six or eight houses in the village, they'd visit you tonight, and then they'd all be visiting me the night after, and then they might be visiting the next neighbor the night after that, and they'd keep going in rotation like that. And they used to have a concertina for a few pounds, and learned how to play it. * 13

The Droney family home, Bell Harbour House, was a popular meeting place for these house dances, and the annual Wren dance was usually held there. The Droneys played reels and polkas for set dances, along with jigs, hornpipes, marches, waltzes, and airs.

By the late 1930s, the house dances had mostly declined, and new halls for dancing were springing up. In north Clare the old sets and waltzes continued, regardless of the desires of the Irish Dancing Commission in faraway Dublin. Chris Droney told of playing at a local hall in Kinvara for his first paid performances as a dance musician:

There was three fellows up the road here when I left school, about fourteen [about 1939], and they used to get half a crown [two shillings and sixpence, or twelve and a half new pence] to play three hours at a little hall in Kinvara....And they told me, "stay playing, stay playing, and in a month or so when you've learned so many tunes off, come with us and you'll get half a crown as well." And I thought a half-crown was the greatest thing there ever was. I kept going with them, and then I stayed at it. * 14

This hall would have been similar to the country dance hall operated by Ella Mae O'Dwyer at the same time on the Beara peninsula in Cork, where sets also continued to be danced.

Chris Droney felt that playing this music was always much easier if it was played for good set dancers, and if it was played in a straightforward style:

Chris Droney with concertina, ca.1948. Courtesy the Irish Traditional Music Archive, Dublin.

> *If you have a set of eight people out on the floor, if they're good dancers, it's twice as easy playing music, if you watch them dancing, as it is listening to the people playing beside you. No problem, if they're good. If they're bad, it's the very opposite. You'll probably mess the whole thing up. Because if you get someone who goes out of time...ten chances to one you'll go out of time too. But if theyre good dancers, you would not miss one note.*
>
> *Now some of these new players - I don't know, maybe I'm wrong, but I don't like that style of playing. If you put eight people dancing a Caledonian set, and put one of these lads playing the tunes, they won't dance. I've seen it happen ... These new players, they have a different style. A different style altogether. Great for concertinas, great for records, great for entertainment, but if you put eight good dancers up on the floor, they won't dance the set.* * 15

Jim Droney and his son Chris were recorded playing together at Bell Harbour House by Ciarán Mac Mathúna of RTÉ in 1956. Jim Droney played a reel, and then recorded two jigs with his son Chris. Both father and son shared a driving, largely unornamented style that was carefully crafted to fit the needs of dancers.

An ***Untitled reel*** was recorded by Jim Droney at that 1956 recording session. The piece is played in a rapid, driving manner in the key of G on a C/G instrument, and was learned from the jew's harp playing of Jim's father, Michael (b. 1829). The A part is played singly, but with a rhythmic pulse added of left hand partial chords. The B part is played partly in octaves, again on the C row. The recording is courtesy of RTÉ, Ireland's Public Service Broadcaster.

Paddy O'Rafferty is a jig, recorded in 1956 of Jim and Chris Droney playing together. It is played in G, entirely on the G row, and nearly entirely in octaves. It has a great driving tempo that shows the tremendous skill of the two players. The recording is courtesy of RTÉ, Ireland's Public Service Broadcaster.

 The two also recorded another jig, the **Three Little Drummers** (also known as *The Rambles of Kitty*) in that 1956 session. Chris Droney plays the same tune, solo, on the 1974 CD *The Flowing Tide*. The recording of this latter version is of an improved quality, and perhaps better for studying the style of the piece, although the version of the two together has a driving force that is undeniable. The tune is played in G, mostly in octaves, and all on the G row. All but one highly pitched phrase (in the A part) is played in octaves. The recording is courtesy of RTÉ, Ireland's Public Service Broadcaster.

Gearóid Ó hAllmhuráin interviewed the Droney family, including Chris's daughter Ann and son Francis, in 1986, and was impressed by the uniformity of melody, variation, phrasing and rhythm of Ann's and her brother Francis's playing as compared with that of their father; clearly this is music that is being faithfully passed down from generation to generation. Francis spoke of learning from his grandfather, Jim Droney:

> *He taught me in the earlier stages, because he wouldn't have had anything much to do around the farm. I was never conscious of carrying on that style. I suppose I did it unknown to myself. We always played as a family and I certainly didn't try to play like anyone else.* * 16

Martin Howley

Martin Howley (1902-1981) of Fanore, in the rocky Burren coast of northwest County Clare, played the German concertina in a fine old octave style, but was better known as a traditional singer. A brief description of him was written by Jim Carroll of Lisdoonvarna, who recorded Howley for a CD entitled *Around the Hills of Clare*, released by Musical Traditions:

> *[He] was somebody we were able to visit on only three occasions, but each time we received a great welcome. He was a general labourer living in a council cottage in north Clare, on the edge of the Burren. Martin was passionately interested in songs from a very early age and was more than happy to share them with anybody. He had an excellent*

memory, not only in being able to remember the songs but also where he first heard them, and he related several anecdotes about learning them. He got a number of them from Travellers, including the extremely rare Fair Margaret and Sweet William, *which he knew as* The Old Armchair. *Our last visit to him, after we had heard he was very ill, was intended to be a short call to let him know we were thinking of him but soon the conversation soon got round to song. On his asking if we had a tape recorder with us, we protested that we were not there to bother him, as he was ill, to which he replied, "But I want to give them to you - I'm a poor man and they are all I have to leave." It was very moving to see the importance Martin attached to the songs he had kept alive for so long, and we proceeded to record him for the last time.*

Martin Howley as a young man, with melodeon. With thanks to Joe Queally and Jim Carroll.

It is difficult to ascertain the precise pitch of Martin Howley's instrument from the recordings; it may be that the old tape used has wobbled in pitch, or that his instrument had an unusual old pitch. What would be concert C on a C/G concertina is approximately B# on the recording. In this discussion, we will assume that it was a C/G concertina.

The version of **Maggie in the Wood**, a polka, that Howley plays is very simple, as befits its likely origins as a concertina tune. It is played in C, all on the C row, and almost all in octaves. He plays several variations on this very common tune which give it an archaic, yet somehow fresh sound. He taps time carefully and audibly with his feet as he plays.

Bothar na Sop. He also plays what he calls a "very old" jig, giving it a title in Irish that means the "Straw Road". He plays it in the key of G, all on the G row. The first part is played singly, and the second part nearly all in octaves.

Finally, he plays a very archaic-sounding **Untitled Jig** in Dm, playing it all on the C row, much of it in octaves.

Group 2: Musicians of the céilí dance era

Following the banning of the house dance and the scorning of 'foreign' round and square dances, the drop in concertina playing was particularly severe. The new parish and community dance halls needed bands, not soloists, and the bulk of the musicians played string and woodwind instruments that were more at home in the keys of G, D, and A than the key of C favored by old-style concertina players. And because the music and dance that followed this banishment took on a nationalistic character, most of the players who continued playing focused on 'native' reels jigs and hornpipes.

One problem was the dearth of these 'native' tunes. Francis O'Neill often mentioned in his writings the general absence of Irish music in the Ireland he visited at the turn of the twentieth century; he observed that the tunes he heard played were relatively few and hackneyed (*Miss McCloud's Reel* was such a tune) relative to the wealth of tunes that left Ireland during the Famine with the emigrating class of former professional musicians.

Such emigrated music soon returned in the form of gramophone records of such émigré musicians as Michael Coleman and Paddy Morrison, and in printed form with the collections of Francis O'Neill. Disregarding for the moment some local deep wells of folklore, an entire generation of Irish musicians relearned an earlier pre-Famine repertoire from such materials. For example, Paddy Murphy the late, well-known player from the Connoly/Kilmaley area, remembered how he and his friends learned new tunes from local postman Hughdie Doohan, a fiddle player who could read music and owned O'Neill's *The Dance Music of Ireland*. Said Paddy:

> *Hughdie used to sit down like any good schoolmaster with the lamp in front of him on the table. The book would be taken down and Hughdie's fiddle tuned to perfection. He would read the music then from O'Neill's book and according as Hughdie read them we learned them off. He was a mighty man for strange and new tunes. It was from Hughdie that we got Kit O'Mahony's Jig, The Flax in Bloom, The Maid of Feakle, The Northern Lasses and loads more. None of them tunes were ever heard of around here until Hughdie started to read them off of the book.* *17

Margaret Dooley (1885-ca.1988) recalled that the changes that had occurred in Irish since the playing days of her youth (as mentioned above, her repertoire included many of the older ballroom-style tunes) were due mainly to the influence of the gramophone and the influence of traditional music played on the radio and television.

It is easy to over-generalize, but the tunes of this group of concertina players, especially those of Elizabeth Crotty, Patrick Flanagan, Michael Doyle and Tom Barry, sound much more modern and familiar than those of the previous group. We hear tunes and, more importantly, settings of tunes that are similar to those of players today. That similarity of settings seems to partly result from the influence of recordings, radio and tune books as the effort to recreate Irish music and dance gained steam. More to the point, these players have for the most part left behind octave playing in the key of C, and play singly in the modern 'fiddle' keys of G and D.

Even Mary Ann Carolan and her father before her would play double reels singly (one note at a time) rather than octaves, because of the relative ease in playing rapidly. With the new *céilí* dance repertoire, reels came to the fore over slower ballroom dance tempos, necessitating the change in playing style.

Elizabeth Crotty

Elizabeth Markham Crotty (1885-1960) was born Elizabeth Markham, in Cooraclare, west County Clare. Although her parents were Irish speakers, she and her generation were not. Her mother was a fiddle player, but she learned to play the concertina, borrowing her older sister's two row German concertina. She married Miko Crotty in 1914, and they owned and operated a pub on the square in Kilrush.

She had a wide exposure to Irish traditional music. Because of poor health, she occasionally travelled to Dublin for treatment, and met many musicians there as well as attended Oireachtas competitions.

When a branch of the Comhaltas Ceoltóirí Éireann was started in Clare, she became a founding member, and later became its first president for life. She played music regularly

Elizabeth Crotty and Kathleen Harrington. Photo courtesy Michael Tubridy.

at the family's pub, meeting many visiting musicians, and was recorded on several occasions in the 1950s by Ciarán Mac Mathúna of RTÉ.

Partly because of the national exposure these recordings, and the broadcasts of them, brought, she was a much-respected celebrity within the traditional music community.

Her birth year, 1885, places her well within the generations that experienced the old house dances, and yet her recorded repertoire reflects very little of it. We know that others in her area, such as Stack Ryan and his musical descendants, Solus Lillis and Bernard O'Sullivan, played many polkas and slides for set dances, as well as waltzes and marches. Her area is just across the Shannon estuary from Kerry, where such music was and is common. And yet her recorded repertoire (as evidenced from the CD produced of her music from the RTÉ recordings of the 1950s) consisted primarily of reels (72%), jigs but not slides (17%), hornpipes (8%) and a single polka.

If we compare her repertoire to that depicted in the chart shown at the beginning of Chapter 6, which compared the concertina repertoires of three women of the house dance era with three modern women, Mrs Crotty clearly resembles the latter rather than the former. As Fred McCormick pointed out in a review of that CD at *Musical Traditions* in 2000:

> *There is ... precious little in the way of any local melodies, most of the items being fairly standard settings of fairly standard tunes. The impression one forms is that Mrs Crotty ended up mothballing many of the tunes she had played in her youth out of a desire to accommodate other musicians.*

It would seem that Mrs Crotty, being a founding member and president of the CCÉ, played tunes that fit with the preferences of that organization and others of the day, which looked askance at the old ballroom dance music (it was noted above that ballroom dance tunes such as schottisches and barn dances are now acceptable at CCÉ competitions, so attitudes are clearly changing).

For whatever reason, there is little of her music that fits within the house dance repertoire.

But the reels! She was a master player. An audio file of a classic medley of hers, *The Wind that Shakes the Barley* and *The Reel with the Beryl*, is included here. It is reproduced from a 1950s recording made by Ciarán Mac Mathúna, courtesy RTÉ, Ireland's Public Service Broadcaster.

A close look at *The Wind that Shakes the Barley* reveals much about both her background and the way in which the old German concertina shaped the way in which a musician played. Although the tune is recorded on the reasonably high quality Lachenal Anglo concertina pitched in C/G that Mrs Crotty played in her later life, she spent her early playing years playing the much less expensive German concertina.

If that earlier German concertina was like those played by Ella Mae O'Dwyer, Katey Hourican and Mary Ann Carolan on their recordings in this archive, it was one made with a double bank of reeds; for every button pushed, two reeds sounded that were pitched an octave apart.

This gave the instrument a much-desired accordion-like sound, and more volume. C/G German concertinas (such as Carolan's) had a deep baritone sound, because the second bank of reeds was tuned an octave below the 'normal' ones.

The inexpensive, mass-produced German concertina was never particularly efficient in its use of air, but playing quick tempo reels on the large double-reeded ones was a bit like running through mud. You could do it, but not as easily as you might have wished. Recordings of Michael Doyle of Ballymakea Mullagh, County Clare (see below) were on such an instrument, and in one recording after a particularly vigorous passage, he groans with the exertion.

The standard version of *The Wind that Shakes the Barley*, it could be said, is the one in O'Neill's *Music of Ireland*, where it was transcribed from the playing of Chief O'Neill himself, who played the flute. The reel was imported to Ireland from France around the mid-eighteenth century, and the instruments that were in use in Ireland at that time were the pipes, fiddle and flute. Accordingly, most of the pre-Famine reel repertoire was composed on these instruments. What is easy for the flute or the pipes, however, is not necessarily what is easy on the German concertina.

The Wind That Shakes the Barley
Comparison, First Four Measures

A comparison of the first four bars of 'The Wind That Shakes the Barley', between that of Francis O'Neill, top (originally in D), and Mrs Crotty, bottom.

The illustration compares O'Neill's version (top) with Mrs Crotty's (bottom). O'Neill's version was originally written in the key of D, and has been changed to G - the key Mrs Crotty plays it in - for the purposes of this comparison. The O'Neill version contains numerous brief scale runs, which are simplicity itself to play on the flute. On a two row German concertina when played along the rows, easy on the flute but less so on the German concertina. Each one step advance up or down the scale requires a change in bellows direction, in effect requiring the musician to switch the bellows direction back and forth, opening and closing.

Given the inefficient nature of the German concertina's bellows, this can be difficult at the rapid tempo desired. No matter that a player like Chris Droney with a high-quality Wheatstone Anglo could drive right through such passages with no bother; the German concertina is less efficient and thus more difficult to play. And no matter that Mrs Crotty herself recorded this piece late in life on a higher quality Lachenal Anglo, and could herself manage the passage without difficulty. Her early experience playing the German concertina has apparently shaped her style in playing the tune.

Mrs Crotty replaced most of those scale runs with interval jumps of varying width. These jumps require fewer direction changes and are hence much easier to play, and at the same time are jaunty and bouncy.

For example, the second bar in O'Neill's version would require four changes in bellows direction when played on a concertina, along the row. Mrs Crotty's version requires none, and yet, with its interval jumps it sounds even livelier than the standard version. This is the work of a musician of some considerable skill, fit within the considerable limits of her instrument, making the setting more concertina-friendly.

Such 'concertina versions' of tunes were once commonplace, and added much spice and individualism to the music of the old concertina players. Today, complex three-row fingering styles have been developed for high quality Anglo concertinas that allow the most difficult passages in arrangements of reels to be managed - no matter that the reels were originally written on flutes or fiddles or pipes.

This is a great advance for the instrument, allowing the concertina to take a seat at the table when playing the most complex tunes of the pre-Famine era. What has been lost, however, are the unique and often quaint or eerie arrangements of the old players.

The tune is in the key of G. The A part is played mostly singly in an along-the-row style, with octave bass notes added in only for emphasis on the longer-held notes. It is played mostly on the C row, moving to the G row only at the end of the A part, as the melody rises. The B part is pitched higher than the A part, like many reels, and Mrs Crotty plays it on the G row, entirely in octaves. It is in this extensive use of octaves in the B part of many reels that she betrays her origins, which stem from a time when the concertina was mostly played in octaves for a slower house dance repertoire.

A second tune, **Dhá Ghabhairín Buí** (*Two Yellow Goats*) is a polka that Mrs Crotty plays in the key of C, all on the C row, and entirely in octaves. It is the only polka that she is known to have recorded, but here she plays it slowly, like an air. It is reproduced from a 1950s recording made by Ciarán Mac Mathúna, courtesy RTÉ, Ireland's Public Service Broadcaster.

Numerous other examples of Mrs Crotty's playing are to be found on an RTÉ CD issued in 2004, entitled *Elizabeth Crotty - Concertina Music from West Clare*.

William Mullaly

William J Mullaly (1884 - ca.1955), born only a year earlier than Mrs Crotty, was the earliest Irish concertina player to record, making a set of recordings in 1926-1927 just after he immigrated to America.

These recordings and the recollections of his relatives constitute nearly all that is known about him. Because of his early recordings, and of course his superb, driving playing, he has occupied a position of importance in Irish traditional music. Like Crotty, however, he recorded none of the old house dance music, and recorded only jigs and reels.

A biography of him, by William Bradshaw, may be found in the Irish Traditional Music Archive's recent release of a CD and booklet of Mullaly's music.*18 He was born near Rathconrath, County Westmeath, not far from the town of Mullingar. One of eleven children, neither of his parents were musicians. Early lessons came from Mrs Anne Heduan of nearby Painstown. Several of his siblings also played music, on other instruments.

After emigrating to America and making his recordings in New York, he disappeared from public view, and ended his days in an institution in the southern United States.

In his youth in Westmeath, house dances were in full swing, and a neighbor, Mrs Kate Doolin, remembered him at one that took place in her home in 1905:

William J Mullaly (1884 - ca.1955) in a photo taken around 1926. With thanks to Nicholas Carolan and Jackie Small at the Irish Traditional Music Archive, Dublin.

> *"Yes, he played in the house that I was born in. He was a great musicianer, lots of tunes, oh, he was great ... To my mind he looked then to be about twenty or so, and it was shortly after that he emigrated."* *19

Mullaly grew up only 50 miles from the Drogheda area, where Mary Ann Carolan's family hosted house dances with polkas, schottisches, waltzes and the like. It seems likely that he was well versed in these types of popular dances, but chose not to record any of them.

Perhaps it was because he knew well the controversy then raging about the scorned ballroom dances in Ireland, and wished to stay above it, or perhaps the Columbia Recording Company wished to keep to more respectable fare. We will likely never know.

From Mullaly's reels, we know that he played in an along-the-row style, and probably owned a Wheatstone Linota concertina pitched in G/D. Like Chris Droney, he heavily favored playing on the bottom row (G for Droney's concertina, and D for Mullaly's).

 One sample track is included in this archive, of two reels, *The Green Groves of Erin* and *The Ivy Leaf*; it is from a Victor 78 rpm recording of 1927. Like Mrs Crotty, he typically played singly, but frequently employed octave phrasing in the higher pitched B parts of reels, as in both of these selections. Both tunes are in the key of A, and are played nearly entirely on the D row.

In many ways, as Jackie Small points out in his analysis of Mullaly's playing for the above-mentioned recent CD, Mullaly's playing presages the techniques of modern players, especially in his frequent use of ornaments. Triplets are perhaps most common and are played in places where a bellows' direction change is not required.

However, there are also generous helpings of cuts, octave notes, and drones in his repertoire that are quite unlike the simpler, relatively unadorned style of earlier Clare players like Stack Ryan and Jim Droney - or for that matter, of Mary Ann Carolan and Mrs' O'Dwyer.

Most of this may be related to the fact that he had a very responsive Anglo-German concertina. At any rate, his playing is perhaps transitional between the old octave players and those who would follow in the late twentieth century revival.

Michael Doyle

Michael (Micho) Doyle (1897-1970) was born in Ballymakea, near Mullagh in west County Clare. His sister, Eileen Doyle Johnston played the fiddle and later the accordion. Michael Doyle was a soldier in the original Irish Republican Army during the Irish War of Independence, and later became a farmer. He travelled in good musical company, frequently playing for house dances in his early years with his neighbor Junior Crehan and with Thady Casey, who was a noted fiddler and dancing master of the area. Famed piper Willie Clancy was the godfather of his daughter Theresa, so presumably there was a musical tie there as well.

Doyle played a simple German concertina all his life, preferring its tone - that of the old country sound - over the 'sharp' sound of an 'English' (meaning Anglo) instrument. He was recorded in the 1960s by the late Clare musician John Joe Healy, whose widow gave the tapes to Jim Carroll; those field recordings are now accessible at the Irish Traditional Music Archive in Dublin. There are only a small handful of these recordings, of seven reels and two hornpipes. Three are included here.

The Doyle family home in Ballymakea, 1940. Like most country cottages of its day, it had a thatched roof. Michael is not pictured, but his sister Eileen holds a fiddle, left. His father James Doyle is at center, and his mother Honor is at right.

The Mount Phoebus Hunt, a hornpipe in the key of G, is shown in the adjacent transcription. Doyle played the tune singly in a cross-row style on his two-row instrument. Although the first part of the tune is played entirely on the C row of his C/G concertina, the second part alternates back and forth between the C and G rows. In general, the higher parts are played on the G row and the lower parts on the C row. This ability to cross the rows is similar to the row-changing in the two-row octave style.

Doyle's ornamentation primarily includes triplets as well as brief runs of octave notes. He played frequently with fiddle players, and probably for that reason most of his recordings are in the key of G.

The Mount Phoebus Hunt

Hornpipe, Ireland

As Played by Michael Doyle
Transcribed for CG Anglo by Dan Worrall

An *Untitled reel* is played very quickly and with great drive, in the key of G and all on the G row. The A part is mostly played singly, with octaves placed for emphasis on the long notes at ends of phrases. The B part is largely played in octaves, not unlike Mrs Crotty's approach in *The Wind That Shakes the Barley*.

A second *Untitled reel* is also played in the key of G, all singly, and almost all on the G row. The tempo is very quick, indeed amazing for a German concertina.

Because there are so few tunes in his recorded repertoire, it is not possible to say much about the breadth of it. His sister Eileen Doyle Johnson, however, played a wide variety of tunes on her accordion in later years, including many waltzes and polkas in addition to reels, hornpipes and jigs. * 20

Patrick Flanagan

Patrick Flanagan (b. ca.1885) lived in Donagore, near Doolin County Clare, where he was a farmer. Micho Russell, the late well known whistle player, his brother Gussie who played the flute, and his brother Packie who played the concertina were neighbors and credited him as a source of many of their tunes:

> *Micho's father had bought him a Clarke's tin whistle when he was eleven years old. All three brothers learned much of their music from a neighbour, Patrick Flanagan. Patrick was a concertina player. To begin with, he simply taught Micho which fingers to lift to play a scale on the tin whistle. After that Micho was more or less left to his own devices and continued learning by ear. He returned to Patrick Flanagan later on to polish his tunes and add to his store.* * 21

It has been noted that Micho Russell's unique style on the whistle had much to do with his learning tunes from the concertina playing of Flanagan who was a generation older than the Russell brothers. Doolin at that time was a poor village in a backwater of west Clare, where scenery abounded but money was scarce; house dance and house sessions were major forms of recreation, and folk customs were strong.

Flanagan was recorded by Shaun Jordan of Lisdoonvarna County Clare, in about 1960, when Flanagan was 75 years of age The recording included five reels and two jigs, and was made in a country house session in Doolin, in a house belonging to a neighbor of Flanagan's named Griffith. Jordan remembers that it was difficult to record Flanagan, as he was a bit uncomfortable with being recorded, regardless of his evident skills on his instrument.

In a very brief *interview,* the soft-spoken Flanagan recalls learning the German concertina as a boy, when concertina playing was very common in his village. Flanagan played a two row C/G German concertina. He played reels singly in a cross-row manner, keeping most of the melody on the right hand and leaving the left mostly with some simple bass drones. Unfortunately, the microphone in this field recording was placed near the left side of the instrument, so the drones tend to overpower the melody; such would not be the case in a live session.

The first of the two **Untitled reels** is played in the key of C, starting on the C row in the A part but moving to the G row as the tune rises in pitch in the B part. The second reel in this melody is played in the key of D minor, mostly on the C row.

The Concertina Reel is played in an old style - all on the C row, including the higher pitched parts. For high parts, Flanagan moves his right hand up one position so that his pinkie is over the right-most button so that the high triplets flow effortlessly.

In the following two **Untitled reels** and another **Untitled reel**, Flanagan is accompanied by a lilter, much to his pleasure. In most of the field recording, his discomfort with being a solo 'performer' is evident, but when the lilter accompanies him his playing reaches a higher level. It is clear that this impromptu recording session did not capture a master concertina player at his best, but it is all we have today of his playing.

Tom Barry

Tom Barry (b. 1890) was from Carhurclough (or Cahruclough), a townland near Ennistymon County Clare, where he was a farmer. Very little is known about him. An entry in the Ennistymon Parish Magazine of 1998 listed his former home, along the road from Glann Cross to Ballagh Cross to the northeast of Ennistymon, as follows:

> *Across the boreen was the home of Thomas Barry, one of our greatest concertina players and his wife Cathy. It was later lived in by Cathy's niece Kathleen and husband Vincent O'Looney and family. They later built a new house and the old one is now closed up."* Barry must have played music with his neighbor Paddy Curran, a flute player who lived a few houses away.

Shaun Jordan of Lisdoonvarna recorded Barry in the 1950s, when he was 70 years of age. When recorded, Barry was playing in a pub in Ennistymon, along with flute player Paddy Mullins, who played in the Kilfenora Céilí Band, as well as some unknown fiddle and spoons players. The recording includes 21 reels, four jigs and no other dances; this was *céilí* country, only a few kilometers from Kilfenora, and Barry's repertoire strongly reflects the music of those dances. *Céilí* dances in Kilfenora began in 1909, when a parish priest, facing financial difficulty, began holding *céilí* dances in the local parish hall; the musicians became the Kilfenora Céilí Band, which in those days played mostly reels and jigs for sets and figure dances (by this time, the old quadrille tunes had been replaced by reels in sets as the trend to 'Irish-ize' the sets continued). In such a setting, it was to be expected that schottisches and barn dances were not appropriate.

In general, Barry sets a very rapid pace for the reels in this recording, regardless of whether playing solo or with other musicians. In most reels he plays singly on his Anglo concertina, which is an appropriate choice for the tempo (and for playing in G and D with fiddles and flutes). On a few tunes, however, he plays in octaves. All of the tunes and their settings in this recording are ones that are familiar to most Irish musicians today, especially those in west Clare.

The Heathery Breeze is a standard setting not very different than that of Packie Russell. It is played in the key of G on a CG concertina, all on the G row (note: the field tape recordings of Barry are all one and one half semitones sharp).

Sporting Nell is a variant of that reel recorded not many years ago by the late concertina player Tommy McCarthy. The tune is in the key of D minor. Although McCarthy played it on the G row, Barry plays it entirely on the C row, at times in octaves, at other times singly. There are two separate recordings of this piece given here, one solo and one with two unknown musicians on fiddle and whistle. This sort of group session playing became more and more common in the era of the *céilí* bands.

An **Untitled reel** is played in the key of G, all on the G row, and makes extensive use of octaves.

A second **Untitled reel** is in the key of C, and here too Barry makes extensive use of octaves. It is played entirely on the C row.

Sally Gardens is played with a group of musicians. It is a familiar setting, played in the key of G. Barry plays it nearly entirely on the G row, resorting to the C row in the A part for an E that he wished to play on the push rather than the pull. He is joined by unknown musicians on the fiddle and spoons.

Notes:

1. Gearóid Ó hAllmhuráin, *The Concertina in the Traditional Music of Clare* (PhD thesis, Queen's University Belfast, 1990), p.166.

2. Gearóid Ó hAllmhuráin, PhD thesis (1990), p.175.

3. Ibid, p.109.

4. Ibid., p.100.

5. Ibid., p.168.

6. That CD is entitled *Madam, I'd Like to Be Tossin' Your Hay*.

7. Note: Riobard's brother Sean has here edited the list of instruments used by the family.

8. Riobard O'Dwyer, The olden days, an unpublished posting on RootsWeb, January 1, 2009.

9. Mary O'Sullivan, as quoted in Larry Lynch, 1991, p.147.

10. Gearóid Ó hAllmhuráin, PhD thesis (1990), pp.166-168.

11. Muiris O Róchain, 1975, in the liner notes to *Clare Concertinas*, Free Reed CD FCLAR 02.

12. Joseph Green, 1995, An interview with Chris Droney: in *Concertina and Squeezebox*, Ithaca, New York, No. 32, p.39.

13. Joseph Green, 1995, p.40-41.

14. Joseph Green, 1995, p.39.

15. Joseph Green, 1995, p.41.

16. Gearóid Ó hAllmhuráin, 1986, p.320.

17. Gearóid Ó hAllmhuráin, 1993, "From Hughdie's to the Latin Quarter: A Tribute to Clare Concertina Player Paddy Murphy", *Treoir* vol. 25, no. 2 (1993), pp. 40-44. This story was quoted by Nicholas Carolan, see Note 104, p.56-57, from which I excerpted my own account.

18. *The Westmeath Hunt: William Mullaly, The First Irish Concertina Player on Record*: CD, Irish Traditional Music Archive, Dublin, 2011.

19. Harry Bradshaw, Biography of William Mullaly, in *The Westmeath Hunt: William Mullaly, The First Irish Concertina Player on Record*: CD, Irish Traditonal Music Archive, Dublin, 2011.

20. Eileen Doyle Johnson was the author's grand-aunt, and Michael Doyle his grand-uncle.

21. Anonymous, 2011, Russell Brothers, Micho, Pakie and Gussie: in Clare People, Clare County Library Website, www.clarelibrary.com

Chapter 9. England

It is one of the ironies of the concertina world, and of English music, that the country where the German and Anglo-German concertinas were most prized and commonly used during the instruments' heyday is the same country where recordings of early players are most scarce.

In the late nineteenth century, concertinas were to be found everywhere where working and middle-class people lived - in the streets, in the pubs, in churches and Salvationist revivals, on board British ships at sea, and perhaps of most importance here, at dances in houses, at village festivals, in taprooms, and in public halls. Of rural Norfolk in 1890 it was said that "almost every house possesses a worn-out concertina or a broken-down accordion." [1]

The poverty which was to be found in nearly all rural areas in the late nineteenth century seemed to favor the German-made concertina, much to the dismay of those in more proper society. The author of this 1885 article bemoaned the state of music in rural England:

> *A show of hands as to the most satisfactory instrument would probably result in favour of the German concertina. This foreigner, with its "fatal facility", has helped drive out the fiddle and to spoil the ears of a rustic people. It is now the concertina that is the rule at rural merrymakings, and the fiddle that is the exception.* * 2

As the concertina grew in popularity in the mid-nineteenth century, it brought its repertoire as well. The 'merrie dances' of old were being replaced by ballroom dancing, both of quadrilles and round dances, especially schottisches, polkas, and waltzes.

In country areas, these newer dances coexisted with older English country dances and step dances (reels, hornpipes and jigs), but the round and square dances were slowly edging out the older ones. A Cambridgeshire account of a platform dance in the late nineteenth century festival gives an idea of the changing mix:

> *Harry Huntley ... was the last harp player known to have played for dancing. He and his father, Jack, who was a fiddler, used to play together at Comberton and other feasts and at the fairs. They took round with them a dancing booth with a sectional floor and a box for the musicians: the two Huntleys, and a concertina player and a drummer. A box was placed in front of the booth for the collection of money. When long-wise country dances were in vogue it was easy for each dancer, as he reached the box, to place in it his fee for the players, but musicians found it more difficult to get their money when round dances, waltzes, etc., became more popular. To ensure that every dancer paid, someone had to be stationed at the door of the booth or other dancing place to collect the money as the dancers arrived.* * 3

As in Ireland, the rural house dance was an important venue for concertina players, as in this account of Christmas in Cornwall, in 1890:

> *[Musical] groups of four or five would come around - we played mainly to the higher class folk, and to the farmers, when we would get a glass of cider and a piece of Christmas cake, but the working class, who were mainly players, would join in with us with their concertinas, and we found many good players. Sometimes they gave us a step dance in*

the kitchen, with a glass of wine. The 'tina was a lovely instrument for quick music. Then at Christmas time we'd have dance parties in the kitchen. We used to have one dance, we would do, "The Polka", and at intervals all dance and meet at the centre. Then we had another dance called "The Heel and Toe", and we finished with a jig. Then of a Saturday night or at Christmas time, many would take their 'tinas to the pubs and after closing time they would do step dancing on a farm wagon with the 'tina, and dance for prizes. * 4

Band with two German concertinas, Saint Blazey, Cornwall, ca.1890. With thanks to Stephen Chambers.

Perhaps the largest impediment to the recording of concertina players in the early to middle twentieth century Britain was the attitude of those whose hands held the purse strings in the music world, such as this correspondent for *The Musical Herald* in 1890 Norfolk:

The merriest time for the labourer is after harvest, when he draws 5 or 6, the amount of his contract for getting in the harvest. His highest flight of merriment at that time is to do a shuffle on the floor to the accompaniment of a concertina. It cannot be called dancing; it is vigorous and rough. The songs that the labourer knows are either negro minstrel songs or the popular ballad two or three years after its death and burial in towns. To such a man, instrumental music is a luxury outside his range. If then, the instrument that a labourer sometimes chooses is cheap and vulgar, we must be content. Better to have a tune on a concertina than a songless people ...

A professional musician in polite society expressed a similar sentiment in 1904, writing that:

"The German concertina is admittedly an inferior instrument. Still, we must not sneer at the thing. I believe it does give a measure of enjoyment to some of our hard working people; it is better for them to listen or to dance to

> *a German concertina than to hear no music at all. In time they will learn to like something better."* *5

Concertina aside, another impediment to collecting recordings was the prevalent attitude to the collection of the material itself, especially the round dance tunes that were the bread and butter of concertina players in England, Ireland, Australia and South Africa.

Reg Hall, in his research into the life and music of Sussex musician Scan Tester, had this to say about the attitude in Britain during the English folk revival of the late nineteenth century toward these dances:

> *The sources of this material [Scan Tester's round dance tunes] have never, to my knowledge, been discussed in print. In fact, within the folk dance communities in England, Scotland and Ireland, with the notable exception of Peter Kennedy's field collecting in the 1950s, the material has been ignored and largely despised.* *6

As was discussed in Chapter 6, the attitude of cultural, political and clerical officials in Ireland toward round dances in the early twentieth century was to ban them outright, resulting both in the loss of much if not most of Ireland's home-grown round dance repertoire, and in the relative paucity of recordings of the early concertina players who played it.

Contrast this situation with Australia, where such dance music was considered part of the country's cultural legacy as early as the 1950s, when large scale collection of rural round and square dances and dance music began with the work of John Meredith. The much larger recorded legacy of early concertina players in Australia as evidenced in this archive is a partial result.

The indifference or even hostility to these dances from music and dance organizations in England meant that recording of those who played it waited until the 1970s, when a revival of English Country Music began to catch the public's attention. This was too late for any but the longest-lasting of the rural musicians of the concertina's heyday, like Scan Tester; nearly all concertina players took their tunes to their graves.

With this situation as a backdrop, it is a source of wonder and joy that out of the scarce handful of concertina players of the instrument's heyday, two who did manage to be recorded were among the most extensively recorded 'traditional' concertinists of that era, anywhere: William Kimber (1872-1961) and Scan Tester (1887-1972). Kimber was recognized and valued mainly for his Morris dances, which by the early twentieth century had gained a measure of widespread respectability, due largely to the efforts of Cecil Sharp.

A British duet, one with German concertina, late nineteenth century. With thanks to Neil Wayne.

Fortunately, Peter Kennedy also sought out examples of both country dance and round dance tunes from Kimber, who was an avid player of such dance music at local social gatherings in rural Oxfordshire, and who was knowledgeable about the dances that each tune accompanied.

It is equally fortunate that Scan Tester lived long enough to catch the interest of Reg Hall in the 1950s and 1960s. Hall was then a young accordion player who was interested in rural dance music and song. In the music of Scan Tester he found a rich mixture of step dance, country dance and ballroom dance tunes.

Of the four others in the English section of the archive, only two played extensively for dancing - either social or Morris. Ellis Marshall (1906-1993) played in the Northwest Morris dance tradition, and like Scan Tester and many others in this archive, he utilized a straightforward octave style. Fred Kilroy (ca. 1910-ca.1976) was born slightly later, but to a changed world in which modern chromatic popular music had taken root in England. In his early years he played for social dances, minstrels, and for the Morris, and as a result his music shows stylistic elements (not least of which is octave playing) of earlier times. However, his recordings also show a strong influence of the brass bands and concertina bands that were so prevalent in northern England.

The last two musicians in this chapter, Bill Link (d.1979) and Eric Holland (ca.1905-1977), might arguably have been left out of this archive, because they played mostly for listeners rather than dancers, with music styles shaped largely by the twentieth century. Nonetheless, they are included here - not only because recorded examples of Anglo players are so rare in England, but because they demonstrate the large changes in playing styles that occurred not only in England but, in different ways, in Ireland and South Africa, as playing for dancing receded and playing for listening, as paid entertainers in pubs and the like, advanced. Both men seem to have largely played in pubs and as musical hires for urban holidaymakers on coach trips, with repertoires primarily consisting of current popular songs.

Their playing exhibits a general lack of a strong, danceable beat, which is understandable given the change in fundamental purpose of their music. They played extended range Anglos of 39 and 40 buttons (three and one half rows) partly in order to smooth out the jerkiness of the Anglo for their listeners. Although they were among the last to play the Anglo in England before the folk revival of the late twentieth century, their use of the Anglo concertina in this newer musical purpose was largely supplanted in urban pubs and cafes during their lifetime by piano accordionists playing even smoother "lounge music."

Holland and Link are closely similar in their relatively smooth legato phrasing and modern tune repertoire to many middle to late twentieth century concertina players in South Africa, who also played 39 to 40 key extended keyboard Anglos.* 7

William Kimber

William Kimber (1872-1961) is remembered most for the role he played with Cecil Sharp in popularizing and helping to preserve a Morris dance tradition that was on the verge of extinction in the early twentieth century. Kimber's story has been well-recounted elsewhere in some detail.* 8

Briefly, he was born at Headington Quarry near Oxford in 1872. Like his father before him, he was employed in the building trade, and he, his father, grandfather and great-grandfather were all Morris dancers. He was 'discovered' by Cecil Sharp in 1899 when he played with the Quarry side in the snow on Boxing Day, and many of his Morris tunes were recorded in the HMV studio in London in 1935 and 1946.

Most of Kimber's 'studio-grade' recordings are of Morris tunes, probably because of the emphasis placed by music collectors on the Morris revival during his lifetime.

William Kimber in Morris regalia, 1906, standing next to his two row Anglo concertina. From Cecil Sharp's 'The Morris Book', 1923.

Kimber, however, was active on many other musical fronts as well. He was a member of the local mummers as well as a handbell ringer at his Parish church, and he belonged to a concertina club that met at a local public house. *9

Moreover, he was an active musician for social dancing. He recorded many English social dance tunes, most of them as field recordings made when he was well into his eighties. Of most interest to the follower of social dance music are the field recordings made in 1951 and 1956 by Peter Kennedy at Kimber's home (Maud Karpeles also helped with the 1951 recordings). These recordings have not been widely distributed, and will form the focus of this discussion.

Here we see another side of Kimber, who recorded schottisches, polkas, jigs, a waltz, a highland fling, a galup, and a barn dance, as well as three and four hand reels. In some of these recordings, Kimber speaks enthusiastically about his experiences with country social dances, and describes some of the dance steps in detail.

Clearly, he played for many social dances, and the list of dance styles reflects the ballroom dances popular during his lifetime. Like Scan Tester, he apparently did not play for many quadrilles, which seem to have gone out of fashion in the English countryside by the end of the nineteenth century.

William Kimber's playing has been transcribed and analyzed in some detail elsewhere,[*10] from which a general picture emerges of his personal style. His playing fits nearly completely within the C and G rows of the instrument, eschewing the top row of accidentals; he learned on a two-row instrument and never shifted his style when, in middle age, he was presented with a three row Jeffries Anglo.

At core an octave player, Kimber moved his two hands in unison as they followed the melody line, with the right hand playing notes an octave higher than the left. He utilized both rows when playing in C, with lower melodic passages played on the C row (e.g., *do-re-mi-fa*), and higher passages on the G row (*so-la-ti-do*). He typically dropped out the lower octave notes on the second and fourth beats of each measure in common time in order to emphasize the first and third beats. This gave a driving beat that is easily heard by dancers.

He also tended to add a third interval partial chord to the left hand lower octave note, making a characteristic harmony that closely follows the melody line. This left hand accompaniment is staccato, minimizing the harsh sound of close chord intervals.

Finally, Kimber tends to add a full chord at the beginning and end of important phrases, again for emphasis and to be heard by the dancers. The use of partial chords within octave playing was not unique among early players; George Bennett in Australia and Faan Harris in South Africa are just two of several others who played in that manner.

Bacca Pipes is a Morris jig that illustrates these basic points of his playing style, including his use of both octaves and partial chords, with both dropped out on the off-beat for rhythmic emphasis. The tune is played on a C/G Jeffries Anglo concertina. The melody line (and octave/partial chord accompaniment) weaves back and forth from the C to the G rows of the instrument. Kimber played this tune for a jig danced over a set of crossed churchwarden-style tobacco pipes placed on the floor. The recording was made in 1946 and is included here courtesy of the English Folk Dance and Song Society.

Bacca Pipes

England
Morris Dance

As Played by William Kimber
Transcribed for CG Anglo by Dan Worrall

House Dance

Getting Upstairs is an American minstrel tune written by Joe Blackburn in the 1830s, and used by Kimber for a Morris dance. It was likely also used elsewhere at that time as a single reel or quadrille tune. Kimber plays this tune in the key of G, almost all on the G row, again using intermittent octave notes with partial chords on the left hand. The recording was made in 1946 and is included here courtesy the English Folk Dance and Song Society.

Over the Hills to Glory is a schottische that Kimber recorded in 1946, and is closely related to both the schottische *The Lass o' Gowrie* and the Irish polka *The Lakes of Sligo*. It and the following schottische, *Moonlight*, both share the rhythmic bounce that Kimber produced by dropping out every other left hand octave note. This technique was very suitable to the needs of noisy dances in houses and public halls. He plays the tune in the key of G on his C/G concertina, frequently crossing rows from C to G to C again. The recording is included here courtesy the English Folk Dance and Song Society.

 The *Moonlight Schottische* is a tune of unknown origin, although there were several schottisches with this same name published between 1880 and 1910. Of it, Kimber said, "This is a good dance, a good tune... [a] plain schottische, four left, four right, eight round." It was recorded in 1951, and it is included courtesy of Topic Records. He plays it in the key of C, in a cross-row manner using both C and G rows.

The following three dance tunes were recorded in 1951 and are included courtesy of Topic Records.

 The *Mayblossom Waltz* is an unusual tune with an oom-pah feel to it; perhaps it was learned from the playing of a fair or carousel organ. It is played in the key of C, and has another unusual feature. Kimber plays two accidentals, F# and Bb, at several times during the piece, the only time he does so in his known recordings. It is the only waltz that he recorded.

 Kimber played the *Little Polly* polka at a smart tempo in the key of C, as always with an intermittent left hand accompaniment of octaves and partial chords, in a cross-row fashion.

 *Kitty Come* is a barndance (a variant of the schottische) of unknown origin. Kimber plays it in the key of C, in a style similar to the above examples.

William Kimber's headstone, at the Parish cemetery in Headington Quarry, Oxfordshire. Photo by Gary Coover, 1979.

Lewis 'Scan' Tester

Scan Tester (1887-1972), the noted Anglo player from Horsted Keynes, Sussex, was born of non-musician parents. He learned to play the Anglo concertina as a boy, from his older brother Trayton, and was an active player for all of his adult life. A relatively large part of that playing life was spent playing for dances as well as in country pubs. An account of his life and times, as well as recordings of his music, have been published by Reg Hall, from which much of the biographical information below was summarized. * 11

Scan Tester with one of his Jeffries concertinas, c.1965.
Photo by Brian Shuel, with thanks to Reg Hall.

Step dances are relatively uncommon in much of England today, although they are still prevalent among travelling people as well as in Suffolk sessions. They were still common in Tester's youth in Sussex, where they were typically danced in country pubs. Much of his early playing was in the all-male preserve of the taprooms of these country pubs. He described these occasions as follows:

> *Course, they used to come in the pubs, you know, with their heavy boots on - the old pelted boots and all - and yorks and all on, and you see 'em out in the room that time of day doing the old stepdances, and they used to, if there was*

enough of 'em, they'd form a figure eight or form a four angles, you know, cross angles, and, you know, there was a lot of different ways they used to dance.

There used to be what we called a reel. It was ordinary four corners, four of them, and they used to step, and then the second part they change over and go in and form the figure-eight. And really, it was old people that done it, mind you. The young ones, they used to join in. Get two in a set, see, and learn 'em. * 12

There were social dance occasions as well, and his repertoire was rich in ballroom dance tunes. After World War I, he played for the occasional hop at a local school, along with a fiddle player. The headmaster who began at that school in 1919, William Byrd, wrote six decades later about those school dances:

Sussex Anglo concertina player Scan Tester (1887-1972), with Daisy Sherlock (piano) and Reg Hall (accordion), playing at a house party in West Hoathly, Sussex, 1957. With thanks to Reg Hall and Roger Digby.

... where the lasses wore their best summer clothes and rather heavy shoes. There was no smart band in those days, but I remember being lulled to sleep by the wheezy tones of the concertina. I remember the smell of the oil lamps and the sound of happy laughter from the dancers. The dances were really happy and joyful, and one wonders, by the doleful looks on the dance floor of today if the young folks are as happy at the dance as we used to be. * 13

Scan Tester formed a family band, *Tester's Imperial Jazz Band*, in the 1920s with his wife Sarah on drums and daughter Daisy on piano. Occasionally Scan's brother Will Tester, who had carried his concertina into the front during the Great War, played with the group. They were quick to pick up the latest dance tunes from their wireless set or from recordings; there was no exclusive adherence to old traditional dance forms here (nor was it , strictly speaking, a 'jazz' band). Daisy remembered some of the dances: schottisches, polkas, fox-trots, waltzes, the *Gay Gordons*, the *Boston Two-Step*, the *Veleta Waltz*, and the *Charleston*.* 14

After the band stopped performing in 1931, Scan and Will Tester continued playing in pubs of the surrounding region, albeit sporadically. By the 1950s, Scan was 'discovered' by musicians Mervyn Plunkett and Reg Hall, who increasingly drew Scan into a series of activities surrounding a revived interest in country pub music. At this time, few in the London folk revival scene had heard the old waltzes, polkas, and schottisches of country pub music, and Scan and his repertoire of old tunes attracted interest from a number of enthusiasts.

An adjacent chart shows the rich mixture of tunes in Scan Tester's recorded repertoire, by percentage; it was compiled from a listing of publically available tunes from Tester's repertoire by Reg Hall.* 15 Besides song tunes, the dominant dances are step dances (jigs, hornpipes, and reels) and ballroom dances: waltzes, marches, schottisches, and especially polkas.

There are a large number of popular songs of his day, in various rhythms including waltzes and one-steps. The large number of step dances reflects the occurrence of step dancing in country pubs during Tester's youth. The overall mix of dance tune types in Tester's repertoire does not greatly differ from that of the three house dance era musicians in Ireland (Carolan, O'Dwyer and Hourican; see bar chart in Chapter 8), except that Tester's reels are primarily single reels, and the Irish reels recorded by those three Irish women are mostly double reels.

Sussex Anglo concertina player Scan Tester's recorded repertoire, displayed as numbers of recorded tunes for each dance type. Compiled from the discography in Reg Hall's 'I Never Played to Many Posh Dances', 1990.

Like most other players in this archive, Scan Tester played predominantly in an octave style; this he seems to have learned from his older brother Trayton, although Scan heard other (apparently much less accomplished) Sussex players in his early days. As Reg Hall wrote:

> *Trayton was in the right position to have been the one who adapted the Fairwarp fiddle stepdance tunes for the concertina. The articulated melody line, dressed by triplets and fill-ins between phrases and underlined by parallel octaves (the two notes of each octave played on different sides of the concertina), and harmony represented by the odd, almost accidental use of thirds in place of octaves, characterize the Tester style. These techniques, together with the lift generated by the attack, staccato notes, the sharp intake of air in the bellows, and the heavy punctuation at the end of an eight bar phrase, were, in all probability, Trayton's gift to his younger brothers.* * 16

Tester was recorded on many occasions from the late 1950s to the early 1970s, and the first six recordings included here are from the archive of Vic Smith, who kindly made them available. The first four of these were recorded in 1971 at the Lewes Arms, Lewes Sussex, and previously were released on the CD *Anglo International*. They appear here courtesy of Graham Bradshaw and Alan Day.

The first track is a medley of three tunes, including a step dance tune and two music hall song tunes. The **step dance tune** is in common time and played all on the C row of a C/G Anglo concertina, and nearly all in octaves. The two songs are **Roamin' in the Gloamin'** and **I Love a Lassie**, written by Harry Lauder in 1911 and 1905, respectively. Both song tunes are played using octaves throughout.

Roamin' in the Gloamin' (see the following transcription) is a good example of the type of music that arrived in the early twentieth century music halls. It has a brief chromatic run in the tenth measure; such phrases were often the "hooks" in these early twentieth-century pieces. Tester plays the tune all on the C row, with the exception of the F#'s needed for the chromatic runs. He adds a considerable number of partial and full chords to this piece, not as separate oom-pahs, as is the fashion with many English Anglo concertina players these days, but as simple added thirds and fifths to the lower octave, in a style not unlike Kimber's.

The recording shows that with this simple playing of the piece he nonetheless held his audience in rapt attention as they sang along. There is no elaborate arrangement of complex left hand chords, and neither is there a piano or a guitar 'interpreting' the background chords for him. Our modern ears have come to expect music with elaborate and sometimes smothering chord arrangements, but Victorian and, apparently, Edwardian ears could do without.

Roamin' in the Gloamin'

Music Hall Song
Written by Harry Lauder, 1911

As Played by Scan Tester
Transcribed for CG Anglo by Dan Worrall

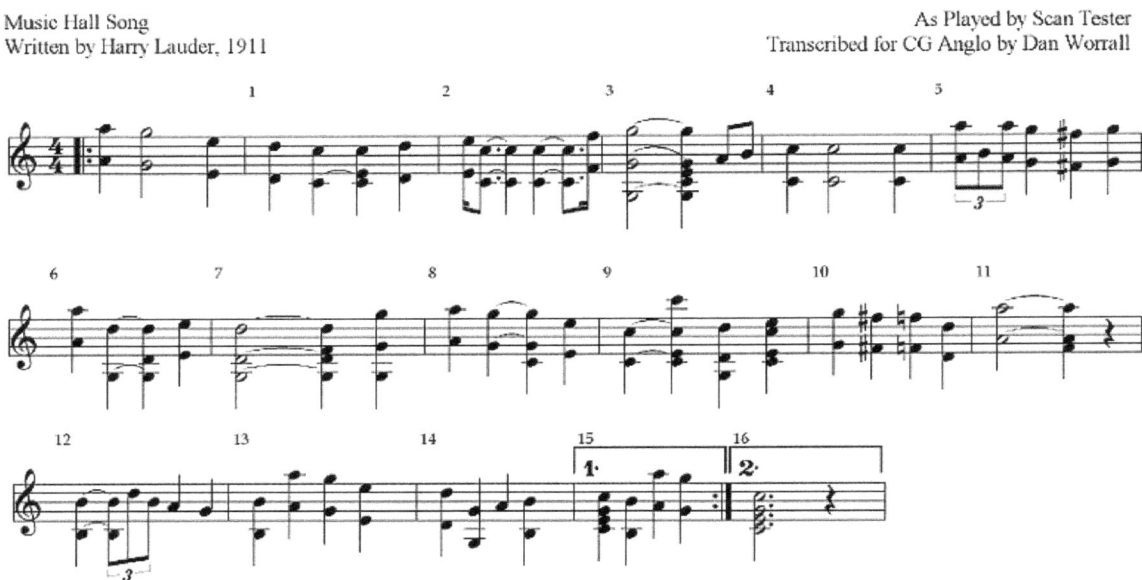

Scan Tester's Schottische is played entirely on the C row, and in octaves; a transcription is attached. In measure seven he runs into difficulty when the tune climbs high in its compass of notes: the upper octave climbs too high for the C row. In situations like this the player has two choices. Tester's choice was to drop an octave down for the remainder of the climb in that measure, thereby remaining on the C row. The other choice, which a player like William Kimber or Dooley Chapman would take, would be to move the higher phrase to the G row.

Scan Tester's Schottische

As Played by Scan Tester
Transcribed for CG Anglo by Dan Worrall

St Patrick's Day (also known as the *17th March Jig*) is a globally common tune; see Chapter 7 for a version played by Australian Charlie Ordish). Tester plays it in the key of C, all on the C row, in octaves. His B part is different from that of the standard setting. As the B part of the standard setting rises significantly in pitch, and hence would be played partly on the G row, it may be that Scan altered the tune rather than be forced to change rows when playing in octaves.

Step Dance Tune is played in C, all on the C row, and in octaves. It is in common time, in hornpipe rhythm.

The following three tune selections, also from the archive of Vic Smith, were recorded in the late 1950s or early 1960s in the Stone Quarry Pub at Chelwood Gate, Sussex, where Tester played nearly every weekend for over forty years. The recording was made by Ken Stubbs.

The first track contains two popular Harry Lauder song tunes, and the singing of pub-goers is evident in the background. ***Stop Your Tickling, Jock*** was written in 1906. ***Keep Right On To The End of the Road*** was written after the death of Lauder's son in France during World War I. Both are played in the key of Bb on Tester's Bb/F Anglo concertina. Like the above three tunes, Tester plays these on the middle row (here, Bb), and in octaves wherever the melody allows.

An ***Untitled Waltz*** is played during the same session, also in Bb on a Bf/F concertina, mostly in octaves. It is played all on the Bb row, except for one chromatic note, B, for which he reaches to the upper row.

The Man in the Moon is a signature waltz tune of Tester's that has become popular in English sessions in the past few decades. He plays it in Bb on a Bf/F concertina, mostly in octaves, and all on the Bb row. The percussion accompaniment was very probably provided by his longtime friend Ernest 'Rabbity' Baxter, who had a very large tambourine, about the size of an Irish bodhran but with jingles.

From the above seven tracks of Tester's playing, one might get the impression that he only played along the middle row of his concertina, but such was not the case as the next two tracks show. They were recorded by Bob Davenport and come courtesy of the archive of Reg Hall.

Tester plays ***See Me Dance the Polka*** in the key of G on a G/D concertina, mostly in octaves. In both the A and B parts of this polka, he begins on the middle (G) row, but crosses to the bottom (D) row as the melody rises in pitch. From this one can only assume that Tester was a skilled cross-row player, but preferred to stick to the middle row wherever possible. This tune requires both rows because of its range.

Alexander's Ragtime Band was written in 1911 by American songwriter Irving Berlin and became a global hit, mainly for its melody. Tester probably played it with his *Tester's Imperial Jazz Band* during the 1920s. One of the new chromatic tunes that were coming from Tin Pan Alley, it had a catchy chromatic lead-in on the beginning of the chorus. In this recording, Tester played the tune in the key of C on a CG concertina, mostly in octaves, using both the C

and G rows. Where the chromatic lead-in would normally be played Eb-E-Eb-E in this key, Tester eschews the accidental, playing D-E-D-E instead; he must have found the Eb awkward, or perhaps just didn't hear that note in the tune. Such chromatic parts ultimately doomed the concertina, especially for those whose instruments only had two rows.

Finally, here is Scan Tester's version of an **Untitled polka** that was compared in Chapter 4 with a similar tune played by Australian Dooley Chapman. The recording was made by Reg Hall and is courtesy of Topic Records.

Ellis Marshall

Ellis Marshall (1906-1993) was born in Oldham, a Lancashire textile mill town. During his working life, he worked in a textile factory, served as a steward for a working man's club, and served as a bomb disposal expert during World War II. Marshall learned to play the concertina from Royton Morris concertina player Lees Kershaw, who had played with the dancers since 1891. He described his tutorship under Kershaw, and the dancing of that team during the post-WWI period in a 1975 interview with Alan Ward

Ellis Marshall in full Morris regalia, 1980. Photo courtesy of Tony Marshall, John Cunniffe and Frances Stott.

> *There was ten of us at the time. We had a concertina apiece. [Kershaw] charged a shilling a lesson. We used to go to his house every night...*

> *I came to Royton when I were seven, and the Royton Morris dancing was going on then. 'Cos they used to go out every Saturday afternoon all round Oldham and Royton - used to make a living out of it practically. They went as far as Blackpool when they were dancing, from here. [They went out] for the day from twelve o'clock till about half past four or five o'clock. [They used to stop at] different pubs - where the money were. They danced all the way.* [17]

While on the Royton Morris side, Marshall teamed with fellow concertina players Peter McDermott, Norman Coleman, and Fred Kilroy (of whom more below). He was a musician for the team that won the English Championships at the Royal Albert Hall in London in 1935. He also played for the revival Royton side of the late 1970s and early 1980s, and played for that side at the Queen's Silver Jubilee in 1977. He was also active in the Oldham Carnival. * 18

The revived Royton Morris team on a visit to Albert Hall, 1936. The concertina players are Peter McDermot (left) and Ellis Marshall (right). With thanks to Tony Marshall.

A recording of Ellis Marshall's playing, from a set of Morris dance performances at the St Paul's Working Men's Institute in Blackpool in 1979, has survived, and Marshall's grandson Tony Marshall has made it available to this collection. The side's musicians at that time included Marshall and Norman Coleman on concertina, with a number of drummers.

At the St Paul's appearance they played a set of tunes starting with the minstrel number *Oh, Susannah*, then a medley of old dance tunes such as *The Girl I Left Behind Me*, and ended with a *cross Morris dance*.

 At a casual recording made at Marshall's home in 1978, he plays through much the same medley, but solo.

Marshall and Coleman, like Scan Tester, played nearly entirely in octaves in those performances. A transcription of the last tune from those tapes, *Cross Morris,* is on the next page. Beyond the ubiquitous octave notes, the tune is adorned with a few very simple along-the-row third-interval partial chords - somewhat like Kimber, but with much more sparse chording.

There is a complete dearth of the oom-pah-like chording favored by revival Morris players. *Cross Morris* is played in a cross-row manner. Starting on the C row, it migrates to the G row for higher passages, such as the last half of measures 2, 4, 5, and 6, as well as measures 7-10.

Cross Morris

England
North West Morris tune, Royton

As Played by Ellis Marshall and Norman Coleman
Transcribed for CG Anglo by Dan Worrall

The use of a simple octave style in playing for Morris dancing was not restricted to the Royton morris side. Caleb Walker (b.1907) played for the Manley Morris dancers, and played with Fred Kilroy on that side (Kilroy earlier played for Royton).

Current day Anglo player Mark Davies learned to play from Caleb Walker, and describes both Walker's playing and the Manley Morris in a way that evokes the above recording of Marshall and the Royton side:

> *Caleb Walker only played in the key of C, playing the tune along the right hand side C row and dropping down to the right hand side G row for the higher notes. He played the roughly corresponding buttons on the left hand side and would often play chords on the left hand side. So basically he was playing in octaves.*
>
> *The Manley concertina players had a unique manner of playing. There could be up to seven concertina players, a bass drum and a side drum in the band. In a carnival procession the dancers and musicians could be marching for up to 2 hours without a break. The concertina players thus held the concertina high almost in front of their faces with the weight of the concertina being taken by the elbows being tucked into the trunk. This in itself was very tiring so at certain stages in various tunes all the concertina players would swing their concertinas in a circle above their heads, making sure they all did this in the same direction to avoid accidents!* * 19

Fred Kilroy

Fred Kilroy (ca. 1910-ca. 1976) played for Morris and other dance groups in the Oldham Lancashire region. Born in Royton, near Oldham, he learned to play in the 1910s and 1920s, at a time when Lancashire was alive with brass bands and concertina bands, and when music halls featured accomplished duet concertina players. He picked up a two-row Anglo-German concertina as a child, later trading it in for a larger model.

As a teenager he joined five concertina players as well as others who played 'bazookas' (a kazoo attached to a horn) and the drum, in the *Westwood Jazz Band*, playing for local dances. He also played for a girl's competition dance team and later with this brother Charlie (also a concertina player) for the *Westwood Prize Morris Dancers*, also a girls' team.

By the 1950s he was playing for his hometown Royton's revival men's Morris side, as well as for the Manley side during their tour of Ireland in 1958.

His musical career was cut short by breathing problems brought on by electrical work in and around a foundry. Retired, he was active in pub appearances during his last decade, the 1970s. * 20

Fred Kilroy in 1929, with some of the Westwood Morris Dancers. With thanks to Alan Ward and 'Traditional Music' magazine.

Kilroy was recorded only on field tapes, and until recently his music has been not commercially available. The *Anglo International* collection of 2005 included three tracks of his playing made by the late Paul Davies in 1976*21, and those plus a fourth track from Davies' field tape are included here.

Kilroy's playing style is dramatically different from that of either Kimber or Tester. He admired the Maccann duet and purchased one early in his playing years, but in the press of money-making appearances with his Anglo he gave up on learning the duet. Nonetheless his approach to the Anglo used decidedly less of the classic push-pull technique of Kimber and Tester (and most Anglo players), as Alan Ward was written:

> *Fred's style is very reminiscent of duet style - he avoids frequent changes of direction on the bellows by fingering the 'repeats' on the instrument - and it appears that this was nothing unusual at the time he learned to play. Fred regarded 'melodeon style' (push-pull) players as under-developed.*22

That search for 'repeats' entails a significant amount of cross-row fingering that took Kilroy often to the third row of his Anglo. Nonetheless, his technique retains much of classic Anglo playing as well, including a tendency toward playing in octaves when extra oomph is needed in the melody line.

A good example of his playing style is the early-twentieth-century march ***Blaze Away***. Written in 1901 by Abe Holzman, an American-born, German-educated composer, the tune uses the highly chromatic style that became common in the ragtime era.

Blaze Away

England
American March and Two-Step, Parts A and B
Composed by Abe Holzmann, 1901

As played by Fred Kilroy
Transcribed for CG Anglo by Dan Worrall

House Dance

This tune was played by Kilroy on a Bb/F instrument in old pitch, and the transcription included here is transposed for a C/G concertina. On the C/G, it is keyed in the key of F, which tends to be a good choice for highly chromatic pieces like this. Played mostly on the C row, the tune requires frequent cross-row ventures to the outer and inner rows. *Blaze Away* is playable on a typical 30-button Anglo, but not with the fluidity of Kilroy. The extra buttons of his 38-key Jeffries allow more options for playing nearly all notes in either a push or pull direction - especially important in playing chorded pieces with chromatic passages. Not surprisingly, not only Fred Kilroy but most current South African players who play 'modern' chromatic music in a chorded style use expanded keyboard instruments, usually with thirty-eight or more buttons.

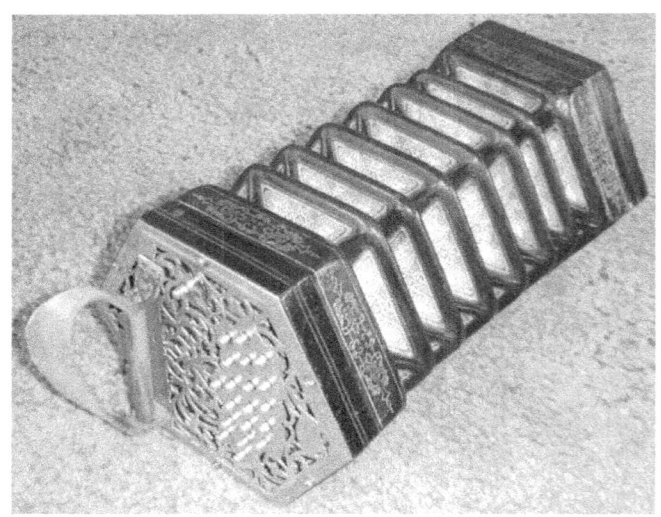

Fred Kilroy's Jeffries G/D Anglo concertina. Photo courtesy of Roger Digby.

The arrival of this sort of highly chromatic music - the chromatic scales of which requires additional development of muscle memory to play - was one of the reasons the Anglo fell on hard times in the early decades of the twentieth century. For the vast majority of players, pieces like this were too difficult to play, or required an upgrade from the usual 20-button instrument - and yet such music was extremely popular with audiences. Only a few 'modernist' Anglo players in England persisted, Fred Kilroy chief among them. In South Africa, Anglo players embraced this new music in much greater numbers, and a sizeable market for 40-button Wheatstone concertinas developed in the early decades of the century.

Kilroy was a break-out player relative to the others in this group of English players, and his playing shows a strong influence of the brass bands (and concertina bands) in the Lancashire area.

The Old Comrades March is a German military march (*Alte Kameraden*) that was composed by Carl Teike in 1889. It was globally popular, even after World War II. Kilroy plays it in the key of Bb on his Bb/F concertina. It was played mostly in octaves, with added

chords. Kilroy's frequent use of third row notes reduced the number of bellows changes in fast passages. This full use of three rows is starkly different than the mostly two-row style of the older players Kimber and Tester, and is generally unlike the styles of nearly everyone else in this archive except for Eric Holland (below) as well as Faan Harris and others of the Boer players.

During the 1920s, Fred Kilroy played for a blackface minstrel show band, *The Kentucky Minstrels*.

This **Minstrel Selection** contains tunes from the standard minstrel repertoire. It begins with a snippet from *The Star Spangled Banner* and is followed by *Yankee Doodle* before delving into more typical minstrel fare: *Dixie*, three Stephen Foster tunes (*Camptown Races, Old Black Joe*, and *Old Folks at Home*), *Old Zip Coon* (a.k.a. *Turkey in the Straw*), and *Marching Through Georgia*. He plays these in a mixture of keys, including both Bb and F (the home keys of his instrument) as well as Eb.

He uses a generous amount of octaves as well as chords, and uses cross-row fingering frequently on all three rows to reduce the frequency of bellows direction changes.

The Great Broughton Darkies Band, c.1912, Northamptonshire. Fred Kilroy played in a similar minstrel band in the 1920s. The combination of concertinas, banjos and drums were a common instrumentation for minstrel and other street bands. With thanks to Sue Allan.

On the Quarterdeck is a British march composed in 1917 by Kenneth Alford (a.k.a Major Frederick Ricketts, bandmaster of the Royal Marines) in order to commemorate the naval Battle of Jutland the previous year. Kilroy plays it from memory in the key of Bb, with all the stylistic flourish of a brass band.

Eric Holland

Eric Holland (c.1905-1977), lived in Crows Nest, Swanage, Dorset, a resort area on the southern English coast. His father taught him to play as a boy, in 1919, and later in his life he played a 40-button Wheatstone Anglo concertina. His playing illustrates the changes in the use of the Anglo that were experienced by those very few English players who continued after the Anglo's heyday was over, and who did not play for the Morris. Such players, including Bill Link as well as Holland, found themselves playing easy listening music in pubs and for coach trips of holidaymakers, rather than for dances, which had by this time become the home of generally concertina-less modern jazz bands.

Eric Holland with 40 button Wheatstone Anglo. Photograph courtesy of Mark Davies.

Little is known about Holland until he joined the International Concertina Association in 1968. At that time, the ICA had a membership that was principally comprised of players of English and Duet concertinas. The humble Anglo was considered by many ICA members in this pre-folk revival era as a step down, for the lower classes. Holland, like Kilroy, used his 40 key, three and one half row Wheatstone Anglo to good advantage for more legato playing, smoothing out bellows direction changes by finding alternate fingerings of notes that kept the playing of the melody all in the same direction for long parts of phrases. This made his playing more acceptable to ICA members, who played concertinas that, being double action, could easily and typically play in such a legato style. From the minutes of the ICA:

> *November 1966: Tommy Williams tells us that he has a recording of Mr Holland, of Crows Nest, Dorset, and has never in his life time of experience heard such excellent Anglo playing. Hr Holland is reported to have a perfect legato phrasing, quite devoid of the jerky accents which are a characteristic of Anglos. Tommy says the sound is indistinguishable from that of a good 'English' player. Mr Holland plays a 40 key Anglo and does not read music.*
>
> *May 1968: Yet another Sound of Music came from Eric Holland, who proved to be an Anglo-player extraordinary. His playing is characterised by a strong melody line, with a true legato rarely heard on an Anglo, and a background of delicate accompanying figures. While we had some reservations in respect of his almost continuous forte in the selection and a waltz encore, his subsequent folk dances had excellent piano effects. As a concertina player we rate him high; as an Anglo player very high indeed.*
>
> *Sept 1977: Mr Holland, of Swanage, Dorset, died on July 15th of a heart attack. Jim Harvey writes: He joined the I.C.A. in January of 1964, but I knew him long before. He was a great friend, and won the 'Ear' Players class at the 1975 Festival. He played the Anglo in his own style and produced music more like a Duet Concertina. We mourn the loss of a great player and friend.* 23

Holland's more legato style was more appropriate for the easy listening venues in which he found himself. The driving beat of earlier Anglo players, who played for dancers who demanded that beat, is largely missing in Holland's playing. His repertoire is a mixture of popular song tunes of the early to middle twentieth century, as well as light classical pieces (Beethoven's *Pathetique Sonata*) and operatic hymns like *Ave Maria*; this was the perfect mix for playing for mid-twentieth century patrons in pubs.

He continuously added new material to his repertoire, as evidenced by large numbers of tunes from the popular film *The Sound of Music*, which was released in 1964.

He was recorded in 1968 by Mark Davies, who has made these recordings available to the archive. Here Holland speaks of his years of Anglo playing, as an introduction to his recording.

He played in a purely octave style, and is said to have learned to play from his father, who very likely played in that manner as well.

These two waltzes *Untitled Waltz 1* and *Untitled Waltz 2,* illustrate his general playing style. He plays them in the key of C on the C row, nearly entirely in octaves, with occasional chords added for accent and as phrase endings.

The march *Scotland the Brave* is likewise played in the key of C and fully in octaves, with a very few rhythmic chords added. He plays the A part on the C row, and the higher-pitched B part mostly on the G row.

The Australian tune *Waltzing Matilda* is played in the same fashion. It is played in a stately, deliberate way that would please listeners but probably not dancers. The bulk of Holland's playing seems to have been done for such listeners. The old days of playing for ballroom dances had long gone, and Anglos were generally not the thing for the groups that played such genres as Henry Mancini tunes or rock 'n roll.

Holland played a variety of light classics and operatic hymns, such as Shubert's version of the Marian hymn *Ave Maria*. Like his other recorded pieces, it is in the key of C, played in octaves with a few added chords for accent.

Bill Link

Little is known of Bill Link (d.1979). He became known at the meetings of the International Concertina Association in the late 1960s, where he typically played medleys of popular songs for its members.

Born ca.1900-1910, he was a Londoner and reportedly retired to a caravan on Jaywick Sands, near Southend-on-Sea, a resort on the southern English coast. During this time he played often in pubs and on coach trips for holidaymakers, just as Eric Holland had done. Link played the Anglo as well as the Crane Duet concertinas. He was recorded in the mid-1970s by Mark Davies, who has made these recordings available.

Here Bill Link speaks about his 52 years of playing his Anglo, which was a Jeffries Bb/F concertina tuned in old pitch.

A holiday party poses in front of an old horse-drawn coach, late nineteenth or early twentieth century. Note the concertina player, near the middle of the front row. Bill Link played for similar festive occasions. From the collection of Stephen Chambers.

Assuming a recording date of about 1975, he learned to play in the early 1920s - a bit later than most in this archive. His recorded repertoire is predominantly a mixture of popular and music hall songs from the 1920s and later, which would be tailor-made for holidaymakers on the coast.

One of these tunes is *My Wild Irish Rose*, written by the American singer and songwriter Chauncey Olcott in 1899. Link plays it in the key of F on his Bf/F concertina. This is the typical key of Link's playing, whereas Eric Holland would usually stick to playing on the middle row in Bb (more properly, in the key of C on Holland's C/G instrument). Link plays in octaves, but adds significantly more chords than Holland. Those chords were a good choice for the casual listener on a beach resort.

That Naughty Waltz is another American popular tune that achieved widespread popularity. It was composed in 1919 by Sol Levy and Edwin Stanley. Link plays it in the key of F and fully in octaves, weaving the melody back and forth from the F to Bb rows.

Putting on the Style is another jazz-era hit, a polka song written by George Wright and Norman Cazden in about 1926. It was resurrected in the 1950s and 1960s by skiffle and folk bands, as well as (even) the early Beatles. Link plays it in F.

Notes:

1. By 'Our Special Commissioner,' 'Musical Life in Norfolk' the *Musical Herald* (London), October 1890, p.508-510.

2. 'The Music of a Village,' in *The Musical World*, (London), April 4, 1885, pp.221-222.

3. Dr R Wortley, 1966, as quoted in Enid Porter, *Cambridgeshire Customs and Folklore* (1969), p.145.

4. F J Collins, 'The Concertina in Cornwall, Around 1890' in *The Concertina Newsletter* 7 (August 1972): pp.9-10. This reference was found in Stuart Eydmann, *Life and Times of the Concertina,* (1995).

5. T L Southgate, *English Music 1604-1904,* (London, 1906), p.339, as quoted by Stuart Eydmann, *Life and Times of the Concertina* (1995).

6. Reg Hall, 1990, *I Never Played to Many Posh Dances*: Scan Tester, Sussex Musician: Musical Traditions supplement No.2, p.83.

7. Such modernist Boer players include, for example, Nico van Rensburg and Neels Mattheus, who play with a complexity and smooth phrasing that approached that of a piano accordion.

8. For example, see Derek Schofield's extensive biography in the liner notes of the CD *Absolutely Classic: The Music of William Kimber* (London: English Folk Dance and Song Society, 1999), and T W Chaundy, 'William Kimber, A Portrait,' *Journal of the EFDSS, vol. 8* (1959), p.209.

9. Keith Chandler, 1993, *Ribbons, Bells and Squeaking Fiddles: The Social History of Morris Dancing in the English South Midlands,1660–1900* (Enfield Lock: Hisarlik Press, Publications of the Folklore Society, Tradition 1), p.17, and Musical Traditions Records CD-ROM MTCD250.

10. Dan Worrall, 2005, *The Anglo Concertina Music of William Kimber*: London, English Folk Dance and Song Society, 86pp.

11. Reg Hall, 1990, *I Never Played to Many Posh Dances*: Rochford, Essex, Musical Traditions, Supplement No.2, and online as a PDF facsimile edition in Musical Traditions (MT Article 215).

12. Scan Tester, as quoted in Reg Hall, *Posh Dances*, 1990, p.77.

13. William J. Bird, 1986, Danehill and Chelwood Gate in 1919: in *Danehill Parish Historical Society Magazine*, vol. III, no. 2, pp.20-21. As quoted by Reg Hall, 1990, p.46.

14. Reg Hall, *Posh Dances* (1990), Appendix A.

15. Reg Hall, *Posh Dances* (1990), p.49.

16. Reg Hall, *Posh Dances* (1990), p.96.

17. Ellis Marshall, as quoted by Alan Ward in 'Fred Kilroy, Lancashire Concertina Maker': *Traditional Music*, nos.1 and 3, 1975 and 1976.

18. Tony Marshall, Ellis Marshall's grandson, kindly provided details of his grandfather's life, as well as tape recordings and a photograph.

19. Mark Davies, 2009, personal communication.

20. Fred Kilroy's biography is paraphrased from Alan Ward, ed., 'Fred Kilroy, Lancashire concertina player,' in *Traditional Music*, nos. 1 and 3 (1975 and 1976). Fred Kilroy's rich playing may be heard on the recently issued CD, *Anglo International* (Folksound Records, Coventry UK).

21. *Anglo International* (Folksound Records, Coventry UK, 2005).

22. Alan Ward, 'Fred Kilroy,' (1975), p.15.

23. I am indebted to Wes Williams for providing these minutes from the International Concertina Association.

Chapter 10. South Africa

In the late nineteenth century, the descendents of the Dutch colonists of South Africa were as dance-mad as were the settlers of Australia and the rural farmers of Ireland and England. Like their conterparts in the Australian bush, they were farmers and ranchers, and lived simply but well.

An American visitor gave the following description of her childhood there in the 1860s, in an address of 1876:

> *Though the Boers have simple habits and few wants, you must not imagine them to be poor. Many of them are very rich, possessing countless herds of cattle and flocks of sheep, and there are many of them whose wool brings them in a very good income. In their homes the Boers are very hospitable, never refusing to entertain a stranger ... They are very fond of music and dancing, and many of them play with much taste on the violin and concertina. This they acquire by ear; their dancing is chiefly confined to reels, and at New Year, when they assemble in great numbers at different houses, they keep up this dancing for two or three consecutive days, not even resting at night.* [1]

An 1899 account by a British visitor, just before the start of the Second Boer War, also describes the Boer passion for concertina music and dancing:

> The Boers are inordinately fond of dancing, reports a London paper. On the smallest pretext, or none at all, they will organize what they call a 'dance-ball-party'. On the afternoon of the pre-arranged day the meisjes, or misses, and the young men roll up from all the surrounding farms, from a distance, maybe, of thirty miles... The living room of the host has been carefully cleared of its never superabundant furniture, a few wooden forms, or planks on empty gin cases, put around the sides, and a couple of reflecting paraffin lamps hung on the walls.
>
> The dancing begins at five in the afternoon to the music of a concertina played by a 'Cape boy', which is to say a half-colored man. Everyone appears in their ordinary dress, uncouth, untidy, and slouchy in the extreme. The women almost invariably wear black with, perhaps, a bit of colored ribbon. The men are in corduroys or cheap tweeds, often wearing their 'smasher' hats and shod in heavy veldtschoens, or boots.
>
> No 'square' dances are performed, but one dance is like another - a slow, jumpy, heavy, monotonous whirl, something between an elephantine waltz and a cumbersome polka. The girls sometimes place their two hands on their partner's shoulders and the men clasp the girls' waists with their two hands.
>
> After a few hours of serious jumping about, the room has to be cleared, for, the floor being of earth, a terrible dust is

A Boer family at home. A young couple is dancing; the man is playing the German concertina while they dance on the dirt floor. Drawing by John Guille Millais in A Breath from the Veldt, 1895.

knocked up and, as the doors and windows are invariably closed, the atmosphere becomes thick with floating clouds of dust. Everyone goes out into the stoep and is refreshed by dop (Boer brandy), lemonade, cookies (cakes) and sweets. In the meantime the room is swept and sometimes a calabash of bullock's blood is brought in with which the floor is smeared by the natives. From time to time - say, every two or three hours - this is repeated, so that intervals of dancing, dusty cloudiness, refreshments on the verandah and smearing of the floor succeed one another periodically.

This sort of thing goes on until about 8 in the morning, when everyone gets a bit sleepy. A general adjournment takes place. The women collect in the side room and snatch a few hours' sleep and the men lie down in the wagon house, or under their carts on the veldt, to smoke and rest. At about noon, after a hearty meal, they begin dancing again until late in the afternoon. At last they go home after about four and twenty hours of it and scatter over the veldt to their far distant homes. * 2

A group of musical Boer soldiers, a few months before the beginning of the Second Boer War. Amongst the rifles and bullet belts they hold a fiddle, button accordion, guitar and concertina. The leader of the band was the concertina player, A Jonas. Photo by Hugh Exton, from the Hugh Exton Photographic Museum in Pietermaritzburg. With thanks to Wilhelm Schultz.

This style of dancing, along with the dust, occurred at the Cape as well, with the Cape Dutch descendants of those who had not made the Great Trek. The following account was written in 1900 about earlier years there:

House Dance

> *And who has not heard of the Dutch dances at the Cape? ... They danced on the mud floor in the voorkammer - the living room of the house, into which the door opens from the outside - and the dust rose thicker and thicker until you could scarcely see across the other room. Then there was a pause, during which they watered the floor, and it, of course, became thick mud, and was ruination to the dresses. But the Boer girls generally change their frocks two or three times during the evening, in order to show off the extent of their wardrobe, and from their youth up are accustomed to dirt in the ballroom, so they do not take their soiled raiment much to heart. On they go, dancing merrily, often to the concertina where they can't get a piano, with their arms entwined around each other's necks in the Dutch fashion.* 3

As in Ireland, dances could occur in the open, too. In the following account of 1897 the dance was held in the open veldt, with a wagon canvas for flooring:

> *We went on by way of Enkeldoorn, where there is a Dutch community, and where a 'bucksail' dance was being held that night... For the uninitiated, I may explain that a bucksail dance is held in the open. The ground is flattened down and the big tent or bucksail, which is used to cover wagons, is spread over it to form a dancing floor. Partners are selected, and these are retained during the whole of the dance, which generally lasts from sunset to sunrise, with intervals for refreshments. The orchestra usually consists of a concertina and guitar or fiddle, but in default of these a mouth-organ or two does suffice. The dance was a very vigorous one.* 4

Even dances indoors could occur on a well-greased wagon sail, as in this account of a 1907 wedding:

> *[T]he stranger will be able to obtain much pleasure by attending, as an invited guest, a typical Boer wedding. Every guest is expected to salute the bride with a loving kiss, and should the festivities conclude with a dance, he will admire the endurance of the meisjes. Dancing will be kept up vigorously in the sweltering voorhuis to the strains of a seemingly tireless concertina. As the floors of many of*

these dwellings are composed of hardened mud, and the stretching of wagon sails, well greased, is the general preparation for dancing, it can be imagined that the 'going' is not easy. * 5

Boer family on a trek to market, late nineteenth century. Note the concertina player on the wagon, and an African servant dancing with a Boer child. From a late nineteenth century drawing by Heinrich Egersdörfer.

By the third and fourth decades of the twentieth century, however, conditions of life had improved, and many towns and villages had community dance halls. At this time, dance bands began to displace the solo concertina or fiddle players of the old days.

The concertina, however, retained pride of place in these bands, and was accompanied largely by chords from guitars and pianos, along with the odd fiddle or banjo player. This was quite different than the situation in Ireland, where the concertinas were edged out by the new *céilí* bands, and reflects the high esteem to which concertina playing had always been held in Boer culture.

There was enough commercial interest in the bands that played for these dances that they were recorded on 78 rpm records beginning in the early 1930s. These recordings were made in the prime of playing years for their concertina players, unlike most recordings in

Ireland, England and Australia, which were made of ageing players during the late twentieth century folk revival.

For this reason, the recordings are startlingly vibrant and danceable, and yet the concertina players who made them were typically born in the 1880s, 1870s and even earlier.

All of the recordings in this chapter are from these old 78 rpm recordings. The *Tradisionele Boeremusiekklub van Suid-Afrika* (Traditional Boer Music Club of South Africa, or TBK), was founded in 1981 for 'the collection, preservation and enhancement of Traditional Boer Music'. They made it an early goal to digitize, preserve, and distribute these old recordings, and their inclusion in this archive is thanks to this organization and especially the work of Danie Labuschagne, Stephaan van Zyl, and Plato Michael.

Boer dances have many similarities with those of Ireland, England and Australia at this time. The Boers mainly danced the *settees* (schottische), *wals* (waltz), polka, and *mazurka* (mazurka), although the country dance, quadrille, and cotillon were not unknown, especially in the nineteenth century. An additional dance that developed in South Africa is the *vastrap*.

As elsewhere, dance music was initially played on a two row German concertina, called a *boerekonsertina* in Afrikaans.

By the time of the early 78 rpm recordings in the 1930s, most of the recorded players had acquired higher quality English-made Anglo concertinas, a sign of the growing prosperity of the Boers relative to counterparts in Ireland or Australia ... or perhaps a sign that the professional dance bands demanded the very best in musicianship.

However, there is a current movement within the TBK to reintroduce the old German two row concertinas that had been so popular before the bands arrived; an example of a modern-day player, Stephaan van Zyl, playing the *boerekonsertina* is included in Chapter 11.

The 1930s saw an explosion of new techniques and styles in Boer music, as the ability to make and distribute recordings inevitably began to change a dancing audience for the music into a listening audience as well.

The oldest of the concertina players on these recordings, Faan Harris, Kerrie Bornman and Chris Chomse, played in a style that was essentially a two row octave style, with simple rhythmic melodies repeated for the dancers. Of these three, Faan Harris acquired a three-row Lachenal Anglo and began to experiment with adding chromatic notes, and he also added significant amounts of improvisation to repeated playings of melodies.

Boer band musicians in Harris's day were no doubt influenced by imported recordings of jazz music that was, by the 1920s, popular in South Africa. Harris's music was the first step in a wave of developments.

Hans Bodenstein and Willie Palm carried this process further, beginning to play in keys other than those of the two 'home rows' on the instrument (which was typically pitched in C/G); they played a number of tunes in the keys of D and A, and yet still played in octaves.

Players like Pietie Prinsloo and Silver de Lange added yet more complexity, devising long fluid and often chromatic phrases that took full advantage of extended range 40 button Anglo concertinas. They also continued to add to the complexity of improvisations. Their tunes were now largely unplayable on the original two row *boerekonsertinas* of a generation earlier. Since their time, the music has continued to grow in complexity.

These seven names were discussed more or less in birth order; Silver de Lange (the youngest, born in 1904) was 18 years younger than the oldest (Faan Harris, born in 1886). Younger players were strongly influenced by the new sounds of jazz and injected a newer style to the old tunes. This newer way of playing was enabled by the 40 button Wheatstone instruments that were imported an relatively large numbers from England, especially by the middle of the twentieth century.

These developments stand in strong contrast to the situation with regard to dance music in England and Ireland, where the concertina was fast disappearing from newer dance bands, be they *céilí* or jazz.

Only a very few players, like Fred Kilroy, experimented with chromatic music, and most simply gave up. Younger Irish players in the *céilí* dance era turned away from octave playing and began to play singly and more along-the-row, in order to keep up with the revived reels that had mostly displaced the round dance and quadrille music of an earlier generation.

In Australia, pockets of old-time dancing continued in certain areas in the 1930s, but without the stimulus of recording 78 rpm records there was no impetus to further develop playing styles beyond what they had been in the nineteenth century. Australian concertina playing continued in a relatively simple, two row style.

The 1930s, when most of the recordings in this chapter were made, mark a high point of Boer music. After World War II, and after the introduction of rock 'n roll, South Africa experienced the same decline in dance and in concertina playing that other countries had seen; efforts to reintroduce dance, and to preserve *Boeremusiek*, are similar to folk revival activities elsewhere today.

Stephen Emil (Faan) Harris

Stephen Emil (Faan) Harris (1886-1950) was one of the very best of the concertina players of South African *Boeremusiek*'s golden years of the 1930s. A biography of him appears on the TBK website, from which the following is summarized. His early years are somewhat mysterious.

A first account of him is when he was a construction worker on the Hartesbeesport Dam project in the early 1920s, where he worked under the name Faan Hakkeveld; while here he played music in the evenings with a guitar player. Rumor has it that he soon moved on to the railroads, and that at this time he lost a son, Frans, to a drunk driver.

Eventually, he moved to Krugersdorp, where he lived for the latter years of his life. His last years were hard ones, and he died of pneumonia.

Faan Harris and Boet Steyn playing music on the market square of Krugersdorp, around 1946. They are standing next to Steyn's 1938 Ford truck. Photo courtesy of the Tradisionele Boeremusiekklub van Suid-Afrika.

His main recordings were made with *Die Vier Transvalers* (The Four from the Transvaal), one of the most popular Boer music bands that ever played. Faan Harris was the leader, along with two guitarists (Josephus Daniël (Sewes) van Rensburg and Frans Hendrik (Frans) Ebersohn) and one cello player (Hendry Frederick (Bossie) Bosman).

They recorded ten tracks in 1932 for the British company His Master's Voice, and the group went on to place second at a 'World Music Competition' in Johannesburg in 1936. After a second recording session in 1937 (for which the recordings are lost), the group broke up.

Three members of Die Vier Transvalers, ca.1934. From left to right, Frans Hendrik Ebersohm, Faan Harris, Henry Frederik Bossman, and Peter Bosman. Bosman was not a member of the group.

Faan went on to record with other groups, but none have had the impact of the recordings with the *Transvalers*.

Harris played a three-row C/G Lachenal concertina. Relative to the playing of recorded contemporaries in Ireland, England and Australia, Harris's playing was more complex, and utilized all three rows of this concertina.

The waltz **Eileen Alannah** was written by American composer John Rogers Thomas in 1873, and became a global hit, well known in Ireland, England and Australia (see discussion, Chapter 5). He plays this tune in the key of G, starting on the C row but using cross-row fingering on the G row for higher passages, and uses the top for frequent chromatic notes used in short chromatic runs. Frequent use of partial chords is made on both the left and right hands. At times, he adds a bellows shake to long notes, to give them more character.

Through all this, however, Harris is basically an octave player, and nearly every note is played in octaves. This is concertina music of the highest quality for his day, and yet is still strongly rooted in the older style of play.

Wals van Tant Sannie (Aunt Sannie's Waltz) was named for Harris's aunt, but is actually the American tune *The Shannon Waltz*. This waltz seems to have been first recorded by the *East Texas Serenaders* in 1926 in Texas.

The Serenaders learned it and a number of other unusual tunes from a traveling fiddle player only known as 'Brigsley.' *6

Faan Harris's version of this waltz was recorded only four years after the piece was first recorded in Texas.

How the tune made its way to South Africa is not known, but recordings of the *Serenaders* were quite popular, and such recordings of the latest dance music were circulated globally.

As Wilhelm Schultz has pointed out, Boers freely imported sheet music and later recordings from abroad throughout the late nineteenth and early twentieth century, especially of American minstrel tunes, popular songs, and dance tunes from Europe and America. These imports were often given new lyrics and renamed in Afrikaans.

The *East Texas Serenaders* were particularly known for their bluesy rags and waltzes, and Faan Harris masterfully adapted this modern tune to his three-row Lachenal Anglo.

Such heavily chromatic twentieth-century material spelled the end of popularity for the diatonic Anglo-German concertina in much of the world, as the typical two-row C/G Anglo could not play most of the required half steps.

The situation was to be much different in South Africa, as demonstrated by this piece and by the preceding *Eileen Alannah*. Harris embraced these new chromatic touches, playing them with relish.

Wals van Tant Sannie is played in the key of G, as can be seen in the adjacent transcription of the A part of the tune. Harris played it mostly in octaves in a cross-row fashion, with lower-pitched parts of the melody played on the C row, and higher notes on the G row. Frequent chromatic notes are played on the top row, in octaves where possible. The chromatic half steps are found in measures two, five, ten, twenty-two, twenty-six, and twenty-seven.

He employed an impressive array of rich chords and triple octave notes (three notes, each an octave apart) in this tune, and used the bellows shake technique - albeit sparingly - on some of the long notes in the piece. *Wals van Tant Sannie* is a superb and complex concertina arrangement.

Wals van Tant Sannie

Waltz

As played by Faan Harris
Transcribed for CG Anglo by Dan Worrall

The *Soutpansberg Settees,* a schottische, was written by Harris during a trip to the northern Transvaal that he took with a friend, where they slept on the open veldt in a homemade tent. Soutpansberg is the name of a mountain range in that area. This tune is played in the key of G and mostly on the C row of his C/G concertina, but he switches to the G row in higher passages - such as measures fourteen and fifteen, and thirty-one and thirty-two - and in measures with octave runs (measures sixteen through most of eighteen). Harris plays it wholly on the two rows of his concertina, without the chromatic complexities of the above two waltzes.

Soutpansberg Settees

Schottische

As Played by Faan Harris
Transcribed for CG Anglo by Dan Worrall

Examples of cross rowing for fluidity in melody can be found in the last notes of measures one, two, and twenty-three, where the fingering drops down to the G row to keep a phrase on the pull. Because strings of eighth notes in the melody are alternately chorded, this cross-row fingering helps keep the passages all in one direction, facilitating the repetitive left hand chords.

Sean Minnie, who plays this tune today, mentions another reason for cross-row fingering:

> *When playing the first phrase of this tune on the Anglo there are a lot of changes in bellows direction to get the syncopation right ... Every alternative note is played on the other side of the concertina, keeping the rhythm to the chords on the left hand. It is a continuous struggle to teach young musicians this style so that they do not play all the notes on the same button with one finger.*

Anna Pop Settees is another schottische. It is played in C, mostly on the C row, except for some places where he drops to the G row to pick up alternate eighth notes to preserve unidirectional passages. There are no chromatic notes.

Kromdraai Mazurka is thought to have been named for a gold mine and associated town just north of Pretoria, near Krugersdorp, where Harris once lived. It is played in the key of G, mostly in octaves, heavily cross-rowed with a number of chromatic runs. Mazurkas have remained popular in South Africa to a greater extent than in the other three concertina countries of this report.

The *Rooidag Toe Polka* (roughly, *Until Daybreak*) is played in the key of G, in octaves and is extensively cross-rowed. It is played entirely on two rows, with no chromatic runs.

Christiaan Willem (Chris) Chomse

Christiaan Willem (Chris) Chomse was born in South Africa of immigrant German parents. He grew up as a farmer, and emigrated to Kenya in 1938, dying there in the town of Eldoret, in 1947.

While still in South Africa, he formed a band, *Die Lydenburg Vastrappers*, named for the town in which the members lived. Besides Chomse on concertina (the group's leader), there were Klaas Alexander Erasmus on clarinet, Geertruida Zacharyda Magdalena (Baba) Winterbach (nee Prinsloo) on piano, and her husband Christiaan Willem (Chris) Winterbach on guitar. The group recorded in 1934 on the Singer label.

Chris Chomse. Photograph with thanks to the Tradisionele Boeremusiekklub van Suid-Afrika.

This group was unusual among *Boeremusiek* bands because of its clarinet, and its smooth rhythm. Both accounts give the group a very German sound, not surprising given their leader's German roots. It may be the closest recording we have to the sound of continental German music played on the concertina, because the two and three row concertinas were quickly replaced there by much larger Chemnitzers and Bandoneons.

The **Noodshulp Vastrap** (possibly, the *First Aid Vastrap*) is played almost entirely in octaves. Chomse seems to have played a three row Bb/F Anglo that allowed him to play with a clarinet in his band; for the purposes of the transcription, this tune has been transposed up a note in order to match the pitch of a C/G Anglo, the system most commonly played today.

(Please note that modern Boer players can play in a great number of keys on their extended keyboard 40 button C/G Anglos, including Ab, A, Bb, C, D, Eb, F and G). He plays the tune in the key of F (G in the transcription), entirely in octaves. The tune is 'crooked' as played - there are only fifteen bars in the A part, and thirty-one in the B.

Like most Boer players in the bands of the 1920s and later, Chomse played with a guitar that functioned as a rhythm backup. With this backup he could hold long notes, whereas a solo player would have to punctuate in every interval to keep the rhythm going for the dancers. Chomse took full advantage of his guitar backup, and clearly didn't care about the effect of long pauses on the number of bars in this polka, so long as the tune had an even number of beats.

Noodshulp Polka

Boer, South Africa
Polka

As Played by Chris Chomse
Transcribed for CG Anglo by Dan Worrall

House Dance

There are prominent chromatic notes in the second, third, and sixth measures - this is clearly a twentieth-century tune, or at the very least a twentieth-century arrangement. Dissonant chords in measures eleven through thirteen are made on the pull on the C row, using the pull F on the top row (as transcribed). Like most Boer tunes, there are only a few grace notes in this polka; these are all in the B part.

As in Australian and early Irish playing, the playing and rhythm of the tune were executed in a relatively simple manner for the purpose of dance. Chording is likewise simple, comprised of just a few third intervals, or of the dissonant second intervals already mentioned.

The *Baba Wals* (Baby waltz) is played in the key of Bb, mostly on the Bb row but with some chromatic notes. It is mostly played in octaves.

The *Bosveld Polka* (Woodland Polka) is played in the key of F on his Bb/F concertina, all on the F row, and mostly in octaves. Bosveld is a town in Limpopo.

The *Mampoer Seties* is played in the key of Bb, mostly in octaves. It is a simple tune, and Chomse makes effective use of phrase-ending partial chords on the right hand. Mampoer is a white spirit made from fermented fruit, and is the Boer equivalent of moonshine.

The *Wissel Polka* (wissel means 'exchange') (Woodland Polka) is played at first in the key of Eb, then modulates to Bb in the B part. Chomse uses extensive cross-row fingering between the Bb and F rows.

Kerrie Bornman

Kerrie Bornman (1891-1968) was born at De Deur, near Vereeniging, about 50km south of Johannesburg. His boyhood was spent under the cloud of the Second Boer War and its aftermath. His father and eldest brother were captured and sent to Ceylon, the farm was burned, and he and his mother were sent to a British concentration camp (one of the unfortunate inventions of that war). After the war, they returned to the ruins of the house. Their only possession other than their land was a family Bible pulled out of the ashes.

Kerrie Bornman and his son Ricardo, ca.1958. Photograph with thanks to the Tradisionele Boeremusiekklub van Suid-Afrika.

His family was deeply musical. Kerrie's grandfather, father and uncle were all concertina players, which brings the family experience back to the very beginnings of the instrument. He began to play for dances by 1904, and at times played for the English for their *Lancers* quadrilles.

He played the German concertina, as did most in Boer South Africa during this time of poverty. He left South Africa to work on the Paris-Dover railway during the depression, then returned to work in the diamond fields at Bakerville.

At this time he was part of a renowned Bornman family band, but the group was never recorded. He did make two recordings however in the 1930s, which are included below. They are of interest as the only boerekonsertina (two row German concertina) recordings made in the early days (by that time most preofessional and semi-professional players had purchased Anglo concertinas), and thus are our clearest link to earliest styles of playing in South Africa.

It was only in the late 1950s that Bornman was again recorded, at the age of 67. Bosman Kock, a local broadcaster, was searching out old Boer concertina players to record. By this time, Bornman had an English-made Anglo concertina, and played his concertina with his son Ricardo on guitar. Bornman died at the age of 77.

The two pieces that Kerrie Bornman recorded in the 1930s are a waltz, **Vrystaat bo wals,** and a Schottische. Bornman plays both pieces in the key of D on a two row German concertina that most likely was pitched in G and D. He also adds a bass note for an oom-pah rhythm. The waltz begins with an opening phrase in octaves, followed by similar oom-pah chords on the left accompanying a right hand melody, with occasional octave phrases that occupy both hands.

In the **Oom Tien se settees** schottische, he plays often in octaves, creating third interval partial chords on the left hand by adding a note up from the lower octave note.

Ou Wessel se Settees (*Old William*) is a schottische in the key of D, in which Bornman is playing on a two row German concertina (*Boerekonsertina*) that is pitched in C/G, like that of his earlier recordings.

The *Pietersburg Mazurka* is played in the key of G; the low octave in this piece indicates that he is playing it on a G/D German concertina. It is a fairly simple but charming tune, mostly in octaves.

Hans Bodenstein

Johannes Pieter (Hans) Bodenstein (1892-1946) was born in the Mooi Valley at Potchefstroom, about 100km southwest of Johannesburg, and lived later in life at Benoni, a suburb of Johannesburg. He and his wife Joe (Johanna Carolina Elizabeth) had four daughters.

He worked in the mines and was active in a 1922 strike that resulted in a reward being placed on his head. He left on a bicycle one night, leaving his wife for two years while he lived in hiding - with his concertina - at first in the Orange Free State, and later in Namibia. With a new administration placed in power in 1924, he could return and resume his life.

He returned with a lot of ideas about how a concertina should be played, and in 1925 joined (and led) a new band that was eventually named *Die Vyf Vastrappers* (The Five Vastrappers), that was being established by Carolina Leeson (1901-1991, piano), along with Stol

Leeson (banjo), Henry Zeller (concertina), and Henry Kruger (guitar). Columbia records (associated with Regal Plate) sent a recording team to South Africa in 1930 to discover Boeremusiek in its native habitat.

The following pen portrait was published in the Rand Daily Mail, 24 July 1930 (with thanks to Wilhelm Schultz and Rob Allingham), and describes a dance in an isolated hall where the Vastrappers (at that time called The Sheepskins) were playing. As a result of this encounter, the band members were invited to Johannesburg, where they were the first Boeremusiek band to make a commercial recording.

Die Vyf Vastrappers in 1926. Hans Bodenstein is second from left. Photograph with thanks to the Tradisionele Boeremusiekklub van Suid-Afrika.

A party of investigators set out last Saturday night to trace Afrikaans dance music to its nature heath ... A young man had offered to lead us to the promised land, which, he gave us to understand, was far removed from the beaten track as to be almost inaccessible to the uninitiated. He was right. From Benoni we twisted and turned, doubled on our tracks, negotiated fearsome ruts like small dongas, and eventually struck what our guide called a main road. To us it seemed that in name only.

Four miles from Benoni [which lies about 30km east of Johannesburg] we passed through a straggling hamlet. Then another mile under the stars with no sign of life about us.

"D`you see the light?" said our guide at length. "That is the hall". Away to the left a solitary gleam sparkled in the darkness. It grew in brilliance as we approached, and finally resolved itself into two prodigeous gas lamps over the door

House Dance

of a large, squat building. This was the hall. To come across it thus planted down in the open veld was like finding a crocus blooming amid the snowy wastes of Kamchatka. We parked our car, paid ten shillings each at the door, and walked inside.

Under the light of a dozen gas flares half a hundred couples were gallivanting gaily. The band sat in a far corner. It mustered only five players, but the joyful noise they made could be heard far into the night. A woman thumped enthusiastically on a piano that bore the marks of many a stern encounter. The melody was being powerfully coaxed from a concertina, while the rhythmic support was being accorded with gusto by two guitars and a banjo. Some of the musical effects had apparently been rehearsed; others definitely had not.

The band continued playing until the "captain of the team" thought the dancers had had enough. Then he clapped his hands, and the music came to a summary stop. A "vastrap" was followed by a "wals", a "polka" and a "tikiedraai lancers", all set to favourite Afrikaans melodies, and then the whole process was gone through again. This was the genuine article without a doubt. The dancers were in their Sunday best. The gentlemen wore notty blue suits, and the ladies coloured costumes that beggared description.

There were no formalities as to introductions, and so forth. You merely approached a girl, clasped her round the waist, and whirled her round the hall. One young fellow varied this procedure by trying to snatch a kiss from an elderly woman. She slapped him cordially in the face, and referred him to her daughter, a dainty little blonde, around whom navigated beaux were clustering like bees around a honey pot. He dutifully took his place in the cue.

Among the trippers might be seen some styles which savoured of the ballroom and others which smacked definitely of the barn dance. The vertical and horizontal arms, and the gracefully cocked head, the stiff leg, the slow shuffle, the gay gallop and the backveld blues - all were there. I saw one of those arms come into violent contact with a passing nose. The owner of the arm spent several minutes to explain it away.

When the interval came round, coffee was served to everybody. Most of the girls smelt it first. After I tested it, I understood why. Every now and then, too, our guide would seek us out to inform us that he was a "cultured gentleman" and that he did not generally come in contact with such people. These protestations become more and more tearful as the evening drew on. Before we left he pulled a bottle from his breast pocket and demonstrated to us just how he was bidding dull care begone. Nor was he alone, it seemed , in this. We bade him good-bye before the general joy had become quite unconfirmed, but the sounds of revelry pursued us far into the night.

The "Sheepskin" Band came to Johannesburg last Tuesday (22 July) and recorded a dozen numbers for posterity.

The recordings were released on Regal, a less expensive subsidiary label of Columbia Records UK. The band disbanded in 1934. Bodenstein died in 1946 in Benoni, but piano player Carolina Leeson lived into the 1980s.

Bodenstein played a three row C/G Wheatstone concertina. An **Untitled Settees** (Schottische) is a fine example of early Boer playing, and is playable on a two-row C/G concertina. As the adjacent transcription shows, Bodenstein plays this piece in the key of C, using a cross-row technique where he plays the lower phrases on the C row and the higher phrases on the G row.

The tune is played nearly completely in octaves. The sparse chords are partial and easily built, as they primarily consist of simple third intervals down from the top octave (right hand) melody notes. Building the partial chords on the right hand contrasts with the technique used by English players like William Kimber, who typically chord on the left; this right-hand chording imparts a continental European sound to the music.

The transcription of the A part represents his second time through the tune; in his first time through, those partial chords were left out, and the playing was purely in octaves.

Bodenstein follows the melody in a cross-row manner as it weaves between the C and G rows. For example, measures one, two, and the first half of three are played on the G row, and then the fingering moves to the C row through measure eight, except for a single excursion back to the G row for the F# in measure five. The B part similarly moves between the two rows.

One characteristic of Bodenstein's playing, evident in all the pieces here, is his jazz-like improvisation of the melody line, in successive repetitions of the piece (the first line is played 'straight'). This takes considerable skill, and the extent of this improvisation is not encountered amongst early recorded players in the other three countries of this study.

It seems reasonable to assume that the rise of improvisation was linked to the jazz recordings the Boers were hearing in the 1920s.

 ***Tweestep Sammie Settees*** (Two-step Sammy's Schottische) was composed by Bodenstein and named for a man named Sam Warren. Warren and his wife often danced to the Vastrappers' music. The tune is played in the key of D on his C/G concertina, fully in octaves. This is somewhat unusual, as D is not one of the two home rows of the concertina that Bodenstein played; it illustrates both his mastery of the instrument and a growing trend to cross row fingering utilizing all three rows of the newer Anglo concertinas.

 ***Barndans met Twee Konsertinas*** *(Barndance with Two Concertinas)* is, like the previous tune played in the key of D, mostly in octaves with phrase-ending chords. It was played by Hans Bodenstein and Henry Zeller.

 Bodenstein's **Untitled Waltz** is similarly played in the key of D, with a few chromatic runs.

 An *Untitled Polka* is a relatively simple tune in the key of G, played in octaves, and almost all on the G row. It is decorated with many partial chords played in the characteristic style on the right hand.

 ***Die Fluister Waltz*** (The Whisper Waltz) is a more complex tune, played in the key of C, again in octaves, with many chromatic runs.

Willie Palm

Willie Palm was born in 1894 in Ficksburg in the former Orange Free State, but moved to Boksburg (a suburb of Johannesburg) as a boy and spent the rest of his life there.

He formed a band named *Die Vier Hugenote* (The Four Huguenots) with his wife Lettie on piano and guitar, and her brothers Alec and Pietie Vermaak on guitar. They were recorded in the 1930s. Their arrangements are stately and straightforward, and deceptively simple. Palm appears to be playing a C/G extended keyboard Anglo concertina in these recordings.

Willie and Lettie Palm. Photograph with thanks to the Tradisionele Boeremusiekklub van Suid-Afrika.

Oom Koos se Mazurka (Uncle Koos's Mazurka) is played in G, in octaves, with some right hand partial chords.

Vergeet Nie (Never Forget) is a waltz in the key of C, played in octaves and in a cross row manner, with a few brief chromatic runs.

Kom ons dans (Come let's dance) is a schottische played in the key of A. This is a rarity amongst early players, and was not seen in the recordings from other countries of this study. It is played in octaves, with considerable amounts of cross-row fingering required. It is deceptively simple, but the style of fingering is complex because of the unusual key. Playing tunes in non-home keys is a hallmark of both early and modern Boer playing.

Mampoer Polka is played in the key of D. Another version of the polka is played by Chris Chomse, above. Mampoer is a white spirit made from fermented fruit, and is the Boer equivalent of moonshine.

Pietie Prinsloo

Marthinus Petrus (Pietie) Prinsloo (1896-1973) was born in Johannesburg, just before the Second Boer War. He met Faan Harris and became a student of the master concertina player. Afterwards, Prinsloo learned to be a joiner, and started working in a mine.

However, underground work did not appeal to him, and within a year he resigned and became a conductor on the tram service, where he met his friend and fellow musician Henry Rex. The two resigned from the tram and purchased a farm near Tuinplaas, in the northern Transvaal, raising peanuts, corn and cattle.

He joined *Die Vier Springbokke* (The Four Springboks), and they recorded in 1932 on the label His Master's Voice. Prinsloo co-led the band with Henry Rex (guitar). Another good friend, George Breval, played piano, and Bossie Bosman played a second guitar.

Pietie Prinsloo in 1932. Photograph with thanks to the Tradisionele Boeremusiekklub van Suid-Afrika..

Prinsloo had no children, but doted on his brother Henry's. **Koekoe my hartjie se Seties** (Koekoe my Heart Schottische) is named for his brother's oldest daughter Koekoe. The tune is played in D in what seems to be a C/G three row Anglo. He plays in octaves in a very fluid style in long melodic runs that attests to intricate cross-row fingering across all three rows. This is technically proficient playing indeed.

Ek hou my Iyf soos 'n ou fisant (I act like an old pheasant) is a polka played at a very brisk tempo, only partly in octaves, in the key of D.

Silver de Lange

Johannes Petrus (Silver) de Lange (1904-1956) was born at Vrededorp, a suburb of Johannesburg. The family was poor, but nonetheless bought musical instruments for the children to learn to play.

He started and led a band called *Die Vyf Dagbrekers* (The Five Daybreakers), with Gert de Lange and Wakkie van Biljon on guitars, Pie du Plooy on piano, and Bobby Pennels on banjo; they made 15 recordings in 1932 for His Master's Voice. It is claimed that he came by his nickname, Silver, because of the pure silver tones he coaxed from his concertina. He was a perfectionist with his music, and demanded high standards from guitar and banjo chording and rhythm.

Silver de Lange in 1932. Photograph with thanks to the Tradisionele Boeremusiekklub van Suid-Afrika.

De Lange taught concertina for a living, and was said to have always been polite, respectful and pleasant with his students. He died of a brain hemorrhage in 1956.

De Lange's music is complex. There is frequent use of chromatic phrases, and complex improvisations are introduced in successive repeats of the tune. His phrasing makes abundant use of cross-row techniques on an extended range Anglo - perhaps a 40 button Wheatstone. For this reason, many of his tunes require more than can be delivered on the normal three-row, 30 button Anglo.

When the Wheatstone Concertina company wished to redesign parts of their Anglo concertinas (South Africa was a big market for 40 button Wheatstone instruments in the early twentieth century), they paid de Lange's way to London for consultation.

Militaire twee-pas vastrap (The Military Two-step Vastrap) was rescued by members of the TBK from a chipped 78 rpm disc by painstaking reconstruction, and the results are well worth their effort. It is played in C on a C/G Anglo concertina. It is mostly played in octaves, and with considerable amounts of cross-row fingering as well as a few chromatic notes. Following a first playing of the straight melody, de Lange then plays successive passes with a considerable amount of improvisation.

 ***Warm Pattat Polka*** (*The Hot Sweet Potato Polka*) is played in the key of D on a C/G concertina, and like all of his pieces contains a significant amount of improvisation in successive repeats of the tune. A 'hot sweet potato' is Boer slang for a fetching and spirited young woman.

 ***Mielieblare Settees*** (Maize Leaves Schottische) is played in the key of G, mostly on the G row except for lower parts of the B part, in octaves. There are numerous chromatic notes added to spice up the melody, and there is a considerable amount of improvisation.

 ***Het Jy My Nog Lief*** (Do You Still Love Me?) is a waltz, played in the key of G, with significant amounts of chromatic notes and improvisation. De Lange uses the bellows shake to good effect in long notes.

 ***Die Hele Nag Deur Vastrap*** (The Whole Night Long Vastrap) is played in the key of C, in octaves, and makes full use of an extended range Anglo keyboard in delivering the tune's complex phrasing.

Notes:

1. Miss Russell, 'The Republics of South Africa,' *Journal of the American Geographical Society of New York* (December 22, 1876), pp.235-251.

2. 'Boers great dancers', *Omaha Daily Bee* (Nebraska), December 14, 1899, p.4.

3. Beatrice M Hicks, *The Cape as I Found It* (London: Elliot Stock, 1900), p.129.

4. Gordon Le Seur, *Cecil Rhodes, The Man and His Work* (New York: McBride, Nast & Company, 1914), pp.157-158.

5. 'Boer Courtship,' *The Otago Witness* (New Zealand), November 6, 1907.

6. Keith Chandler, 'The East Coast Serenaders', extended notes to document release: *Musical Traditions*, article MT020 (1998), http://www.mustrad.org.uk.

Chapter 11. Modern players in the old style

Concertina playing in all four countries of this study today is nearly unrecognizable from the music made by most of the early players in this archive. A key reason for this change has been the general demise in social dancing, at least of the types of ballroom dance that were prevalent in the heyday of the Anglo concertina. The repertoire of the Anglo in its heyday consisted principally of the music for these round dances and quadrilles.

The general early- to middle-twentieth century demise of concertina playing paralleled the loss of ballroom dance; the two were symbiotic. In some places, like Australia and South Africa, these dance styles lived on a bit longer, and in South Africa these dance tunes were captured at the onset of commercial 78rpm recording.

These early recordings from the 1930s seem to have instigated a move toward more complexity in playing styles. In South Africa, this complexity included the use of chromatic notes and improvisation taken from jazz, as well as experimentation with cross-row playing in new keys beyond the two 'home row' keys of the instrument.

Although a few players in England experimented with chromatic playing, they were few in number and overall impact. However, with the Morris dance revival of the 1960s and 1970s, a move toward complexity in chording and phrasing began that moved the playing of the instrument far beyond its humble two-row roots.

In Ireland at the same time, the development of competitions at festivals spurred the use of cross-row fingerings across all three rows to enhance phrasing, as well as the addition of complex ornamentation, to an extent not seen earlier. As we have seen, these changes accompanied an abrupt change in the Irish repertoire, where a renewed emphasis on reels and other step dance tunes replaced the round dance repertoire of an older generation.

For this reason, it is difficult to find concertina players today who can and do play in the earlier style that was so attuned to house dancing during the heyday of the concertina - a style that was known in all four study countries by its simple phrasing, octave playing, and general lack of ornamentation.

This chapter presents a few recordings by concertina players found in the author's travels who still play largely and/or convincingly in the octave style. By and large, the musicians of this group play for social dances, either as their main way of approaching the concertina or as a significant adjunct.

Australia

The largest single group of such players are located in Australia, for several reasons. There has never been a significant commercial recording industry or significant competitions to influence concertina playing in Australia, allowing it to remain close to its dancing roots. In some areas, notably the Nariel Valley area of Victoria, old time dancing has continued in relatively uninterrupted fashion to the present day, and many bands contain concertina and one row button accordion players.

Also, there is in Australia a very strong 'colonial dance' and 'bush dance' revival movement that has is active and well-researched. The organizations there that hold dances endeavor to preserve older music and dances in relatively unaltered form.

Ian and Ray Simpson are brothers who were raised in Nariel. Their father was Neville Simpson, a concertina and accordion player and regular in the old Nariel band, where both brothers gained their appreciation of Australian dance music. A grandfather, Charlie Ordish, is among the players featured in Chapter 7, and they are related as well as to Con Klippel.

Ray moved to the Melbourne area some years back for work, and has been very active there in playing for colonial and bush dances. Ian and his wife Diane continue to live in Nariel and play for the old Nariel dances, along with their good friend Keith Klippel (below). Ian makes high quality wooden whistles and builds Anglo concertinas, and plays the button accordion and the saw in addition to Anglo concertina.

In the following two recordings, Ian plays a C/G Anglo concertina of his own manufacture. Ian's playing is closely related to that of the Klippels and of course that of his father.

Tickets, Please is a tune heard by his grandfather Charlie Ordish while attending a circus in Wodonga Australia.

As the story goes, an accordion player was playing the tune while Ordish was standing near the ticket booth. Not knowing the tune's title, Ordish called it *Tickets, please* for the sounds with which he associated the tune. On the way home, Ordish visited the circus encampment and made sure he learned the tune from the circus musician.* 1

Ian plays the tune at a stately pace so that it closely adheres to the tempo used for the Nariel dances. He plays much of it in octaves, with frequent use of partial chords as well as sparse ornamentation. He plays it all on the C row, dropping the melody an octave at times to enable it to be played all on that row.

Ian plays the slow waltz ***The Rose of Tralee*** along with his wife Di, who accompanies a second verse on a wooden whistle made by Ian. He plays it in C, just like he plays *Tickets, please*. The key of C is a favorite in the Nariel band, because it has always been led by concertina and button accordion players with instruments tuned in C. He plays it all on the C row, at times in octaves, and at times not, as befits the passages in the melody. It is a lovely version, in harmony with the rural setting of their lives.

Ray Simpson has strong roots in rural Nariel but was separated by the press of employment from that area. He has been a city dweller for a number of years, in Melbourne, and is an accomplished musician for dances in that city. The tempo of urban life is much quicker than that in rural Nariel, and one can imagine hearing that in his playing. It is not often that one can hear music from two brothers, separated and living for years in very different environments, playing the same tune from their childhood.

Ian and Di Simpson standing in the entry of their Nariel home, 2011.

Here is Ray Simpson's version of the very same tune included above from Ian, **Tickets, Please**. Ray plays it primarily on the C row, as does Ian, but his tempo is quicker, he adds fewer partial chords than his brother, and he adds a considerably larger amount of ornamentation, including very rapid duplets of notes. Ray and his children all play Irish music - popular in Melbourne - in addition to Australian music, and the ornamentation appears to have originated from that experience.

Here Ray plays a Nariel variant of the old minstrel favorite, **Golden Slippers**. As in the above piece, he plays it in the key of C and all on the C row. In the B part, he raises the tune an octave when a low passage curbs his ability to continue to play the tune in octaves whilst remaining on the C row, thus signaling his Nariel roots; his brother Ian as well as their relative Con Klippel frequently use this technique (as did Scan Tester in England).

Ray Simpson at the National Folk Festival, Canberra, 2011. Ray, with a serape over his suit and a mask, was leading a large column of masked musicians and dancers to the festival's annual masked ball.

Keith Klippel is a third-generation Australian concertina player and fourth generation free reed player who grew up in the Nariel valley, and now lives in nearby Tallangatta. The recordings of his father, Con Klippel, are featured in Chapter 7.

Keith has played in the Nariel band for all his adult life, along with his friends Ian and Di Simpson and others, and today he mostly plays the button accordion in that band.

Keith Klippel at home in early 2011. He is playing his father Con Klippel's Lachenal concertina.

For the purposes of this project, Keith has dusted off his father's Lachenal two row C/G Anglo concertina and plays a tune used for quadrille dancing in Nariel, *The Little Old Cabin in the Dell*. He plays it all on the C row and nearly all in octaves, in the manner of his father.

Peter Ellis lives in Bendigo, Victoria and is a founder of the Emu Creek Bush Band as well as a leader in the revival of Australian old-time dance, both through his activity in playing for, teaching, and calling dances for the Bush Dance and Music Club of Bendigo,*2 as well as for his many books on traditional Australian music and dance published by that organization. He knew Jim Harrison, who was featured in Chapter 9.

Peter Ellis waving a concertina, 2011.

Here Peter plays the *Varsoviana* in the Harrison style, complete with arms swinging the concertina in windmill-like circles. The recording demonstrates the sound of that popular old swinging technique. He plays the tune in the key of G on a C/G Anglo, all on the C row, and adds a large number of partial chords to the piece.

Peter also knew the late Harry McQueen (1910-1994) of Castelemaine, Victoria, and collected a number of dance tunes from him, including the *Garibaldi's Waltz March.*

McQueen played the two-row button accordion for many a dance, but his father and grandfather played the concertina. Peter here plays two tunes collected from Harry, but which originated from Harry's grandfather. As Peter tells it:

> *As a child, Harry watched his grandfather play 'Garibaldi's March Waltz' on the front verandah of his miner's cottage in Daylesford. He would walk up and down the verandah playing, and stopping and bowing at certain phrases. The tune has Varsoviana type 'holds', part A is in 4-4, part B in 3-4 and even more Varso style ...*

Years later, Harry was visiting an old friend, in hospital dying. This friend, Len Teague I think, hadn't been to dances since when 15 years, with his parents. These dances were held in the 'stone house', ancestral home of the Gervasoni's of Yandoit. Italians settled there in the 1850s or 60s. He asked Harry about his continuing to play for dances and whether they still 'danced the Garibaldi March Waltz'. Harry was ecstatic, he'd never come across the dance except for the snippets of his grandfather when playing the tune. He wrote down Teague's description and we have revived the dance from that, lucky to have Jim's original tune. * 3

Dave de Hugard grew up on a tobacco farm in rural Queensland, and began playing folk music as a college student in the early 1960s. He has since worked as a folklore collector and researcher, and has published several highly regarded CD recordings where he plays and sings Australian music, including *On the Wallaby Track* and *Magpie Morning*. He plays the accordion, fiddle and banjo as well as the concertina, and is a frequent musician at old time dances.

Dave de Hugard, 2011.

Here he plays an old schottische tune called ***Kate Perrett's*** learned from his friend, musician Kath McCaughey (1901-1989), who in turn learned it from Kate Perrett, of Guy Fawkes, up in the New England area of Australia. Dave plays the tune in Bb on a Bb/F concertina, and crosses back and forth from the Bb to the F rows as needed to fit the pitch of the melody.

England

Most players in England today use a richly chorded style developed by listening to traditional English melodeon players. In the 'revival' of the concertina there in the 1960s and 1970s there were few living role models for the Anglo concertina played in the traditional octave style, and many young concertina players took their musical cues from melodeon players as a result. Scan Tester however influenced several young concertina players during his later years, and still others came by octave playing the natural way: it evolved naturally in their playing as they began to play for dances.

Will Duke lives in Sussex. He began playing the Anglo concertina in 1971, and had the great good fortune to meet and learn from Scan Tester in the last years of his life. He has played in a number of English country music and dance bands, and is also is a traditional singer.

Sussex player Will Duke. With thanks to Katie Howson and the East Anglia Traditional Music Trust.

He has released several CDs of traditional Sussex song and concertina music, including *Out of the Box* and *Scanned*. He acknowledges a great debt to Scan Tester in his training on the concertina, and plays in a modified octave style that builds on the lessons learned from Tester.

Here he plays two schottisches learned from Tester, **High Low Schottische** and another that is **Untitled**. Will plays tribute to Tester's octave style, and adds in some embellishments and stylistic elements of his own. He plays these on a G/D Dipper concertina.

Dave Prebble comes from East Sussex, and bought his first concertina in 1979, unfortunately after Scan Tester had passed away. With no one to teach him, he rather naturally began to play octaves on his left hand, pleased with the fuller sound.

After hearing John Kirkpatrick, he began to layer in chords in his playing as well. This mix has served him well in years of playing at pub sessions, with Morris and clog dance sides, and for English country dances in rural community halls.

Dave Prebble plays his Jeffries Anglo concertina, 2011.

He plays a medley of three tunes here. The first, ***Jackie Donnan's Mazurka No.2***, is played in straight octave fashion; the second, ***The Shrewsbury Waltz***, drops out some octave notes to emphasize the beat; the third, ***Sally Sloane's Mazurka***, is a mixture of octaves and chords.

Harry Scurfield, from Otley, West Yorkshire, is another revival era player but with a world music bent, playing blues, jazz, Cajun, and even South African (Zulu) squashbox for over 38 years. With no Anglo players in most of those styles to learn from - squashbox excepted - Scurfield's approach is unique, although he acknowledges octave playing as a thread that has always run through his technique, a trait picked up from listening to recordings of Scan Tester.

Harry plays in a five-piece group, *Bayou Gumbo*, and at times with another Anglo player, Matt Dennis. When playing for dances, he often turns to what he terms the 'power and punch' that octave playing releases, to say nothing of the richness of its sound'.

Harry Scurfield, in a recent concert with Bayou Gumbo. Photo by Ani McNeice.

Here he plays three tunes. The first is *Si C'était à Refaire* by the well-known New Orleans musician Sydney Bechet; the second is *Kit White's Two Couple Square*, named for a Yorkshire melodeon player; and the third is *The Bells of Hell*, taken from the playing of Jim Eldon of Hull and the late Billy Harrison of the East Riding of Yorkshire. All three are played in the key of C on his C/G Anglo concertina, mostly in octaves.

Ireland

It would seem that Ireland, where the tradition of music and dance is so revered, and which is the well-spring of so much of today's traditional concertina music, would have a number of concertina players who play in the old octave style. There seem to be few, however. Most of the dwindling generation of pre-revival concertina players belong more to the céili era of reels rather than the earlier house dance era of round dances and quadrilles, when playing in octaves in the key of C, usually on German concertinas, was much more prevalent.

Sean O'Dwyer grew up playing in a family dance band in his parent's dance hall in Ardgroom, and is well steeped in the set tunes, polkas, slides and marches of that region. His mother, Ella Mae O'Dwyer, was a big influence; her playing was featured in Chapter 8. Sean now lives in Dublin, and following a multi-decade lapse from public playing, he is now playing again, and has released a CD, *Irish Traditional Music from Beara*.

Although he plays mostly in a single-note fashion these days, along with most of the Anglo players of his generation, he well remembers his mother's octave repertoire used in the Ardgroom dances of long ago. For this project, he unearthed his mother's inexpensive C/G German concertina from his sister's storage, and carefully and methodically brought it back to playing condition. Here he plays two selections on it.

Sean O'Dwyer, holding his mother's German concertina.

 The first includes a medley of tunes played by his mother in the Ardgroom dance days: *The Centenary March and the Ardgroom Two-step*.

 The second is an air, ***Port na bPúcaí*** *(Tune of the Faeries)*.

For those owners of high-priced hand-crafted Anglo concertinas who are prone to dismissing the German concertina as a 'big step down,' this version of the air may cause reflection. The old instrument has a rich and ancient-sounding tone, that result from the double sets of brass reeds (one set an octave lower, giving a baritone sound) as well as from the octave playing style employed by Sean; at times, four reeds are sounding for each note of the melody. His use of bass drones is worthy of an uillean piper, and adds much to the piece.

South Africa

The Traditional Boer Music Club of South Africa (TBK) has worked in recent decades to restore the *boeremusiek* playing styles of nearly a century ago. One of the first steps taken by that club in its early days in the 1980s was the restoration of the classic 78 rpm *boeremusiek* recordings of the 1930s, and the distribution of these recordings to its members. Two of the chief participants in that effort were Stephaan van Zyl and Danie Labuschagne.

A second step was the restoration of the old *boerekonsertina*, the German concertina of the sort played in Ireland by Ella Mae O'Dwyer, in Australia by Charlie Ordish, George Bennett and others, and in South Africa by Kerrie Bornman, to say nothing of tens of thousands of rural players in all of these countries who preceded these musicians. The quality of current versions of this instrument, manufactured in Germany and China, are not nearly equal to those of a century ago, presenting a problem to those who value the old sound. To solve this problem, South African Danie Labuschagne now builds two row concertinas in the German style, albeit with an improved metal action.

A third rung in the restoration of old time *boeremusiek* in South Africa is the encouragement of old time dancing with live music.

Stephaan van Zyl in the early 1980s, holding a boerekonsertina. With thanks to Kalie de Jager.

Stephaan van Zyl lives in the Pretoria area and plays both the two-row *boerekonsertina* and the Crane duet concertina. He has been instrumental in reviving the old Boer style on the concertina, and has released a tutorial for old-time *boerekoncertina* on Youtube.

The old style, as we have seen in Chapter 10, consisted of playing in octaves, with simple partial chords added for occasional emphasis along with phrase-ending full chords.

In ***Oupa se Wals*** *(Grandfather's Waltz)*, he plays one of Labuschagne's German-like newly constructed *boerekonsertinas*, in this old style. The concertina is pitched in G/D, and the tune is played in the key of G.

Notes:

1. Peter Ellis, personal communication 2011. Peter heard the story from a recording of Con Klippel.

2. www.bendigobushdance.org.au

3. Peter Ellis, personal communication, 2011.

Chapter 12. Playing in octaves: a brief tutorial

Playing in the traditional octave style, as we have seen above, has a rich history of application to dance, as well as a rich sound, but resources for learning it are rare indeed.

In Ireland, England, South Africa and Australia, the best players used a cross-row technique of playing in octaves on two-row concertinas that was best learned from a concertina teacher or another player; some players never learned it.

In modern day weekend schools of Irish- or English-style Anglo concertina playing, one may hear of playing in octaves as an occasional ornament for a phrase, but not as a general approach to the instrument, at least not as most of the early recorded players in this archive would have seen it. In this section, a few useful tips are offered for those wishing to learn how the old-timers played.

I recorded a series of nine tutorial clips in a brief sitting. No attempt has been made to polish them or present in a formal way, nor am I a professional musician. They are offered as a casual meeting with one who enjoys playing in octaves.

Playing in octaves is counter-intuitive, because when moving up a scale, the fingers on the left hand advance from button to button at a different time than the fingers on the right. For that reason, it is a task for muscle memory that must be practiced for some time before it becomes second nature.

There is a cross-row transition to be learned as well, which is of course alien to the beginning player, who tends to play - and think - along the row. It is these two skills together that the late Irish concertina and fiddle player John Kelly (1912-1989) referred to when he discussed his early tuition in the instrument, from a woman in his area:

> *[Mary Houlihan] was supposed to have been the queen of [the older players here]. It was like going to high school. When I graduated from home I went to her and got a good bit of instruction from her. She learnt the double [octave] style of playing from a man by the name of Patrick Murphy from Frure ... 'T was he showed her the double style of goin' across the keys, and she had it very good. She had a beautiful concertina, wherever in the name of God she got it, I don't know. There was a great sound in it . 'Twas a high-class German concertina.*＊1

Playing octaves in such a cross-row manner is a very simple procedure - once someone shows it to you.

A button numbering scheme for the basic Anglo-German concertina is shown in the adjacent figure. For the purposes of this discussion, the top (third) row of buttons will be neglected; most of the early recorded players (excepting the more advanced of the Boer players as well as Englishman Fred Kilroy) typically had and used only two rows.

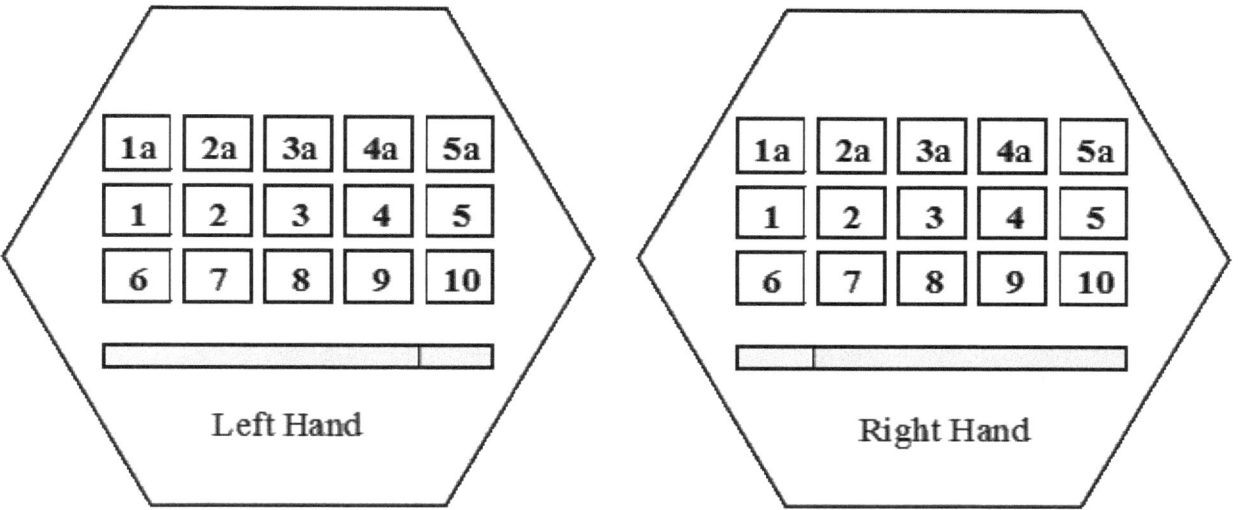

Button numbering convention, three-row Anglo-German concertina. Most early players had only two-row instruments, which consisted of the bottom two rows shown here. The second (middle) row is in the key of C (buttons 1-5), and the bottom (inside) row is in the key of G (buttons 6-10).

Please note: the audio examples are played on two instruments: a 30 button, three row Anglo concertina in the keys of C/G by Colin Dipper in England, and a 20 button, two-row German-style concertina in the keys of C/G by Danie Labuschagne in South Africa. The latter instrument is doubled in octaves, meaning two notes an octave apart play for each single button pushed; this baritone instrument is very similar to those played by Mary Ann Carolan and by Ella Mae O'Dwyer, among others, in the archive recordings.

It should be noted that a 20 button two-row instrument is perfectly adequate for the examples and tunes in this tutorial.

1. Playing in the key of C

The basic two-row octave scale in the key of C is illustrated in the figure below as well as in *Tutorial 1*.

In the C scale, the first four notes (*do-re-mi-fa*) are played on the C row, with the right hand playing the upper octave while the left plays the lower octave. For the last four notes (*so-la-ti-do*), both hands drop down to the G row. It will be seen that as the fingers move up the keyboard from button to button, the fingers on the right hand change buttons at a different place in the scale than do the fingers on the left hand. This takes some practice to execute proficiently, but once learned it becomes second nature. It may help the beginner to keep in mind the image shown in the second Figure below: one's fingers trace the pattern of a 'double Z' on the keys when working up the scale.

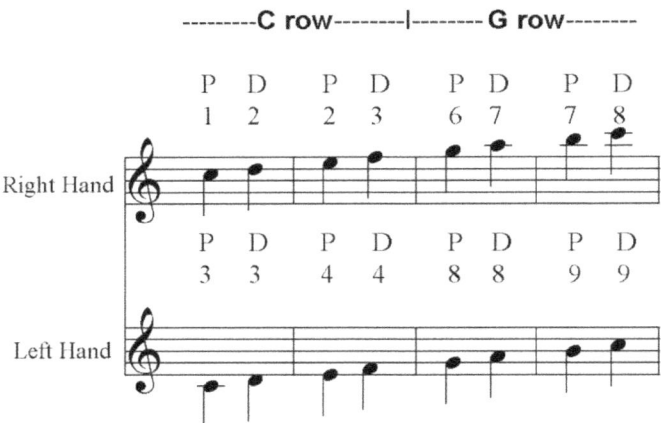

The basic two-row octave scale in C. The numbers represent the buttons on the keyboard in the previous figure on the right (upper staff) and left (lower). The two hands play in unison. P = Press, D = Draw. Buttons are numbered as in Figure 1.

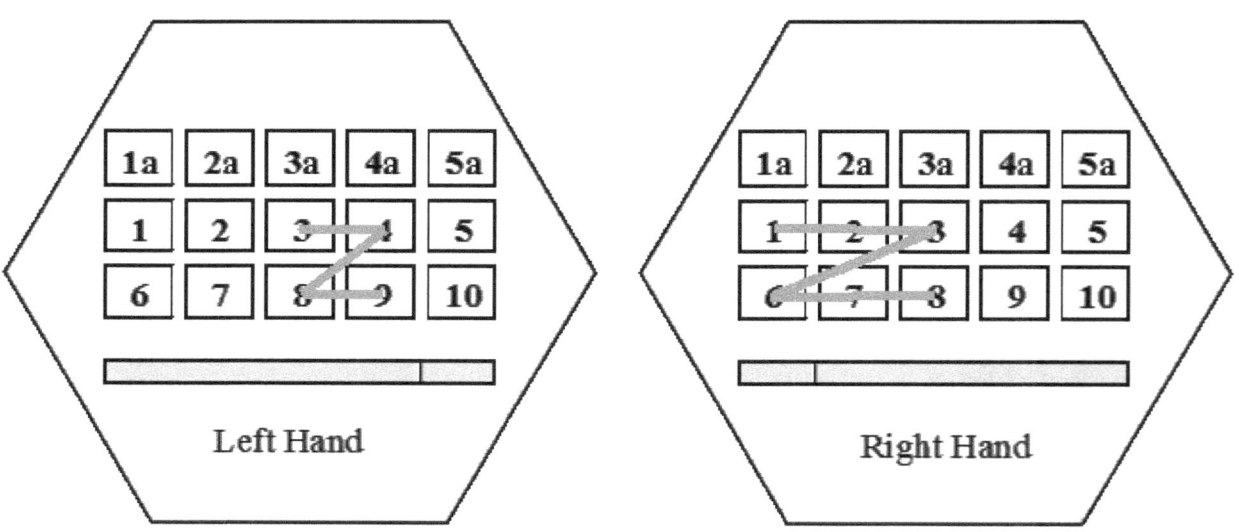

The path of the ascending octave scale in the key of C, where the fingers trace out a 'double Z' on the buttons.

It will be noted that it is quite easy to continue to play the *so-la* on the C row rather than moving to the G row, and it is also possible to play the last two notes (*ti-do*) in octaves on the C row. However, the fingering changes necessary to play the latter two notes on the C row are quite awkward, which is why the two-row octave technique was developed - it is much easier to move down to the G row to play them.

So-called single-row octave players will play on the C row for an entire tune, but in that case, either a) the tune does not use a high-end *ti-do* in its range of notes, b) the musician will simply eliminate the upper octave notes in the high part of the tune, or c) the musician will drop the higher-pitched part of the melody abruptly down an octave. More on this latter option in the example of Scan Tester's playing style.

Dooley Chapman's version of the song tune **Ring the Bell, Watchman**, is a good first tune to learn in the octave style in C. Chapman played a Bb/F concertina, and hence he plays the tune in the key of Bb, but it is here transcribed into the key of C for a C/G instrument (we shall attempt to match his fingering, however).

Tutorial 2 goes slowly through the tune with commentary. The score is shown with a dashed line that indicates when the melody should be played on the G row; all other parts are played on the C row.

Ring the Bell, Watchman

Australia
Breakdown

As Played by Dooley Chapman
Transcribed for CG Anglo by Dan Worrall

Ring the Bell, Watchman as played by Dooley Chapman. Parts shown with an accompanying dashed line are played on the G row, and parts without that line are played in the C row.

2. Playing in the key of G

Playing in the key of G in octaves is similar to playing in the key of C, except for the addition of the necessary F#, which is located of course on the G row. The following Figure and the audio file with commentary, *Tutorial 3*, illustrate the scale of G in two complete octaves; these two complete octaves can be played in the octave style without a great deal of difficulty. The lower note A may not be as shown on all concertinas, as the lower notes of the left hand vary quite a bit from brand to brand.

A two-row octave scale in G, in octaves, for a Jeffries-style two-row concertina.

Bernard O'Sullivan's version of the polka *I Have a Bonnet Trimmed with Blue*, which was probably learned from Stack Ryan, is a simple tune played in the key of G in a two-row octave style (note: the phrase 'two-row' means a tune played in octaves where both rows of buttons are used; in other words, cross-row playing).

The next page shows the transcription of O'Sullivan's playing. The dashed line indicates where the melody should be played on the G row, and the notes without such a dashed line are to be played on the C row.

Tutorial 4 goes slowly through the tune with commentary.

I Have a Bonnet Trimmed With Blue

Ireland
Polka

As Played by Bernard O'Sullvan and Tommy McMahon
Transcribed for CG Anglo by Dan Worrall

Transcription, I Have a Bonnet Trimmed With Blue. Parts shown with a dashed line are played on the G row, and parts without that line are played in the C row.

3. Octave jumps

Some old-time players learned how to play in octaves but somehow never got the hang of cross-row playing, and kept all their tunes played on a single row. Others had the skill of cross-row playing, but enjoyed the extra discipline imposed by forcing octave playing upon a single row.

The English musician Scan Tester was one such player, and one of his schottisches, here called ***Scan Tester's Schottische***, provides an excellent example of how a single-row player would approach octave playing.

As was mentioned above, when a melody, played in octaves and confined to a single row, reaches either too high or too low for octaves to be comfortably played, one could either drop one octave and continue to play singly, or one could jump the entire melody an octave up or down, and keep sailing through. That is what Tester does in this schottische, which is played entirely on the C row.

Tutorial 5, illustrates the process of octave jumps in that tune, with commentary. In the Figure below, the octave jumps are clearly visible in measures 2, 6, 7, 12, and 16.

It should be pointed out that an octave jump such as that in measure 7 is entirely unnecessary, as one could drop down to the G row, in cross-row fashion, and continue to ascend the run of notes without the jump. Tester's other playing show that he indeed *could* do that, but that was not his choice here; he apparently enjoyed playing an occasional tune full of jumps.

Transcription, Scan Tester's Schottische. It is played entirely on the C row.

4. Adding a beat

The old-time musician had two challenges in playing for dancing, either inside a house during a noisy party, or outside, where the sound of the instrument could evaporate in the open air. The first challenge, volume, was met by playing in octaves as much as possible.

The second challenge was to provide a danceable beat that inspired the dancers. One way of doing that was to drop out some of the notes in the lower octave left hand, thereby emphasizing the beat of those octave notes that remained. Usually, the remaining lower octave notes were on the first and third beats of each measure, giving an audible downbeat that matched the dancers' steps.

One could also accentuate that beat even further, by adding some simple partial chords to the remaining lower octave notes. Englishman William Kimber was a master of this style, as well as South African Faan Harris and Australian George Bennett.

The A part of Kimber's version of the *Bacca Pipes* jig illustrates his technique.

Tutorial 6, describes the basic procedure. The A part is played slowly, proceeding from 1) melody played singly on right hand, 2) melody played in octaves throughout, 3) lower octave notes dropped out on second and fourth beats, and 4) partial chords added to remaining left hand octave notes (typically, a third interval up is added to each lower octave note).

This basic technique of emphasizing the downbeat by dropping out lower octave notes is essential to nearly all of Kimber's style of playing; it is prominently featured in his schottisches, for example the *Moonlight Schottische* and *Over the Hills to Glory* (see Chapter 9).

Bacca Pipes

England
Morris Dance

As Played by William Kimber
Transcribed for CG Anglo by Dan Worrall

Transcription for William Kimber's version of Bacca Pipes. The A part (measures 1-16) is played all on the C row, and the B part is played in a cross-row fashion.

Providing the downbeat in this manner in time with the downward steps of dancers, as Kimber did, was a commonly employed device, but was hardly universal. Some players provided accentuation of the off-beat instead, to provide lift to help the dancers *raise* their feet. There are likely multiple origins for off-the-beat playing, where the second and fourth beats, rather than the first and third, get the emphasis.

However, American minstrel music picked up off-beat emphasis from African-American musicians and popularized it around the globe during the middle to late nineteenth century. In particular, the African banjo was principally strummed on the off-beat, and was the key instrument for the minstrel genre. Period writings in England describe the fascination of people when they heard these 'wild' and intoxicating rhythms for the first time.

The playing of Irishwoman Mary Ann Carolan provides an example of such lift. Mrs Carolan was no stranger to minstrel music; one of her traditional songs, **Young Bob Ridley**, originated in American minstrel shows in the middle of the nineteenth century. In the middle of the A part of her version of the polka **The Lass of Gowrie**, played on the German concertina, she drums the lower C note on the off-beat.

In **Tutorial 7** the tune is dissected slowly, with commentary. The tune is played entirely on the C row, and largely in octaves.

Her version is at a sprightly tempo and is fairly easy to play on a modern Anglo concertina. One should recall however that she plays it on a German concertina, which demands a great deal more energy and strength in order to pump its bellows that rapidly. One is reminded of the late Texas Governor Ann Richard's description of the actress and dancer Ginger Rogers: "Ginger did everything Fred Astaire did, only backwards and in high heels."

 Another example of off-beat emphasis is provided by the tune *Dick Cribb*, as played by the Australian and (at the time of recording) octogenarian George Bennett. The A part emphasizes the off-beat in a way that is reminiscent of a strumming banjo.

 William Kimber's version of **Getting Upstairs** also has an off-beat pulse, in a tune that was originally an American minstrel show breakdown.

Two musicians with fretless banjos with Anglo concertina player, Australia, ca.1870. Fretless banjos entered Australia and elsewhere by way of the minstrel shows, and had a large impact upon repertoire and musical rhythm amongst amateur musicians. Photo courtesy Peter Cuffley and Peter Ellis.

Note how South African musician Faan Harris employs a left hand beat in the A part of his *Soutpansberg Settees*, as in the attached transcription, below. Although he provides octave notes on both the beat and off-beat, it is the off-beat that gets most of the emphasis.

Soutpansberg Settees

Schottische

As Played by Faan Harris
Transcribed for CG Anglo by Dan Worrall

5. The 'Australian Scale'

Several Australian players, all of whom played in a cross-row manner using both rows of the instrument, were enamored of substituting an F# for an F when playing in the key of C, which gives an odd, modal sound to the scale and to tunes played in that manner.

Amongst the tunes of this archive, Dooley Chapman's versions of *Old Dan Tucker* and the *Lancer's Tune* exhibit this trait, as does Jim Harrison's *Princess Polka*. It is heard often enough in old-time playing there to give some of their tunes a certain identifiable Australian sound.

Tutorial 8 demonstrates the modified scale in the key of C, here casually termed the 'Australian scale'.

Chapman's version of **Old Dan Tucker** is played on a Bb/F concertina. In the Figure below, it is transcribed to the key of C (it modulates to G in the B part).

In *Tutorial 9,* the tune is played slowly and with commentary on how the F# was inserted; it is a side-effect of playing in octaves in a cross-row manner. It is not a modification that is necessary to the music, as it is just as easy to play the normal F; clearly these musicians liked the sound of the F#. Australian players like Con Klippel and Fred Holland, who typically stuck to single-row playing, did not employ this modification.

In the tutorial, I played measure 7 all on the C row and all in octaves, giving it a bounce. Dooley however preferred a more subtle legato phrasing here, precisely as written. The octaves are dropped, and the two phrases in that measure are played mostly singly and across the rows, which takes out two bellows direction changes.

Old Dan Tucker

With these few lessons and a little practice, any Anglo player should be able to master the old art of octave-style playing.

Its emphasis is on simplicity for dancing, rather than showy musical virtuosity, and it was this fit-for-purpose simplicity that made it so universal a technique in so many varied settings around the globe.

When learning by ear from the archived recordings of early musicians, it helps to utilize slow-down software. With appropriate software (like Roni Music's *The Amazing Slow-Downer®*), one can not only slow the tempo down, but change the pitch. For example, recordings of players using Bb/F concertinas can be brought into compliance with a concertina in C/G pitch simply by raising the pitch one semitone. In addition, pitch variance caused by primitive tape recorders used in field recordings can be cured by adjusting the pitch more finely, in cents.

In the final analysis, traditional styles of concertina playing can survive only in the presence of dancing, and most especially the old time round dances and quadrilles, for which the concertina's classic repertoire was created. Playing this old music well may require that one finds a house dance or community dance to listen to, dance for, and finally play for.

Note:

1. John Kelly, as interviewed by Gearóid Ó hAllmhuráin, *The Concertina in the Traditional Music of Clare* (PhD thesis, Queen's University Belfast, 1990), p.109.

Chapter 13. Resources

Printed music for old time ball-room dance - both for round dances and the earlier tunes for quadrilles - is at times difficult to find. There is no shortage of sheet music that was commercially published at the time for these dances, as there are a number of libraries and archives around the world that carry this material. These are usually composed for orchestra or for pianoforte, and were intended for high society ballrooms.

For music that has made its way, at least part of the way, through anything like a 'folk process', however - meaning the tunes as they would have been played in rural and working-class dances, for example, with tunes both from global tune sources as well as from local compositions - the pickings are decidedly slimmer.

In Ireland, the only significant, known printed source for the full range of dances that were once danced there in country houses - including schottisches, barn dances, waltzes, mazurkas, quadrilles and the like - is to be found in *The Roche Collection of Traditional Irish Music*, first published in 1929 and reprinted by Ossian Publications. There are only a few pages there, however, of these dance tunes, which Roche rather ironically put into a section called 'Old Dances' to separate them from the more numerous reels and jigs.

Irish polkas, most of them of the later form used in set dances, can be found in several printed sources, most notably in the Breathnach's *Ceol Rince na hÉireann*, volumes 2 and 3 (published by An Gúm, Dublin), and in the book *Johnny O'Leary of Sliabh Luachra: dance music from the Cork-Kerry border*, published in 1994 by The Lilliput Press.

For ear players, there is the extensive digital online archive of Comhaltas Ceoltóirí Éireann. A search on the word schottische, for example, will turn up a number of archived examples from early players on various instruments.

The Topic Records CD entitled *Round the House and Mind the Dresser: Irish Country-House Dance Music* provides a number of early twentieth century recordings of Irish house dance music as well as a commentary on the style's near-disappearance in Ireland.

The online *Set Dancing News* of Bill Lynch documents the return of set dancing in Ireland and abroad, and mentions many social evenings that now often include a schottische, a barndance, or a *Shoe the Donkey* varsoviana.

In England, ballroom-style dance was (and perhaps still is) viewed unfavorably by many in the folk music community. An article entitled *English Country Music - A Personal View* by Roger Digby, to be found on the website: *www.concertina.net*, lists many old-time traditional groups who played, and in some cases still play, this music.

The Topic CD of 2000 entitled *English Country Music* has many examples of this dance music played by stalwarts of the genre (including Scan Tester), and comes with an informative booklet by Reg Hall.

Perhaps the most significant British commentary on the topic is to be found in Chapter 5 of the book *I Never Played to Many Posh Dances*, which is a celebration of the life and times of Scan Tester written by Reg Hall, published in 1990 by Musical Traditions and now available for free download on their online website: *www.mustrad.org.uk/articles/r_hall.htm*

In South Africa, the two main boeremusiek societies, the *Tradisionele Boeremusiekklub van Suid-Afrika* (TBK) and the *Boeremusiekgilde*, both operate websites with much information on the topic, and both can provide many CDs of early performers as well as their modern counterparts. There is however not a lot of printed music.

A key reference on the history of boeremusiek and its dances (in Afrikaans) is Wilhelm Schultz's *Die Ontstaan en Ontwikkeling van Boeremusiek*, published in 2001 by A.V.A. Systems in Pretoria.

Australia has a rich array of both printed music and audio files of pre-folk revival musicians. The National Library of Australia is the principal site for sound files of early players, and the two books of John Meredith that they published are primary references on bush music and musicians.

The Bush Dance & Music Club of Bendigo & District has compiled a large number of finely detailed publications, many of them by concertina player and dance master Peter Ellis, that contain many hundreds of dance tunes as well as comprehensive instructions on how to do the dances themselves.

Because the tunes of ballroom dance are often of global origin, these are important if not essential resources for all (in particular, Ellis's *The Waltz, the Polka, and all Kinds of Dance Music* (2007) as well as his *The Merrie Country Dance* (2005)).

There are a number of other societies that provide information on colonial and bush dancing, among them the Bush Music Club of Sydney, the Wongawilli Colonial Dance Club, Bush Traditions, and the Australian Folklore Unit.

Discography

Musician	Country	Year	Tune	Source
Barry, Tom	Ireland	1950s	Heathery Breeze (reel)	Private recordings made by Shaun Jordan, Lisdoonvarna
Barry, Tom	Ireland	1950s	Sporting Nell (reel)	ditto
Barry, Tom	Ireland	1950s	Sally Gardens (reel)	ditto
Barry, Tom	Ireland	1950s	Untitled reel 1	ditto
Barry, Tom	Ireland	1950s	Untitled reel 2	ditto
Bennett, George	Australia	1960s	Dick Cripp (breakdown)	Disc 3067077, pt. 2, National Library of Australia
Bennett, George	Australia	1960s	Two Little Girls in Blue (waltz)	ditto
Bennett, George	Australia	1960s	Black Cloud (schottische)	ditto
Bennett, George	Australia	1960s	Rakes of Mallow (single reel)	ditto
Bennett, George	Australia	1960s	Ring the Bell Watchman (song tune)	ditto
Bennett, George	Australia	1960s	What'll They Do When the Billy Boils Over (jig)	ditto
Bennett, George	Australia	1960s	George Redder's Step (jig)	ditto
Bennett, George	Australia	1960s	Lancer's Tune (jig)	ditto
Bennett, George	Australia	1960s	All smiles tonight (waltz)	ditto

Bennett, George	Australia	1960s	Varsoviana	ditto
Bennett, George	Australia	1960s	Old Time Schottische	ditto
Bennett, George	Australia	1960s	Turn That Old Man Around (polka)	ditto
Bennett, George	Australia	1960s	My Mother Said I Never Should (polka)	ditto
Bennett, George	Australia	1960s	Darling Wait 'Til Morn (waltz)	ditto
Bennett, George	Australia	1960s	The capture of the Kelly Gang (song)	Disc 3067140, part 3, National Library of Australia
Bennett, George	Australia	1960s	My Pretty Girl (waltz)	ditto
Bennett, George	Australia	1960s	Break the News to Mother (waltz)	ditto
Bennett, George	Australia	1960s	Gundawindi Waltz	ditto
Bodenstein, Hans & Die Vyf Vastrappers	South Africa	1930	Untitled Settees GR 28 (schottische)	re-recorded from Regal (HMV) 78s by *Tradisionele Boeremusiekklub van Suid-Afrika*
Bodenstein, Hans & Die Vyf Vastrappers	South Africa	1930s	Die Fluister Wals (waltz)	re-recorded from Columbia 78s by *Tradisionele Boeremusiekklub van Suid-Afrika*
Bodenstein, Hans & Die Vyf Vastrappers	South Africa	1930	Untitled Polka Settees GR 54 (schottische)	re-recorded from Regal (HMV) 78s by *Tradisionele*

				Boeremusiekklub van Suid-Afrika
Bodenstein, Hans & Die Vyf Vastrappers	South Africa	1930s	Barndans met Twee Konsertinas (barn dance)	re-recorded from Columbia 78s by *Tradisionele Boeremusiekklub van Suid-Afrika*
Bodenstein, Hans & Die Vyf Vastrappers	South Africa	1930s	Tweestap Sammie Settees (schottische)	ditto
Bornman, Kerrie	South Africa	1950s	Ou Wessel se Settees, with Ricardo Bornman (schottische)	*Tradisionele Boeremusiekklub van Suid-Afrika*
Bornman, Kerrie	South Africa	1950s	Pietersburg Mazurka, with Ricardo Bornman	ditto
Bornman, Kerrie	South Africa	1930s	Oom Tien se Settees (schottische)	re-recorded from Regal (HMV) 78s by *Tradisionele Boeremusiekklub van Suid-Afrika*
Bornman, Kerrie	South Africa	1930s	Vrystaat Bo Wals (waltz)	ditto
Carolan, Mary Ann	Ireland	1980s	The Lass Of Gowrie/Mary Ann's/Try And Help Him If You Can (polkas)	Disc 400-RTE-RR CD R 113, Raidió Teilifís Éireann
Carolan, Mary Ann	Ireland	1980s	The Perfecture/The Morning Glory (slides)	ditto
Carolan, Mary Ann	Ireland	1980s	Mary Ann Carolan speaks about dances	ditto

Carolan, Mary Ann	Ireland	1980s	Veleta Waltz	Private recordings made by Jim MacArdle, Drogheda
Carolan, Mary Ann	Ireland	1980s	Lady Mary Ramsay (schottische)	ditto
Carolan, Mary Ann	Ireland	1980s	You're welcome home Prince Charlie (jig)	ditto
Carolan, Mary Ann	Ireland	1980s	Quadrille #3 (single reel)	ditto
Carolan, Mary Ann	Ireland	1980s	Napoleon's March	ditto
Carolan, Mary Ann	Ireland	1980s	Bonny Kate (reel)	ditto
Chapman, Albert (Dooley)	Australia	1981	Dooley speaks about playing to the step	Australian Folk Masters CD1 and Disc 33605, National Library of Australia
Chapman, Albert (Dooley)	Australia	1981	Dooley speaks about the demanding dancers	ditto
Chapman, Albert (Dooley)	Australia	1981	Untitled Polka	ditto
Chapman, Albert (Dooley)	Australia	1981	Old Dan Tucker (breakdown)	ditto
Chapman, Albert (Dooley)	Australia	1981	Lancer's Tune (quadrille single reel)	ditto

Chapman, Albert (Dooley)	Australia	1981	Ring the Bell Breakdown	ditto
Chapman, Albert (Dooley)	Australia	1974	Starry Night Waltz	Private recording by Bob Campbell, 1974
Chomse, Chris & Die Lydenburg Vastrappers	South Africa	1930s	Baba Wals (waltz)	re-recorded from Singer 78s by *Tradisionele Boeremusiekklub van Suid-Afrika*
Chomse, Chris & Die Lydenburg Vastrappers	South Africa	1930s	Bosveld Polka	ditto
Chomse, Chris & Die Lydenburg Vastrappers	South Africa	1930s	Mampoer Seties (schottische)	ditto
Chomse, Chris & Die Lydenburg Vastrappers	South Africa	1930s	Noodschulp Vastrap	ditto
Chomse, Chris & Die Lydenburg Vastrappers	South Africa	1930s	Wissel Polka	ditto
Colley, Susan	Australia	1973	Varsoviana	Private recording made by Warren Fahey, 1973
Colley, Susan	Australia	1973	The Wild Colonial Boy (song)	ditto
Colley, Susan	Australia	1973	Susan Colley speaks about dances	ditto

Crotty, Elizabeth	Ireland	1956	Wind the Shakes the Barley, Reel with the Beryl	Tape T448, Raidió Teilifís Éireann (housed at CCÉ Archive)
Crotty, Elizabeth	Ireland	1956	Dhá Ghabhairín Buí (polka)	Tape T223, Raidió Teilifís Éireann (housed at CCÉ Archive)
Doyle, Michael	Ireland	1960s	Mount Phoebus Hunt (hornpipe)	Private recordings made by John Joe Healy, Miltown Malbay
Doyle, Michael	Ireland	1960s	Untitled Reel	ditto
Doyle, Michael	Ireland	1960s	Untitled Reel 2	ditto
Droney, Jim	Ireland	1956	Untitled Reel (with Chris Droney)	Tape T222, Raidió Teilifís Éireann (housed at CCÉ Archive)
Droney, Jim	Ireland	1956	Three Little Drummers (jig, with Chris Droney)	ditto
Droney, Jim	Ireland	1956	Paddy O'Rafferty (jig; with Chris Droney)	ditto
Flanagan, Patrick	Ireland	1961	Two Untitled Reels	Private recordings made by Shaun Jordan, Lisdoonvarna
Flanagan, Patrick	Ireland	1961	The Concertina Reel	ditto
Flanagan, Patrick	Ireland	1961	Two reels with lilting	ditto

Flanagan, Patrick	Ireland	1961	Untitled Reel with Lilting	ditto
Flanagan, Patrick	Ireland	1961	Patrick Flanagan speaks about the German concertina	ditto
Harris, Stephen (Faan) & Die Vier Transvalers	South Africa	1932	Soutpansberg Settees (schottische)	re-recorded from Regal (HMV) 78s by *Tradisionele Boeremusiekklub van Suid-Afrika*
Harris, Stephen (Faan) & Die Vier Transvalers	South Africa	1932	Eileen Alannah (waltz)	dittoa
Harris, Stephen (Faan) & Die Vier Transvalers	South Africa	1932	Anna Pop Settees (schottische)	ditto
Harris, Stephen (Faan) & Die Vier Transvalers	South Africa	1932	Rooidagtoe Polka	ditto
Harris, Stephen (Faan) & Die Vier Transvalers	South Africa	1932	Kroomdraai Mazurka	ditto
Harris, Stephen (Faan) & Die Vier Transvalers	South Africa	1932	Wals van Tant Sannie (Shannon Waltz)	ditto

Harrison, Jim	Australia	1986	Princess Polka (with George Klippel on piano)	Disc TRC 2222, National Library of Australia
Harrison, Jim	Australia	1986	Why did my Master Sell Me (waltz, with Neville Simpson)	ditto
Harrison, Jim	Australia	1986	Untitled Schottische	ditto
Harrison, Jim	Australia	1986	The Mill Belongs to Sandy (polka)	ditto
Holland, Eric	England	1968	Eric Holland speaks, 1968	Private recordings, Mark Davies, Bradfield, Yorkshire
Holland, Eric	England	1968	Scotland the Brave, march	ditto
Holland, Eric	England	1968	Untitled waltz	ditto
Holland, Eric	England	1968	Untitled waltz 2	ditto
Holland, Eric	England	1968	Waltzing Matilda	ditto
Holland, Eric	England	1968	Ave Maria	ditto
Holland, Fred	Australia	1957	Untitled Schottische	Disc TR 4/24, National Library of Australia
Holland, Fred	Australia	1957	Write Me a Letter from Home (waltz)	ditto
Holland, Fred	Australia	1957	Mudgee Schottische	ditto

Hourican, Katey	Ireland	1970s	Untitled Polka	Tape T395, Comhaltas Ceoltóirí Éireann Archive
Hourican, Katey	Ireland	1970s	Merry Blacksmith (reel)	ditto
Hourican, Katey	Ireland	1970s	Spanish Lady (polka)	ditto
Hourican, Katey	Ireland	1970s	Moneymuck (schottische)	ditto
Hourican, Katey	Ireland	1970s	Mammy Will You Buy Me A Bow Wow (schottische)	ditto
Howley, Martin	Ireland	1970s	Maggie in the Wood (polka)	Private recordings made by Jim Carroll, Miltown Malbay
Howley, Martin	Ireland	1970s	Bothar na Sop (jig)	ditto
Howley, Martin	Ireland	1970s	Untitled Jig	ditto
James, Ernie	Australia	1974	Bullfrog Hop (jig)	Disc TRC 2221 C-14, National Library of Australia
James, Ernie	Australia	1974	Cornflower Waltz	Disc TRC 2221 C-5, National Library of Australia
James, Ernie	Australia	1974	Untitled Schottische	ditto
James, Ernie	Australia	1974	Berlin Polka	ditto
Kilroy, Fred	England	1976	Blaze Away (march)	Private recordings

				made by Paul Davies, London
Kilroy, Fred	England	1976	Minstrel Selection	ditto
Kilroy, Fred	England	1976	Old Comrades March	ditto
Kilroy, Fred	England	1976	On the Quarterdeck (march)	ditto
Kimber, William	England	1946	Bacca Pipes (jig)	EFDSS CD 03, English Folk Dance and Song Society, London
Kimber, William	England	1946	Over the Hills to Glory (schottische)	ditto
Kimber, William	England	1935	Getting Upstairs	ditto
Kimber, William	England	1951	Mayblossom Waltz	Folktrax 382, Topic Records, London
Kimber, William	England	1951	Kitty Come (barn dance)	ditto
Kimber, William	England	1951	Little Polly (polka)	ditto
Kimber, William	England	1951	Moonlight Schottische	ditto
Klippel, Con	Australia	1969	Con Klippel speaks	Disc TRC3606/2, National Library of Australia
Klippel, Con	Australia	1969	Me Smokey Smokey (song tune)	ditto
Klippel, Con	Australia	1969	Arthur Byatt's Schottische	ditto

Klippel, Con	Australia	1969	Grandmother Klippell's Schottische	ditto
Klippel, Con	Australia	1969	The Mill Belongs to Sandy (polka)	ditto
Klippel, Con	Australia	1969	Manchester Galop	ditto
de Lange, Johannes (Silver) & Die Vyf Dagbrekers	South Africa	1932	Die Hele Nag Deur Vastrap	re-recorded from HMV 78s by *Tradisionele Boeremusiekklub van Suid-Afrika*
de Lange, Johannes (Silver) & Die Vyf Dagbrekers	South Africa	1932	Het Jy My Nog Lief (waltz)	ditto
de Lange, Johannes (Silver) & Die Vyf Dagbrekers	South Africa	1932	Mielieblare Settees (schottische)	ditto
de Lange, Johannes (Silver) & Die Vyf Dagbrekers	South Africa	1932	Militaire Twee-pas Vastrap	ditto
de Lange, Johannes (Silver) & Die Vyf Dagbrekers	South Africa	1932	Warm Pattat Polka	ditto
Link, Bill	England	1970s	Bill Link speaking	Private recordings made by Mark Davies, Bradfield, Yorkshire
Link, Bill	England	1970s	Untitled waltz	ditto

Link, Bill	England	1970s	My Wild Irish Rose (waltz)	ditto
Link, Bill	England	1970s	Untitled polka	ditto
Marshall, Ellis	England	1979	Royton Morris at St. Paul's Working Men's Institute, Blackburn Lancashire, with Norman Coleman	private recordings; Tony Marshall
Marshall, Ellis	England	1978	Royton Morris tunes (recorded at Marshall's home)	ditto
Mullaly, William	Ireland	1927	The Green Groves of Erin/The Ivy Leaf (Reels)	Victor 78rpm recording
O'Dwyer, Ella Mae	Ireland	1974	Mrs O'Dwyer's Fancy (polkas)	Free Reed Records CD AnClar 06
O'Dwyer, Ella Mae	Ireland	1974	The Ardgroom Set (polkas)	ditto
O'Dwyer, Ella Mae	Ireland	1974	The Stack of Barley (barn dance)	ditto
O'Dwyer, Ella Mae	Ireland	1970s	Old Set Tunes (slides)	Tape T223, Raidió Teilifís Éireann (housed at CCÉ Archive)
O'Dwyer, Ella Mae	Ireland	1970s	Untitled March	ditto
O'Neal, Clem	Australia	1970s	Untitled Schottische	Cassette tapes, Bush Music Club of Sydney
O'Neal, Clem	Australia	1970s	North Wind Schottische	ditto
O'Neal, Clem	Australia	1970s	Tom Mitch's schottische	ditto

O'Neal, Clem	Australia	1970s	All By Yourself in the Moonlight (Barn Dance)	ditto
O'Neal, Clem	Australia	1970s	Kick Your Leg Up Sal Brown (Varsoviana)	ditto
O'Neal, Clem	Australia	1977	Untitled Schottische and the Boston Two Step	Private recording made by Dave de Hugard, 1974
O'Neal, Clem	Australia	1977	Bird in a Gilded Cage (waltz)	ditto
Ordish, Charlie	Australia	1957-63	Turn Around and Then Stop, Varsoviana	Disc TRC 2539/17, National Library of Australia
Ordish, Charlie	Australia	1957-63	Untitled Polka Mazurka	ditto
Ordish, Charlie	Australia	1957-63	So Early in the Morning (polka)	ditto
Ordish, Charlie	Australia	1957-63	St. Patrick's Day in the Morning (jig)	ditto
Palm, Willie & Die Vier Hugenote	South Africa	1930s	Oom Koos se Mazurka	re-recorded from HMV 78s by *Tradisionele Boeremusiekklub van Suid-Afrika*
Palm, Willie & Die Vier Hugenote	South Africa	1930s	Mampoer Polka	ditto
Palm, Willie & Die Vier Hugenote	South Africa	1930s	Kom ons Dans (schottische)	ditto
Palm, Willie & Die Vier Hugenote	South Africa	1930s	Vergeet Nie (waltz)	ditto

Prinsloo, Marthinus (Pietie) & Die Vier Springbokke	South Africa	1932	Koekoe My Hartjie Settees (schottische)	ditto
Prinsloo, Marthinus (Pietie) & Die Vier Springbokke	South Africa	1932	Ek Hou My Lyf Soos 'n Ou Fisant (polka)	ditto
Ryan, Stack	Ireland	1950s	Eamonn a' Chnoic (air)	Tape T508, Raidió Teilifís Éireann (housed at CCÉ Archive)
Ryan, Stack via Bernard O'Sullivan	Ireland	1974	Stack Ryan's Polka	Free Reed Records CD AnClar 02
Ryan, Stack via Bernard O'Sullivan	Ireland	1974	My Heart's in the Highlands/The Dewdrop (waltzes, with Tommy McMahon)	ditto
Ryan, Stack via Bernard O'Sullivan	Ireland	1974	I Have a Bonnet Trimmed with Blue/The Rakes of Mallow (polka and single reel, with Tommy McMahon)	ditto
Teahan, Terry	Ireland	1976	Poll Ha'Penny (fling/schottische	Topic LP 12TS352
Teahan, Terry	Ireland	1976	Sword Dance (slide)	Topic LP 12TS352
Tester, Scan	England	1960s	Untitled Polka	Topic Records CD TSCD581D, *I Never Played to*

				Many Posh Dances
Tester, Scan	England	1950s	Untitled waltz	private tape made at Stone Quarry pub, Chelwood Gate Sussex, recording by Ken Stubbs
Tester, Scan	England	1950s	Man in the Moon waltz	ditto
Tester, Scan	England	1950s	Harry Lauder Song Tunes	ditto
Tester, Scan	England	1960s	See Me Dance the Polka	Private recording made by Bob Davenport
Tester, Scan	England	1960s	Alexander's Ragtime Band	ditto
Tester, Scan	England	1971	St Patrick's Day (jig)	Private recording made at Lewes Arms, Sussex, recorded by Vic Smith; Folk Sound Records
Tester, Scan	England	1971	Step Dance Tune (hornpipe)	ditto
Tester, Scan	England	1971	Scan Tester's Schottische	ditto
Tester, Scan	England	1971	Step Dance Tune/Roaming in the Gloaming/I Love a Lassie	ditto
Yarnold, Percy	Australia	1985	Wooly Tale Foxtrot	Disc TRC2222, National Library of

				Australia/ John Meredith
Yarnold, Percy	Australia	1985	Keightley's Schottische	ditto
Yarnold, Percy	Australia	1985	Early in the Morning (polka)	ditto
Yarnold, Percy	Australia	1985	Percy speaks on dances	ditto

About the Author

Dan Michael Worrall is one of a fifth generation of his family to live in the Houston area. Trained in regional geology, he enjoyed a career in petroleum exploration research and management. He holds a bachelor's degree from Rice University, a master of arts from the University of Wyoming, and a PhD from the University of Texas at Austin, all in geology.

Two of Dan's grandparents immigrated to America from County Clare, Ireland, and his wife Mary also hails from that country. Perhaps as a result, he has long followed Irish (and English and American) traditional music as a hobby. He has played the concertina for over 45 years, and has published a number of works for that instrument, including *The Anglo Concertina Music of William Kimber* (English Folk Dance and Song Society, London, 2005); *The Anglo-German Concertina: A Social History* (2 vols., Concertina Press, Fulshear Texas, 2008); and *Tripping to the Well: Six Clare Women and Mrs. O'Dwyer's Old German Concertina* (CD, Oidhreacht an Chláir, Miltown Malbay, Ireland, 2014). He has been an editor of the online *Concertina Journal* since its inception in 2016, and has led an annual concertina workshop at the Palestine (Texas) Old Time Music Festival since 2004.

He is also an avid avocational historian, with two recent books on local history: *Pleasant Bend: Upper Buffalo Bayou and the San Felipe Trail* (2016) and *A Prehistory of Houston and Southeast Texas: Landscape and Culture* (2021). Both books, as well as his two-volume social history of the Anglo-German concertina, are available at:

    www.amazon.com

He lives with his wife on a farm in the lower Brazos valley just west of Fulshear, Texas. They have two grown children and two grandchildren.

Dan Worrall (left) and Peter Ellis serenade the statue of Australian folk icon Ned Kelly in Glenrowan, Victoria, 2011. The song, The Ballad of Ned Kelly is sung by concertina player George Bennett in Chapter 7.

Other concertina publications by Dan Worrall

Tripping to the Well: Six Clare Women & Mrs. O'Dwyer's Old German Concertina: CD, published in 2014 by Oidreacht an Chláir, Miltown Malbay.

House Dance, 2011 edition, published as CD-ROM, available at Musical Traditions, Stroud, Gloucestershire, UK and the National Library of Australia, Canberra; or as downloadable music file from The Concertina Journal:

>   www.concertinajournal.org/House_Dance_Text/

The Anglo-German Concertina: A Social History: 2008, two volumes, available in print at www.Amazon.com, or as a free online digital version at Google Books.

The Anglo Concertina Music of William Kimber: 2005, English Folk Dance and Song Society, London (out of print, but to be reprinted in 2022 by Rollston Press, Honolulu, HI).

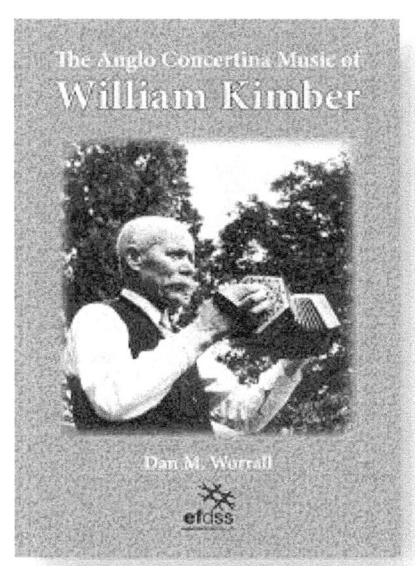

www.ingramcontent.com/pod-product-compliance
Lightning Source LLC
Chambersburg PA
CBHW080545230426
43663CB00015B/2713